Michigan's Bicycle Trails

An American Bike Trails Publication

Michigan's Bicycle Trails

Published by   American By Trail

Copyright 2005 by American Bike Trails

All Rights Reserved. Reproduction of any part of this book in any form without written permission is prohibited.

Created by   Ray Hoven

Design by   Mary C. Rumpsa

American Bike Trails assumes no responsibility or liability for any person or entity with respect to injury or damage caused either directly or indirectly by the information contained in this book.

Table of Contents

This book provides a comprehensive, easy-to-use reference to most of the off-road trails throughout Michigan. It contains over 150 detailed trail maps. The book is organized by geographical sections: Eastern Southern Michigan, Western Southern Michigan, Eastern Northern Lower Michigan; Western Northern Lower Michigan; Eastern UP, and Western UP. Each section begins with a map of that section showing trail locations together with a reference listing of trails within the section. The back of the book provides indexes in alphabetical sequence of all the trails illustrated, plus separate listings by leisure and mountain biking, and cross references by city to trail and county to trail. The trail maps include such helpful features as locations and access, trail facilities, and nearby communities.

Terms Used

Length   Expressed in miles. Round trip mileage is normally indicated for loops.

Effort Levels **Easy**   Physical exertion is not strenuous. Climbs and descents as well as technical obstacles are more minimal. Recommended for beginners.

Moderate/More Difficult   Physical exertion is not excessive. Climbs and descents can be challenging. Expect some technical obstacles.

Most Difficult/Expert Physical exertion is demanding. Climbs and descents require good riding skills. Trail surface may be sandy, loose rock, soft or wet.

Directions   Describes by way of directions and distances, how to get to the trail areas from roads and nearby communities.

Map   Illustrative representation of a geographic area, such as a state, section, forest, park or trail complex.

Forest   Typically encompasses a dense growth of trees and underbrush covering a large tract.

Park   A tract of land generally including woodlands and open areas.

DNR   Department of Natural Resources

Types of Biking

Mountain   Fat-tired bikes are recommended. Ride may be generally flat but then with a soft, rocky or wet surface.

Leisure   Off-road gentle ride. Surface is generally paved or screened.

Tour   Riding on roads with motorized traffic or on road shoulders.

ROAD SYMBOLS

- 🛡39 Interstate Highway
- 🛡12 U.S. Highway
- 26 State Highway
- K County Highway

AREA LEGEND

- City, Town
- Parks, Preserves
- Waterway
- Mileage Scale
- ★ Points of Interest
- – – County/State
- 🌲 Forest/Woods

TRAIL LEGEND

- ▪▪▪▪▪ Trail
- ▪ ▪ ▪ ▪ ▪ Skiing only Trail
- ▪▪▪▪▪▪▪ Hiking only Trail
- ▪ ▪ ▪ ▪ ▪ Planned Trail
- ▪ ▪ ▪ ▪ ▪ Alternate Trail
- ——— Road
- +++++++ Railroad Tracks

TRAIL USES

- 🚴 Mountain Biking
- 🚴 Leisure Biking
- ⛸ In Line Skating
- 🎿 Cross-Country Skiing
- 🚶 Hiking
- 🐎 Horseback Riding
- 🛷 Snowmobiling

SYMBOL LEGEND

- Beach/Swimming
- Bicycle Repair
- Cabin
- Camping
- Canoe Launch
- First Aid
- Food
- GC Golf Course
- ? Information
- Lodging
- Overlook/Observation
- P Parking
- Picnic
- Ranger Station
- Restrooms
- Shelter
- T Trailhead
- Visitor Center
- Water

Hypothermia

Hypothermia is a condition where the core body temperature falls below 90 degrees. This may cause death.

Mild hypothermia

1. Symptoms
   a. Pronounced shivering
   b. Loss of physical coordination
   c. Thinking becomes cloudy
2. Causes
   a. Cold, wet, loss of body heat, wind
3. Treatment
   a. Prevent further heat loss, get out of wet clothing and out of wind. Replace wet clothing with dry.
   b. Help body generate more heat. Refuel with high-energy foods and a hot drink, get moving around, light exercise, or external heat.

Severe hypothermia

1. Symptoms
   a. Shivering stops, pulse and respiration slows down, speech becomes incoherent.
2. Treatment
   a. Get help immediately.
   b. Don't give food or water.
   c. Don't try to rewarm the victim in the field.
   d. A buildup of toxic wastes and tactic acid accumulates in the blood in the body's extremities. Movement or rough handling will cause a flow of the blood from the extremities to the heart. This polluted blood can send the heart into ventricular fibrillations (heart attach). This may result in death.
   e. Wrap victim in several sleeping bags and insulate from the ground.

Frostbite

Symptoms of frostbite may include red skin with white blotches due to lack of circulation. Rewarm body part gently. Do not immerse in hot water or rub to restore circulation, as both will destroy skin cell.

Heat Exhaustion

Cool, pale, and moist skin, heavy sweating, headache, nausea, dizziness and vomiting. Body temperature nearly normal.

Treatment: Have victim lie in the coolest place available— on back with feet raised. Rub body gently with cool, wet cloth. Give person ½ glass of water every 15 minutes if conscious and can tolerate it. Call for emergency medical assistance.

Heat Stroke

Hot, red skin, shock or unconsciousness; high body temperature.

Treatment: Treat as a life-threatening emergency. Call for emergency medical assistance immediately. Cool victim by any means possible. Cool bath, pour cool water over body, or wrap wet sheets around body. Give nothing by mouth.

West Nile Virus

West Nile Virus is transmitted by certain types of mosquitoes. Most people infected with West Nile Virus won't develop symptoms. Some may become ill 3 to 15 days after being bitten.

Protect Yourself: Wear property clothing, use insect repellents and time your outdoor activities to reduce your risk of mosquito bites and other insect problems. Most backyard mosquito problems are caused by mosquitoes breeding in and around homes, not those from more natural areas.

Bicycle Safety

Bicycling offers many rewards, among them a physically fit body and a pleasant means of transportation. But the sport has its hazards, which can lead to serious accidents and injuries. We have provided rules, facts and tips that can help minimize the dangers of bicycling while you're having fun.

Choose The Right Bicycle

Adults and children should ride bicycles with frames small enough to be straddled easily with both feet flat on the ground, and with handlebars that can be easily reached with elbows bent. Oversize bikes make it difficult to ride comfortably and maintain control. Likewise, don't buy a large bike for a child to grow into-- smaller is safer.

Learn To Ride The Safe Way

When learning to ride a bike, let a little air out of the tires, and practice steering and balancing by "scootering" around with both feet on the ground and the seat as low as possible. The "fly-or-fall" method-where someone runs alongside the bicycle and then lets go-can result in injuries.

Training wheels don't work, since the rider can't learn to balance until the wheels come of. They can be used with a timid rider, but the child still will have to learn to ride without them. Once the rider can balance and pedal (without training wheels), raise the seat so that the rider's leg is almost straight at the bottom of the pedal stroke.

Children seldom appreciate the dangers and hazards of city cycling. Make sure they understand the traffic laws before letting them onto the road.

Use This Important Equipment

Headlight A working headlight and rear reflector are required for night riding in some states. Side reflectors do not make the rider visible to drivers on cross streets.

Safety seat for children under 40 lbs. Make sure the seat is mounted firmly over the rear wheel of the bike, and does not wobble when going downhill at high speed. Make sure the child will not slide down while riding. The carrier should also have a device to keep the child's feet from getting into the spokes.

Package rack Racks are inexpensive, and they let the rider steer with both hands and keep packages out of the spokes.

Obey Traffic Laws

Car drivers are used to certain rules of the road, and bicyclists must obey them too. The following rules should be taught to a child as soon as he or she can ride a bicycle:

Make eye contact with a driver before entering or crossing lanes.

Signal and glance over your shoulder before changing lanes.

Watch for openings in the traffic stream and make turns from the appropriate lane.

When riding off-road, be sure you are on a trail that permits bicycles.

Before riding in the road, these rules should be practiced until they become habit and can be performed smoothly. Adults must set good examples-children imitate them regardless of verbal instructions.

Beware Of Dangerous Practices

Never ride against traffic. Failure to observe this rule causes the majority of car-bicycle collisions. Motorists can't always avoid the maneuvers of a wrong-way rider since the car and bike move toward each other very quickly.

Never make a left turn from the right lane.

Never pass through an intersection at full speed.

Never ignore stop light or stop signs.

Never enter traffic suddenly from a driveway or sidewalk. This rule is particularly important when the rider is a child, who is more difficult for a motorist to see.

Don't wear headphones that make it hard to hear and quickly respond to traffic.

Don't carry passengers on a bike. The only exception is a child under 40 lbs. who is buckled into an approved bike safety seat and wears a helmet as required by law.

Passenger trailers can be safe and fun. Be aware, though, that a trailer makes the bike much longer and requires careful control. Passengers must wear helmets.

Find Safe Places To Ride

Most cities have some bicycle-friendly routes, as well as some high-traffic areas that require skill and experience. It's safest to ride on secondary roads with light traffic. When choosing a route, remember that the wider the lane, the safer the cycling.

Get A Bike That Works With You

Skilled riders who use their bikes often for exercise or transport should consider buying multi-geared bikes, which increase efficiency while minimizing stress on the body. (These bikes may not be appropriate for young or unskilled riders, who may concentrate more on the gears than on the road.) The goal is to keep the pedals turning at a rate of 60-90 RPM. Using the higher gears while pedaling slowly is hard on the knees, and is slower and more tiring than the efficient pedaling on the experienced cyclist. Have a safe trip!

Bicycle Helmets

"It's as easy as falling off a bicycle." The adage has been around for decades. Unfortunately, it makes light of the potential for tragedy if you should take a serious fall while riding a bicycle.

With an increasing number of people riding bicycles on our streets and highways, the risk of injury-in particular, head injury--continues to rise. Each year, nearly 50,000 bicyclists suffer serious head injuries. According to the most recent statistics, head injuries are the leading cause of death in the approximately 1,300 bicycle-related fatalities that occur annually. To a large extent, these head injuries are preventable.

Wearing a helmet can make a difference. Until recently, advocates of the use of protective headgear for cyclists found their stance lacked scientific support. But wearing protective headgear clearly makes a difference. Recent evidence confirms that a helmet can reduce your risk of serious head and brain injury by almost 90 percent should you be involved in a bicycle accident.

Bicycle riding is an excellent form of aerobic exercise that can benefit your musculoskeletal and cardiovascular systems. Make the investment in a helmet and take the time to put in on each time you ride.

Reprinted from July 1989 "Mayo Clinic Health Letter" with permission of Mayo Foundation, for Medical Education and Research, Rochester, Minnesota.

What To Look For In A Bicycle Helmet

We endorse these guidelines for bicycle helmets recommended by the American Academy of Pediatrics:

The helmet should meet the voluntary testing standards of one of these two groups: American National Standards Institute (ANSI) OR Snell Memorial Foundation. Look for a sticker on the inside of the helmet.

1.) Select the right size. Find one that fits comfortably and doesn't pinch.
2.) Buy a helmet with a durable outer shell and a polystyrene liner. Be sure it allows adequate ventilation.
3.) Use the adjustable foam pads to ensure a proper fit at the front, back and sides.
4.) Adjust the strap for a snug fit. The helmet should cover the top of your forehead and not rock side to side or back and forth with the chain strap in place.
5.) Replace your helmet if it is involved in an accident.

Emergency Toolkit

When venturing out on bicycle tours, it is always smart to take along equipment to help make roadside adjustments and repairs. It is not necessary for every member of your group to carry a complete set of equipment, but make sure someone in your group brings along the equipment listed below:

1.) Standard or slotted screwdriver
2.) Phillips screwdriver
3.) 6" or 8" adjustable wrench
4.) Small pliers
5.) Spoke adjuster
6.) Tire pressure gauge
7.) Portable tire pump
8.) Spare innertube
9.) Tire-changing lugs

A Few Other Things

When embarking on a extended bike ride, it is important to give your bike a pre-ride check. To ensure that your bike is in premium condition, go over the bike's mechanisms, checking for any mechanical problems. It's best to catch these at home, and not when they occur "on the road." If you run into a problem that you can't fix yourself, you should check your local yellow pages for a professional bike mechanic.

When you are planning a longer trip, be sure to consider your own abilities and limitations, as well as those of any companions who may be riding with you. In general, you can ride about three times the length (timewise) as your average training ride. If you have a regular cycling routine, this is a good basis by which to figure the maximum distance you can handle.

Finally, be aware of the weather. Bring plenty of sunblock for clear days, and rain gear for the rainy one. Rain can make some rides miserable, in addition to making it difficult to hear other traffic. Winds can blow up sand, and greatly increase the difficulty of a trail.

Rail-trail Courtesy & Common Sense

1.) Stay on designated trails.
2.) Bicyclists use the right side of the trail (Walkers use the left side of the trail).
3.) Bicyclists should only pass slower users on the left side of the trail; use your voice to warn others when you need to pass.
4.) Get off to the side of the trail if you need to stop.
5.) Bicyclists should yield to all other users.
6.) Do not use alcohol or drugs while on the trail.
7.) Do not litter.
8.) Do not trespass onto adjacent land.
9.) Do not wear headphones while using the trail.

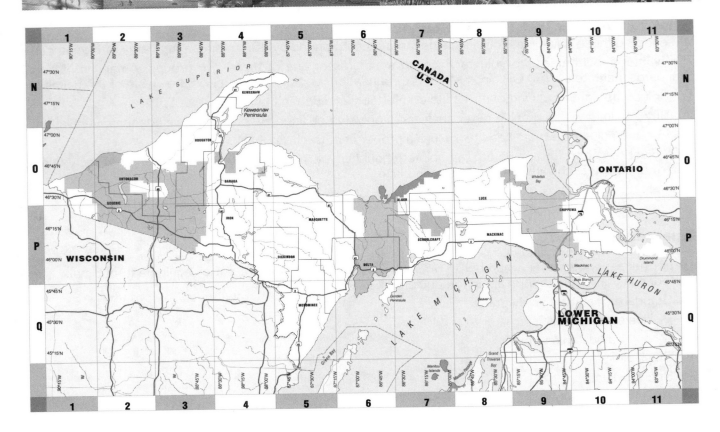

Mileage between principal cities

	Flint	Detroit	Ann Arbor	Lansing	Kalamazoo	Grand Rapids
Alena	179	237	229	214	289	248
Ann Arbor	55	38		62	97	131
Battle Creek	101	113	75	50	25	67
Detroit	57		38	84	142	156
Benton Harbor	174	183	145	123	49	85
Flint		57	55	51	128	107
Grand Rapids	107	156	131	66	52	
Ironwood	555	613	607	550	600	548
Jackson	88	80	36	38	64	107
Kalamazoo	128	142	97	75		52
Lansing	51	84	62		75	66
Mackinaw City	227	285	279	222	272	218
Menominee	428	488	480	423	473	421
Mt. Pleasant	87	149	127	85	137	85
Muskegon	143	189	187	102	84	39
Pontiac	32	25	47	70	144	139
Port Huron	70	56	93	127	202	183
Saginaw	37	101	89	72	147	113
Sault Ste. Marie	283	341	335	278	328	276
Traverse City	188	249	240	176	190	138

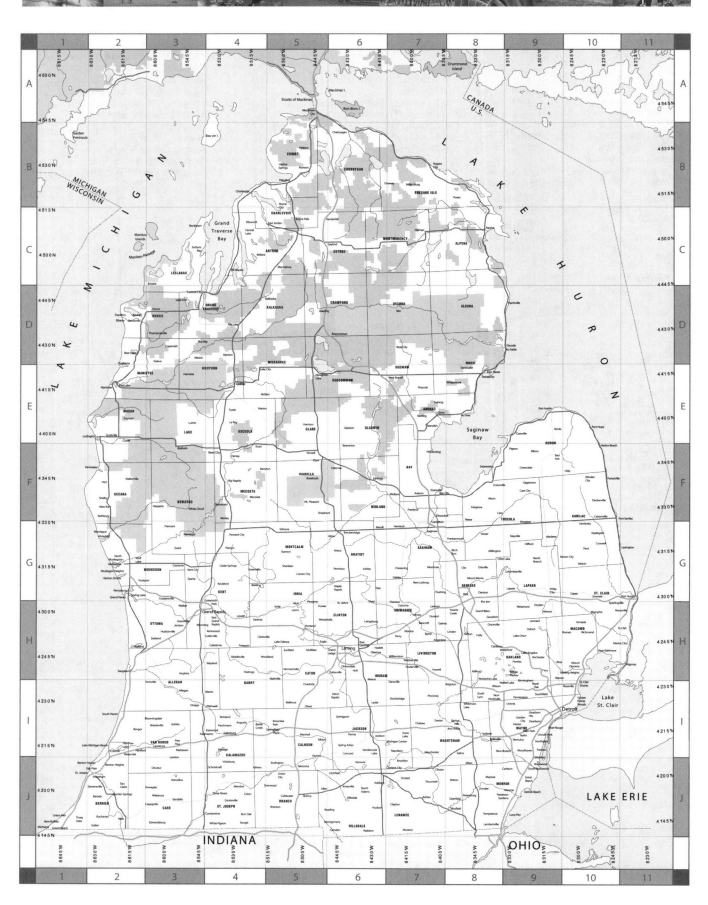

Southeast Michigan's Trails Overview

Legend:
- ■ Recreational Trail
- ▲ Fat Tire Trail
- ◆ Recreational & Fat Tire Trail

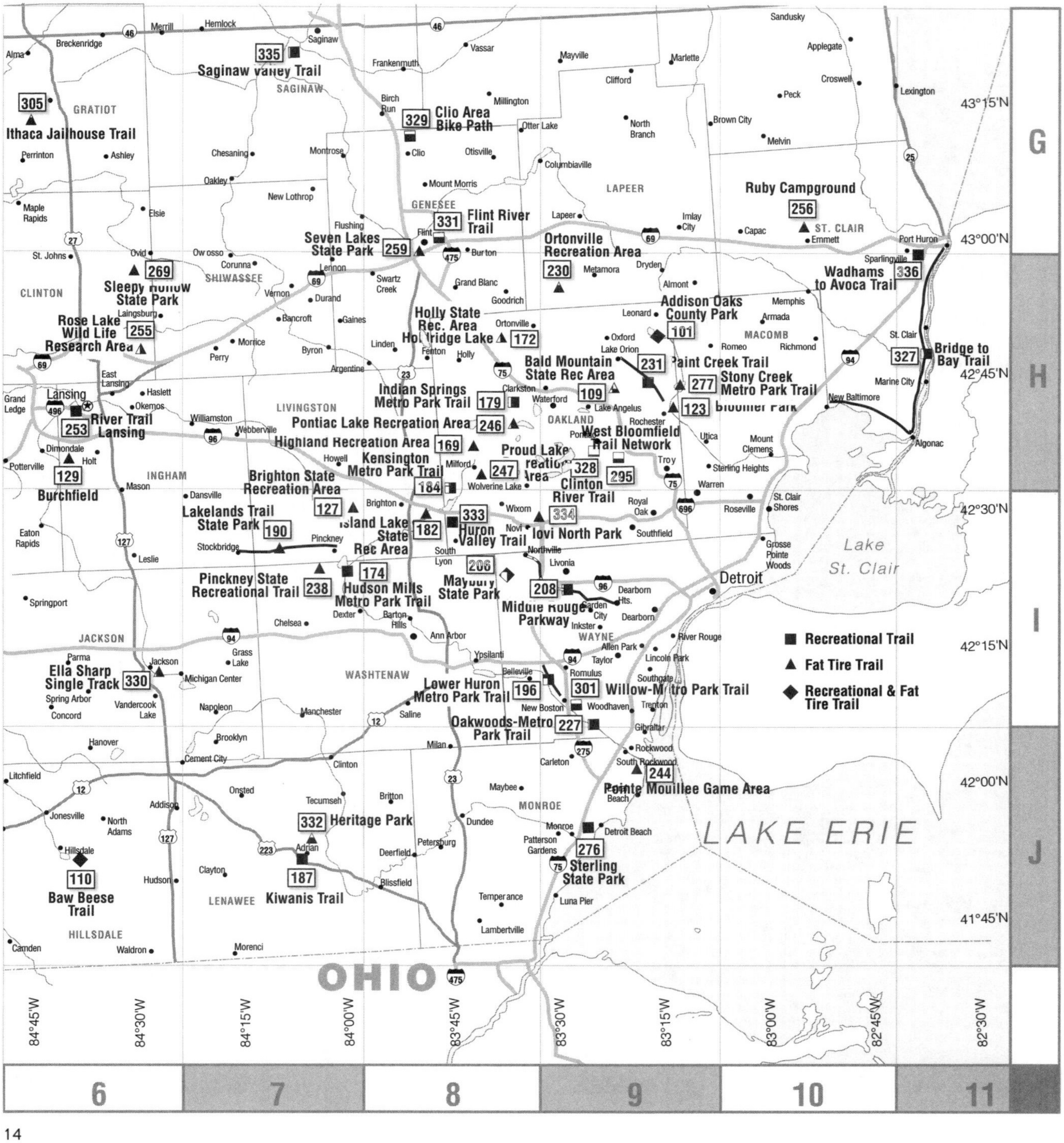

Addison Oaks County Park

Trail Uses	(icons)	**Setting**	Wooded, fields
Grid	H9, **Trail ID** 101	**Location**	Near cities of Lake Orion and Rochester
Length	8.5 miles	**Lat/Long**	42-48 / 83-10 Park concession
Surface	Paved, dirt	**County**	Oakland
Difficulty	Easy to difficult	**Contact**	Oakland County Parks 248-856-4647
Acres	794	**Fees**	Vehicle entry

Getting There Located about 7 miles north of Rochester and 4 miles east of Lake Orion. From I-75, take M-24 (exit 81) and proceed north to Clarkston Road. East on Clarkston road to Lake George Road for ½ mile to Predmore Road, and then east to Kline Road. North on Kline Road to the park entrance, a short distance off West Romeo Road. From there, take Rochester Road north and exit west on Romeo Road for 2 miles. Park entrance is on the north side.

Trail Notes Paved, natural (groomed). Wooded trails with varied flat and hilly terrain with 6 miles of marked mountain bike trails, and 2.5 miles of paved trails (Buhl Lake Trail). Bike & ski rentals are available. Effort level is easy to moderate, except that some of the newer track would be rated difficult.

Facilities (icons: P, ₹, ♿, ⛺, 🚲, 🏊, GC)

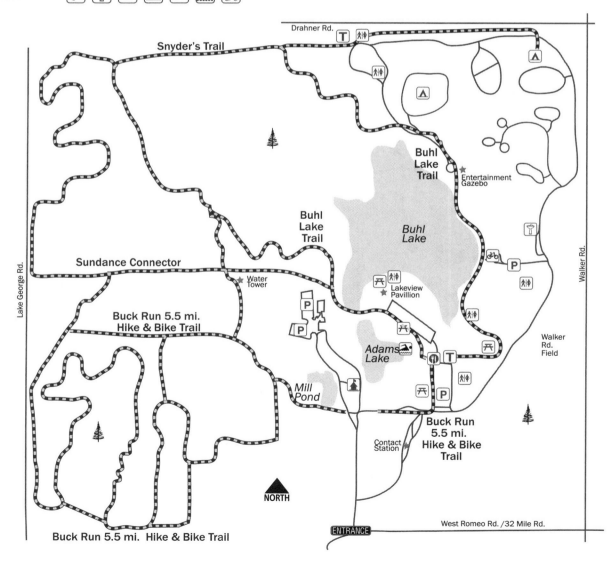

15

Bald Mountain State Recreation Trail

Trail Uses	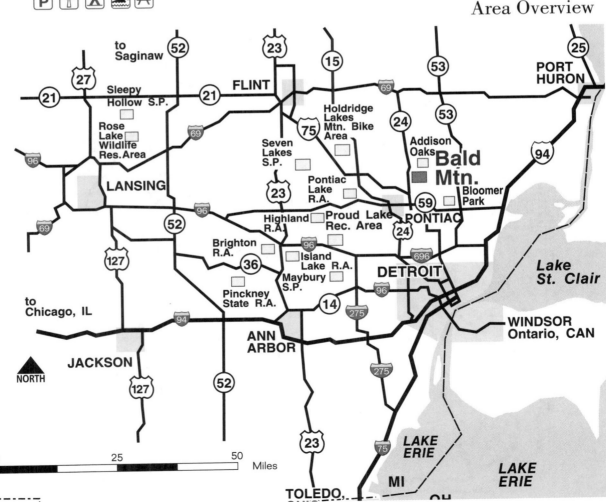	**Setting**	Woods, lakes, scenic vistas
Grid	H9 **Trail ID** 109	**Location**	Lake Orion and Pontiac
Length	15 miles	**Lat/Long**	42-47 / 83-12 Parking-Predmore & Harmon Rd.
Surface	Natural	**County**	Oakland
Difficulty	Easy to moderate	**Contact**	Bald Mountain Recreation Area 248-693-6767
Acres	4,637	**Fees**	Vehicle entry

Getting There   North Unit - Take I-75 to M-24 (exit 81), and proceed north on M-24 for 6 miles to Clarkson Road. East on Clarkson Road to Adams Road, then north to where it ends at Stoney Creek Road. East on Stoney Creek Road a short distance, and then north on Harmon Road until it junctions with Predmore Road. There is a trailhead off the west parking lot.

South Unit - Take I-75 to M-24 (exit 81), then north to Greenfield Road. East on Greenfield Road for a 1/2 mile to the parking lot on the north side of the road. Park Headquarters are a little east on Greenfield Road.

Trail Notes   Loops with easy to moderate effort level. Terrain varies from moderate to hilly. Trails are well-signed, single track and run clockwise. To the north the trails are signed White, Blue and Orange. To the south the trails are signed Red, Yellow, Orange, Blue, Green and White. The South Unit stays wet and muddy into late spring while the North Unit is normally dry.

Facilities

Area Overview

Northern Section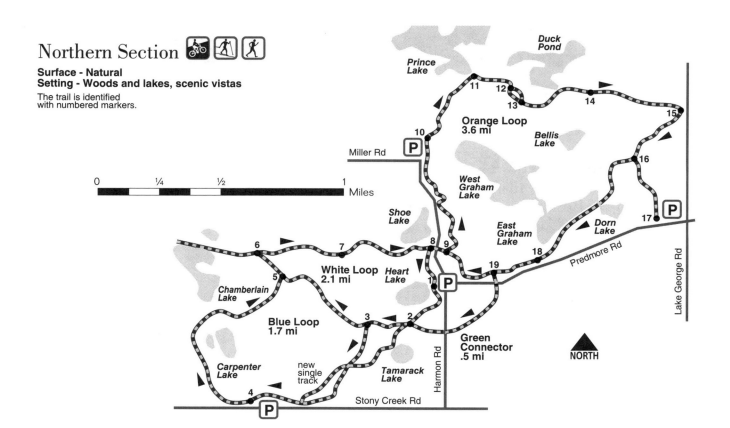

Surface - Natural
Setting - Woods and lakes, scenic vistas

The trail is identified
with numbered markers.

Prince Lake

Duck Pond

Orange Loop
3.6 mi

11 12 13 14 15

Bellis Lake

10

Miller Rd

West Graham Lake

16

17

Shoe Lake

East Graham Lake

Dorn Lake

6 7 8 9

White Loop
2.1 mi

Heart Lake

18

19

Predmore Rd

Lake George Rd

5

Chamberlain Lake

Blue Loop
1.7 mi

3 2

Green Connector
.5 mi

▲ NORTH

Carpenter Lake

new single track

4

Tamarack Lake

Harmon Rd

Stony Creek Rd

0   ¼   ½   1   Miles

Bald Mountain Recreation Area Overview

24

Indian Lake Rd

Manito Lake

Lake Orion

Long Lake

Miller Rd

Conklin

Stony Creek Rd

Lake George Rd

LAKE ORION

Clarkston Rd

Clarkston Rd

Lapeer Rd

Scripps Rd

Greenshield Rd

24

Orion Rd

Adams Rd

Kern Rd

Waldon Rd

Gunn Rd

Joslyn Rd

Lower Trout Lake

Silver Bell Rd

0   ½   1   2   Miles

Southern Section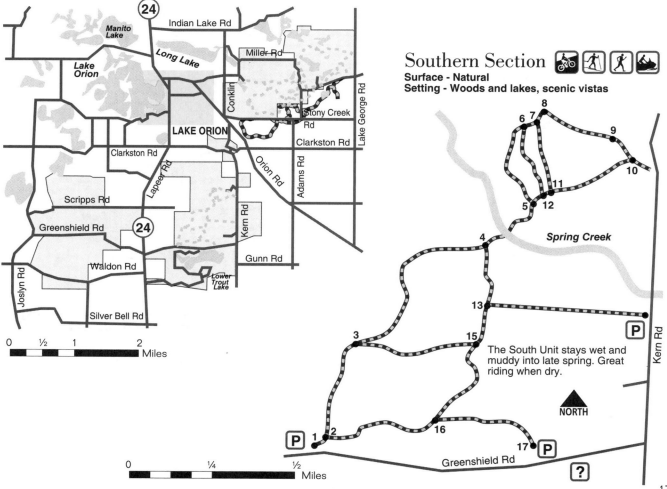

Surface - Natural
Setting - Woods and lakes, scenic vistas

8

6 7

9

10

11

5 12

Spring Creek

4

13

3

15

The South Unit stays wet and
muddy into late spring. Great
riding when dry.

▲ NORTH

Kern Rd

1 2

16

17

Greenshield Rd

[?]

0   ¼   ½   Miles

17

Baw Beese Trail

Trail Uses		**Setting**	Open
Grid	J6 **Trail ID** 110	**Location**	Hillsdale , Osseo
Length	6 miles	**Lat/Long**	41-54 / 83-12 Trailhead-Baw Beese Lake
Surface	Asphalt, ballast	**County**	Hillsdale
Difficulty	Easy	**Contact**	Hillsdale Parks & Recreation Dept. 571-437-3579

Getting There For the east trailhead follow Water Works Avenue on the north side of Baw Beese Lake past several parks to Sandy Beach Park. Take a dirt road about .3 miles east to the trailhead. The trail begins on the northeast side of Baw Beese Lake and ends at Lake Pleasant Road, just north of Hudson Road, southeast of Hillsdale.

Trail Notes The trail was named in honor of Chief Baw Beese of the Potawatomi. The trail runs between Hillsdale and Osseo, and was built on old railroad corridor.

Facilities P T ♦♦

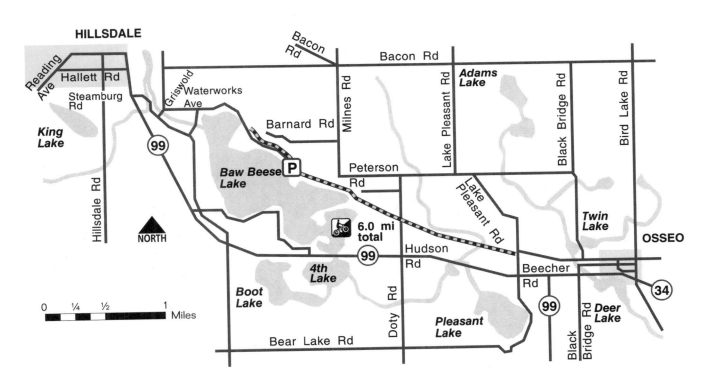

Bay City State Park

Trail Uses	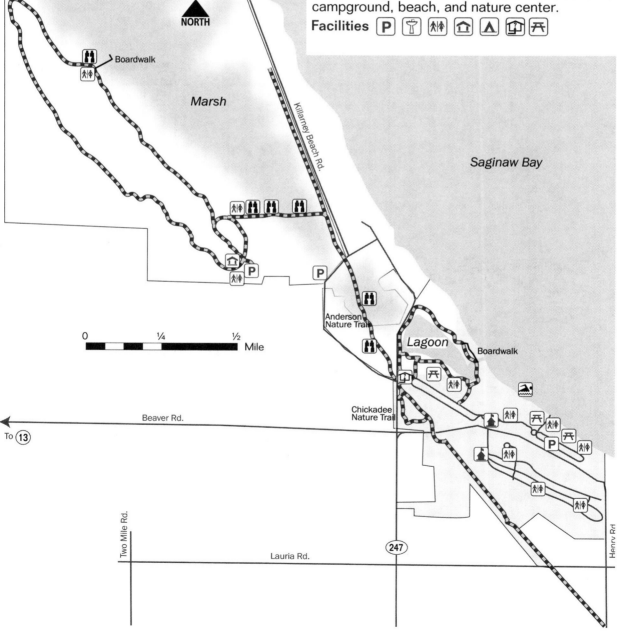	**Setting**	Marsh, forest, beach
Grid	F7 Trail ID ❶	**Location**	Bay City
Length	5 miles	**Lat/Long**	43-40 / 83-54 Park area
Surface	Paved, gravel, natural	**County**	Bay
Difficulty	Easy	**Contact**	Bay City State Recreation Area 989-684-3020
Acres	1,800	**Fees**	Vehicle entry

Getting There Located 5 miles north of Bay City in Bay County. Exit I-75 at Beaver Road (exit 168) and proceed east 5 miles to the park entrance at Euclid Road.

Trail Notes The park encompasses Tobic Lagoon, just west of Saginaw Bay. The setting is predominantly flat, with marsh, forest, and beach area. Effort level is easy. The park has two 30-foot observation towers, a campground, beach, and nature center.

Facilities P ⛲ 🚻 🏠 ⛺ 🏚 🏕

Bloomer Park

Trail Uses		**Setting**	Open areas with some hills and wooded areas

Trail Uses

Grid	H9 **Trail ID** 123
Length	6 miles
Surface	Natural
Difficulty	Moderate

Setting	Open areas with some hills and wooded areas
Location	Rochester Hills
Lat/Long	42-41 / 83-07 Trailhead at John Rd.
County	Oakland
Contact	Bloomer Park 248-656-4753
Fees	Vehicle entry fee

Getting There Bloomer Park is located in the City of Rochester Hills. From Hwy 59, proceed north on John R Road for 3 miles. The park entrance with parking and trail access is a ¼ mile north of Bloomer Road.

Trail Notes Consists of 6 connecting loops, ranging in length from 1.2 to 1.5 miles. Effort level is easy with a terrain that is mostly flat to moderately hilly. The trail offers a beautiful scenic ride along the Historic Canal and Clinton River. Other park facilities include canoeing, tobogganing and a multi-purpose sports field.

Facilities P T ♀♂

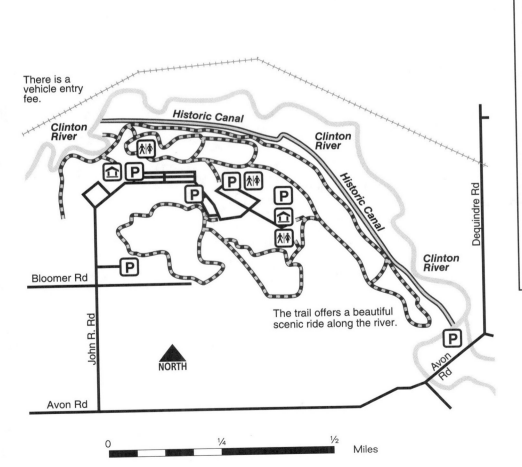

SYMBOL LEGEND

🏊	Beach/Swimming
🚲	Bicycle Repair
🏠	Cabin
▲	Camping
🛶	Canoe Launch
+	First Aid
🍴	Food
GC	Golf Course
?	Information
🛏	Lodging
👤	Overlook/Observation
P	Parking
🚻	Picnic
🏕	Ranger Station
♀♂	Restrooms
⌂	Shelter
T	Trailhead
🏛	Visitor Center
🔻	Water

There is a vehicle entry fee.

Clinton River

Historic Canal

Clinton River

Historic Canal

Clinton River

Dequindre Rd

Bloomer Rd

John R. Rd

The trail offers a beautiful scenic ride along the river.

NORTH

Avon Rd

Avon Rd

0   ¼   ½   Miles

Bridge to Bay Trail

Trail Uses	(icons)
Grid	H11 **Trail ID** 327
Length	54 miles
Surface	Paved
Difficulty	Easy
Setting	Open, rural
Location	Algonac, Marine City, Marysville, New Baltimore, Port Huron, St. Clair
Lat/Long	42-37 / 82-33 Algonac area
County	St. Clair
Contact	St. Clair County Parks 810-989-6960
Getting There	There are many accesses along its route. To get to New Baltimore, take CR 29 east for 2.5 miles from its junction with I-94.
Trail Notes	Over 20 miles of this 54 miles proposed trail has been completed. From New Baltimore it parallels the north shoreline of Lake St. Clair and then continues north along the west side of the St. Clair River between Algonac, past Port Huron, to the St. Clair/Sanilac County line. Its sections consist of boardwalks, river walks, rail trails and bike paths, connecting communities, parks, beaches, and tourist attractions.
Facilities	(icons)

TRAIL LEGEND

▪▪▪▪▪▪▪▪	Trail
– – – – –	Skiing only Trail
▪▪▪▪▪▪▪▪	Hiking only Trail
– – – – –	Planned Trail
▪ ▪ ▪ ▪	Alternate Trail
────────	Road
++++++++	Railroad Tracks

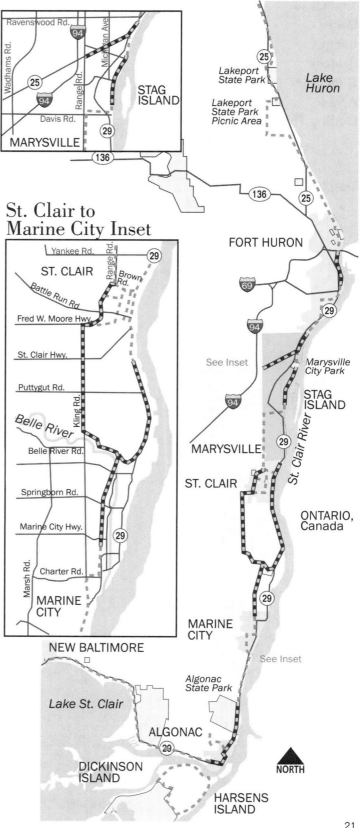

21

Brighton Recreation Area

Trail Uses

Grid I7 **Trail ID** 127

Length 18 miles

Surface Natural

Difficulty Easy to moderate

Acres 5,000

Setting Rolling hills and meadows, woods, marshes, lakes, streams

Location Brighton

Lat/Long 42-29 / 83-50 Bishop Lake parking area

County Livingston

Contact Brighton Recreation Area   810-229-6566

Fees Vehicle entry

Getting There Five miles southwest of the I-96 and I-23 interchange in Livingston County. From Brighton, take Brighton Road 4 miles to West Chilson Road, then south 1.5 miles to Bishop Lake Road. East on Bishop Lake Road to the trailhead at the south end of the Bishop Lake parking lot.

Trail Notes Brighton Recreation Area consists of nearly 5,000 acres. The trails are maintained in part by the Michigan Mountain Biking Association. Generally hardpack, with occasional patches of sand. Terrain varies between hilly, moderate and flat, with some steep area. Restrooms and drinking water are located in the parking area. Concessions and camping is both rustic and modern.

Facilities

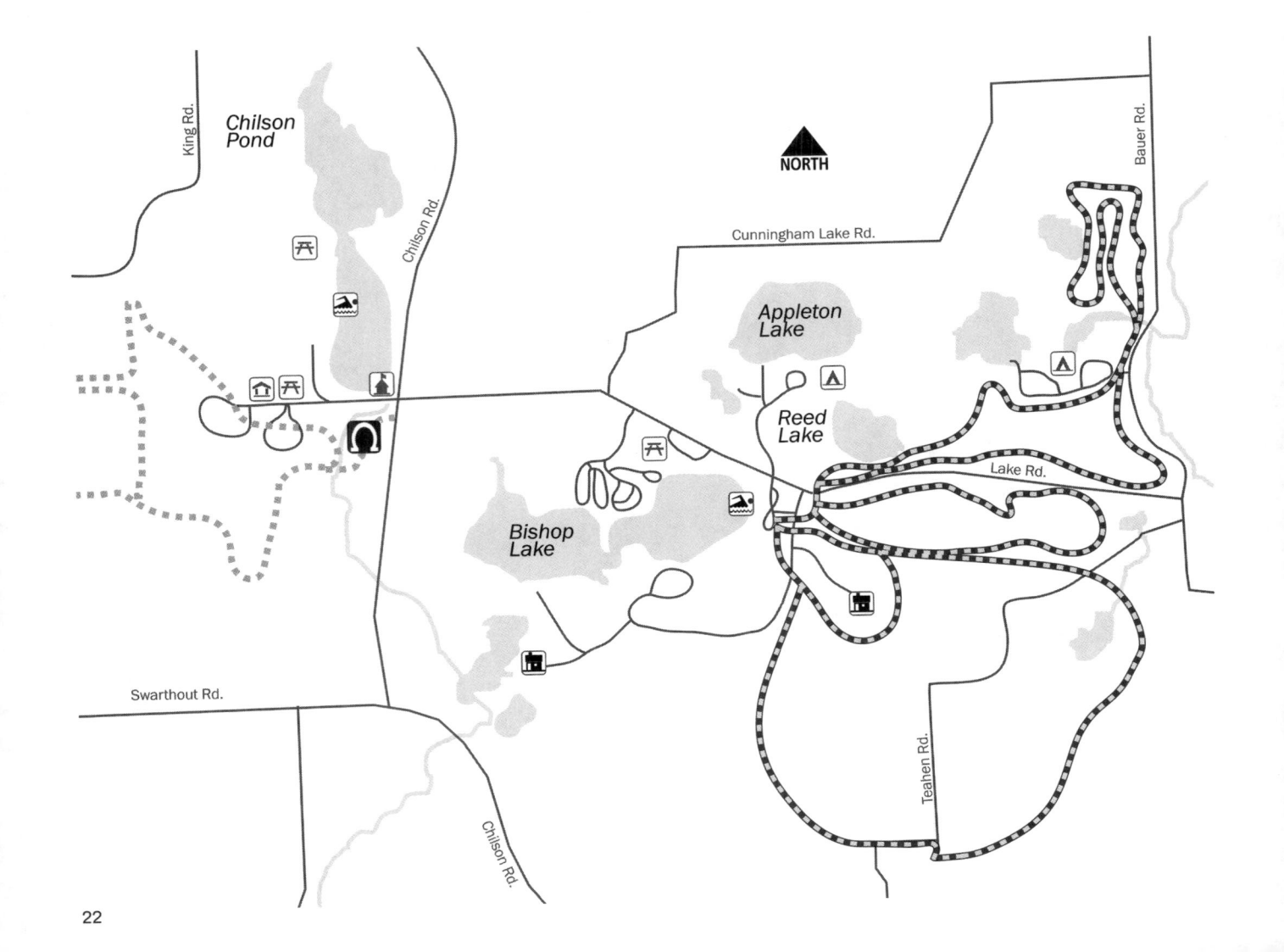

William M.Burchfield Park
Grand River Park

Trail Uses	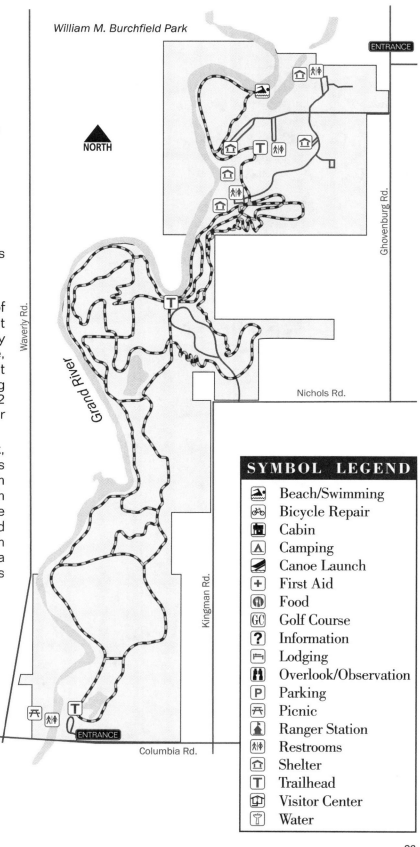
Grid	H6 **Trail ID** 129
Length	4.5
Surface	Natural
Difficulty	Easy to moderate
Setting	Woods, meadows
Hours	Half hour before sunrise to a half hour after sunset
Location	Mason
Lat/Long	42-37 / 84-35 Parking area
County	Ingram
Contact	Ingram County Parks Dept. 517-676-2233
Fees	Vehicle entry
Getting There	From I-96, south of Lansing, exit on M-99 (exit 101), south to Waverly Road, then left for a mile, and left again onto Holt Road. At Grovenburg Road, head south for 2 miles to the Grand River Park entrance.
Trail Notes	The trail is single track, clockwise, and is considered easy with few climbs. The north trailhead is located at the northern end of Grand River Park, and the south trailhead by McNamara Landing. The trail is posted.
Facilities	P ⊤ ⚹ ⛱

TRAIL LEGEND

▪▪▪▪▪▪	Trail
▬ ▬ ▬ ▬	Skiing only Trail
▪▪▪▪▪▪▪▪	Hiking only Trail
- - - - -	Planned Trail
▬ ▬ ▬ ▬	Alternate Trail
▬▬▬▬	Road
+++++++	Railroad Tracks

William M. Burchfield Park

NORTH

Waverly Rd.

Grand River

Ghovenburg Rd.

Nichols Rd.

Kingman Rd.

ENTRANCE

Columbia Rd.

ENTRANCE

SYMBOL LEGEND

🏊	Beach/Swimming
🚲	Bicycle Repair
🏚	Cabin
⚠	Camping
🛶	Canoe Launch
➕	First Aid
🍴	Food
GC	Golf Course
?	Information
🛏	Lodging
🔭	Overlook/Observation
P	Parking
⛱	Picnic
🏛	Ranger Station
⚹	Restrooms
🏠	Shelter
T	Trailhead
🏢	Visitor Center
⊤	Water

Clinton River Trail

Trail Uses	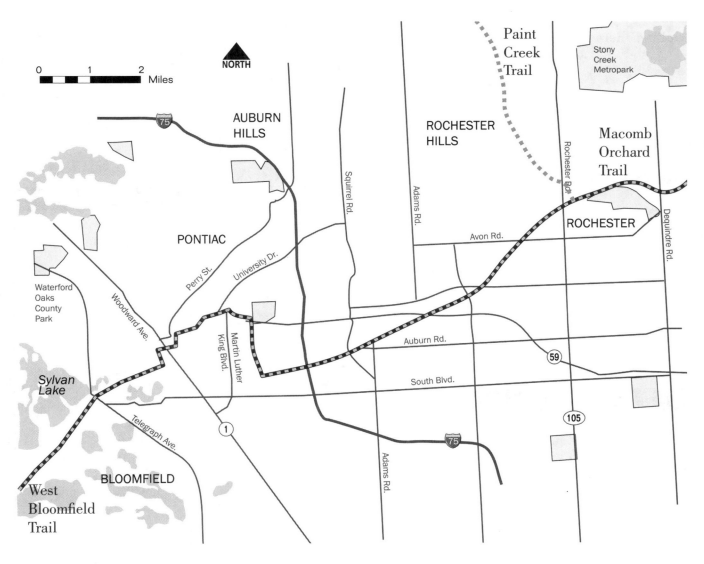	**Setting**	Urban, parks, open
Grid	H9 **Trail ID** 328	**Location**	Bloomfield Hills, Rochester
Length	12	**Lat/Long**	42-38 / 83-15 Rochester area
Surface	Paved (partially open)	**County**	Oakland
Difficulty	Easy	**Contact**	The Green Collaborative 734-668-8848

Getting There   The eastern trailhead is located in Bloomer Park by Rochester. There are many access points along the route.

Trail Notes   This is a multi-use path through the eastern half of Oakland County, and primarily located on abandoned railroad grade. It passes through the cities of Sylvan Lake, Pontiac, Auburn Hills, Rochester Hills and Rochester, and connects with the existing West Bloomfield trail to the west and the Macomb Orchard Trail to the east. The landscape includes downtowns, industry, residential areas, parks, and open land.

Facilities

Clio Area Bike Path

Trail Uses	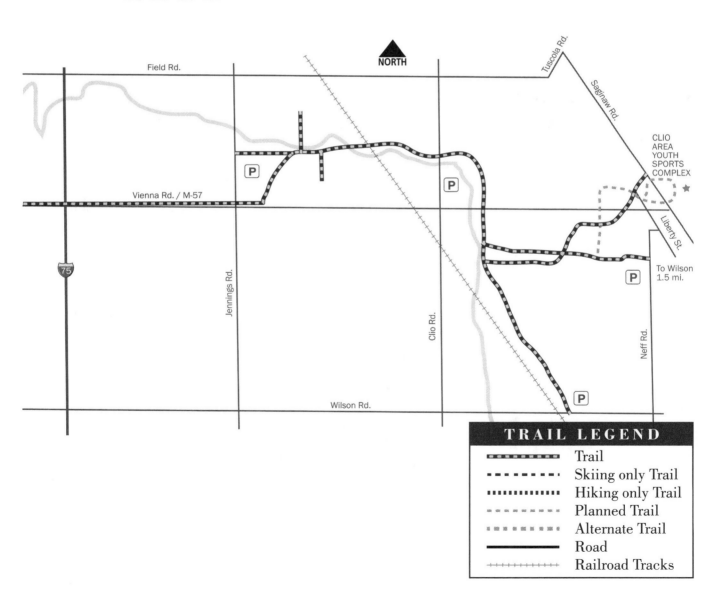	**Setting**	Woods, open
Grid	G8 **Trail ID** 329	**Location**	Clio
Length	5 miles	**Lat/Long**	43-11 / 83-44 Clio area
Surface	Paved	**County**	Genesee
Difficulty	Easy	**Contact**	Clio Chamber of Commerce 810-686-4480

Getting There   The path is easily accessible from parking lots off Jennings, Wilson, and Neff Road, as in the Clio City Park.

Trail Notes   The Path is located along the scenic Pine Run Creek in the City of Clio in northern Genesee County. It is a 5 mile long, 10-foot wide concrete surfaced path. It meanders through woodlands, parks, residential, and commercial area.

Facilities

TRAIL LEGEND

· · · · · · · · · Trail
- - - - - - - Skiing only Trail
· · · · · · · · · · Hiking only Trail
- - - - - - - Planned Trail
- - - - - - - Alternate Trail
———————— Road
++++++++++ Railroad Tracks

Ella Sharp Single Track

Trail Uses		Setting	Woods, open, flat to rolling	
Grid	I6 **Trail ID** 330	Location	Jackson	
Trail ID	330	Lat/Long	42-14 / 84-27 Jackson area	
Length	13 miles	County	Jackson	
Surface	Natural, paved & dirt road	Contact	Ella Sharp Park 517-789-7533	
Difficulty	Moderate	Fees	Vehicle entry	

Getting There   Go north on Stonewall Road about a quarter mile from Horton Road. The Park entrance is left (east). Go to the stop sign, and then north on Oakwood Street to Birchwood Drive. Turn east to the parking area a quarter mile further.

Trail Notes   There are 13 trail loops in all. They are clearly signed. The trail system is easy to follow and mostly open with occasional gravel and loose rocks. The vehicle entrance fee is paid at park headquarters.

Facilities   P

SYMBOL LEGEND

- Beach/Swimming
- Bicycle Repair
- Cabin
- Camping
- Canoe Launch
- First Aid
- Food
- GC Golf Course
- Information
- Lodging
- Overlook/Observation
- P Parking
- Picnic
- Ranger Station
- Restrooms
- Shelter
- T Trailhead
- Visitor Center
- Water

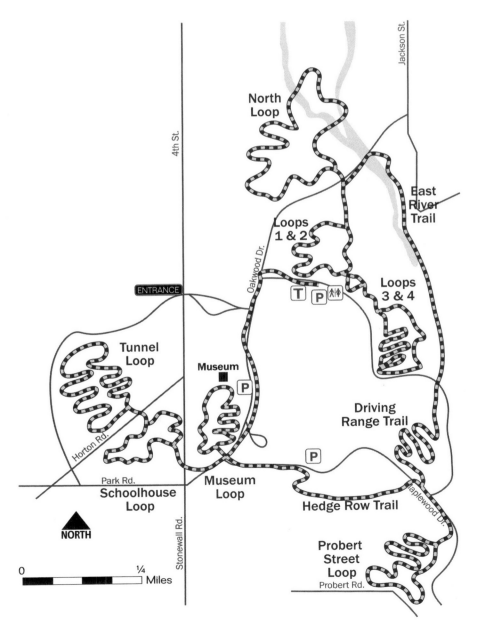

Flint River Trail

Trail Uses	🚴 🛼 🏃	**Setting**	Woods, open, urban
Grid	G8 **Trail ID** 331	**Location**	Flint
Length	13 miles	**Lat/Long**	43-02 / 83-41 Flint area
Surface	Paved, dirt roads	**County**	Genesee
Difficulty	Easy	**Contact**	Flint River Watershed Coalition 810-767-6490

Getting There The trail can be accessed from I-475 at Robert T. Longway or Carpenter Road.

Trail Notes The Flint River Trail is a multi-use trail running along one or both sides of the Flint River from downtown Flint through Flint and Genesee County Park to the City of Genesee. The trail is mostly asphalt with some undeveloped area on road or dirt tracks.

Facilities P 🍸 🚻 🎧

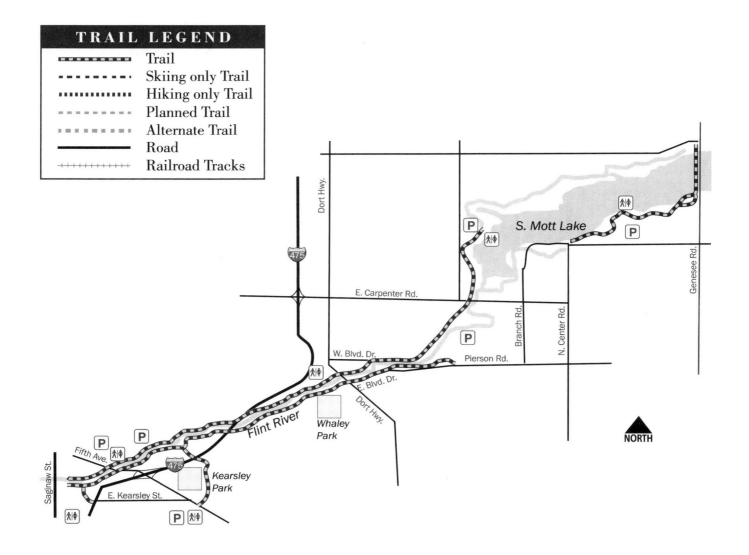

TRAIL LEGEND

▪▪▪▪▪▪▪	Trail
▪ ▪ ▪ ▪ ▪	Skiing only Trail
▪▪▪▪▪▪▪▪	Hiking only Trail
▪ ▪ ▪ ▪ ▪	Planned Trail
▪ ▪ ▪ ▪ ▪	Alternate Trail
————	Road
+++++++++	Railroad Tracks

Heritage Park

Trail Uses			
Grid	J7 **Trail ID** 332	**Setting**	Flat to rolling, farmland
Length	9.5 miles - loops	**Location**	Adrian
Surface	7.5 miles natural, 2 miles of dirt road	**Lat/Long**	41-56 / 84-00 Adrian area
		County	Lenawee
Difficulty	Easy to difficult	**Contact**	City of Adrian 517-268-2161

Getting There   Located in the City of Adrian in southeastern Michigan about 2 miles north of the city limits. From Hwy 52, north on Main Street for about 2 miles, then right on North Adrian Drive. Follow the signs to Heritage Park. Turn left (east) to the parking area.

Trail Notes   The trail varies from wide to twisting singletrack. It is well designed and generally marked with white arrows. Most of the trail is singletrack, with some doubletrack and dirt road. The setting is made up of farmland and tree-lined knolls and is generally flat. The Michigan Mountain Biking Association assists in the maintenance of this trail.

Facilities   P

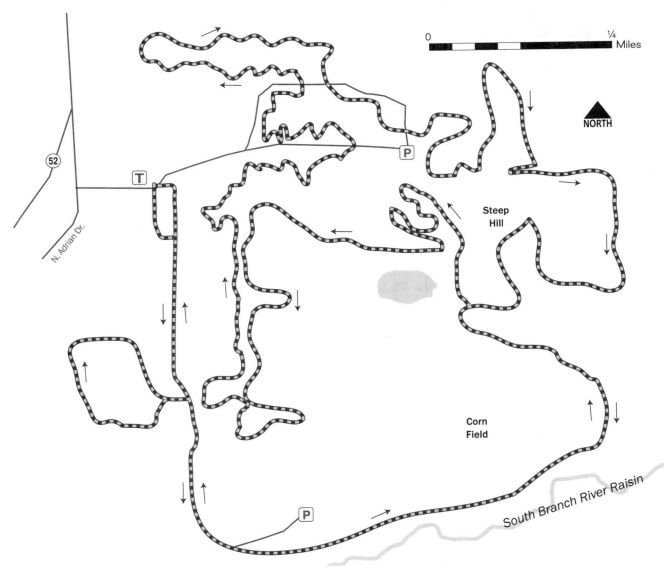

Highland Recreation Area

Trail Uses		**Setting**	Rolling, hilly
Grid	H8 **Trail ID** 169	**Location**	Highland, Milford
Length	17 miles	**Lat/Long**	42-38 / 83-34 Haven Hill Lake parking
Surface	Natural	**County**	Oakland
Difficulty	Moderate to difficult	**Contact**	Highland Recreation Area 248-889-3750
Acres	5.900	**Fees**	Vehicle entry

Getting There The Recreation Area is located approximately 17 miles northeast of the I-96 and I-23 intersection in Brighton, or 15 miles west of the M-59 and I-24 intersections in Pontiac. From M-59, exit south on Duck Lake Road for a mile to Livingston Road. Proceed west (right) for .2 miles to the entrance on the south side of the road, where there is access to the trail across the parking lot, and Park Headquarters nearby.

Trail Notes There are 4 connecting loops, ranging in length from 3.0 to 4.5 miles. The biking trails are ridden clockwise. Effort level is difficult. Hilly, with heavy woods, some open areas, and numerous ponds along the route. You will experience marsh in Loop A and swamp in Loop C. There is a separate horse trail except for the initial stretch on Loop A. Toilets are located at the trailhead, but drinking water is not available. Bring repellent during the hot summer months.

Facilities P   👫   🏕   🔺   🏊

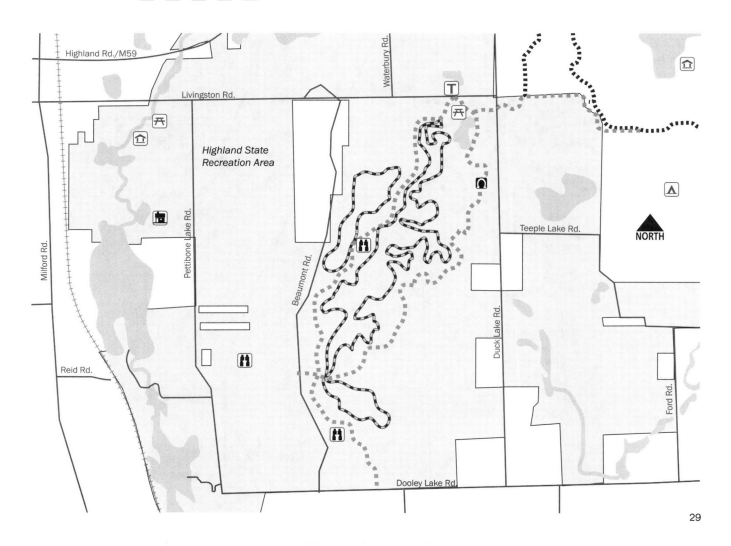

Holly State Recreation Area
Holdridge Lakes

Trail Uses

Grid   H8 **Trail ID** 172

Length   23 miles, loops

Surface   Natural

Difficulty   Easy to difficult

Setting   Flat, rolling, woods, meadows, beach

Location   Holly, Waterford

Lat/Long   42-50 / 83-35   Parking off Hess Rd

County   Oakland

Contact   Holly Recreation Area   248-634-8811

Fees   Vehicle entry

Getting There   Located about 18 miles northwest of Pontiac and 12 miles south of Flint in Oakland County. Exit I-75 westbound at Grange Hall Road (exit 101) for less than a half mile to Hess Road. Go north on Hess Road for 1.4 miles to parking and the trailhead.

Trail Notes   The loop trails are single track. There is a ¾ mile loop called Turtle Trail, the North Loop is 2.2 miles long; and the West Loop is 5 miles long. The Long and Short loops run clockwise, and the North loop runs counter clockwise. The more advanced trail is 15 miles long and is called Gruber's Grinder. The setting is rolling hills with woods, low marshes, and beach area. It is generally hard packed, and there are some floating bridges in the marsh areas. The trail system was built and is maintained by members of the Michigan Mountain Biking Association.

Facilities   P ⛱ ⛺ 🏊

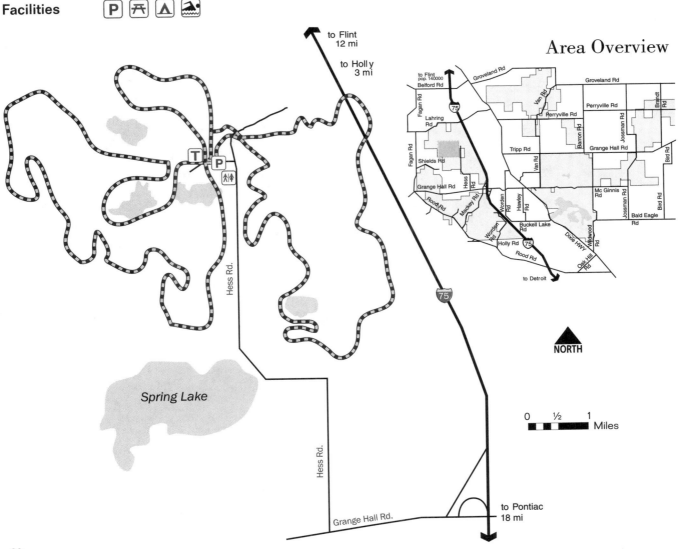

Hudson Mills MetroPark

Trail Uses	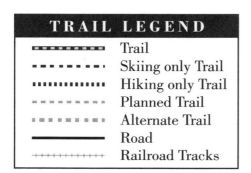	**Setting**	Woods, meadows, lagoon, flat
Grid	I7 **Trail ID** 174	**Location**	Dexter, Hudson Mills
Length	2.7 miles	**Lat/Long**	42-22 / 83-54 Parking area
Surface	Paved	**County**	Washenaw
Difficulty	Easy	**Contact**	Hudson Mills Metropark 313-477-2757
Acres	1,600	**Fees**	Vehicle entry

Getting There From the junction of I-23 and I-14 just north of Ann Arbor, take I-23 north for 4.5 miles north to North Territorial Road, then west for 8 miles to the park entrance.

Trail Notes Hudson Mills is a 1,600-acre park located 12 miles northwest of Ann Arbor. The west side of the loop trail parallels the Huron River. There is a separate nature trail and an Activity Center.

Facilities P T ♦♦ ⓜ ⊼ ◸ GC

TRAIL LEGEND

▪▪▪▪▪▪	Trail
▪ ▪ ▪ ▪	Skiing only Trail
▪▪▪▪▪▪▪	Hiking only Trail
▪ ▪ ▪ ▪	Planned Trail
▪ ▪ ▪ ▪	Alternate Trail
———	Road
++++++++	Railroad Tracks

SYMBOL LEGEND

🏊	Beach/Swimming
🚲	Bicycle Repair
🏠	Cabin
ⓐ	Camping
◸	Canoe Launch
+	First Aid
ⓜ	Food
GC	Golf Course
?	Information
🛏	Lodging
🛉	Overlook/Observation
P	Parking
⊼	Picnic
🏛	Ranger Station
♦♦	Restrooms
🏠	Shelter
T	Trailhead
🏛	Visitor Center
T	Water

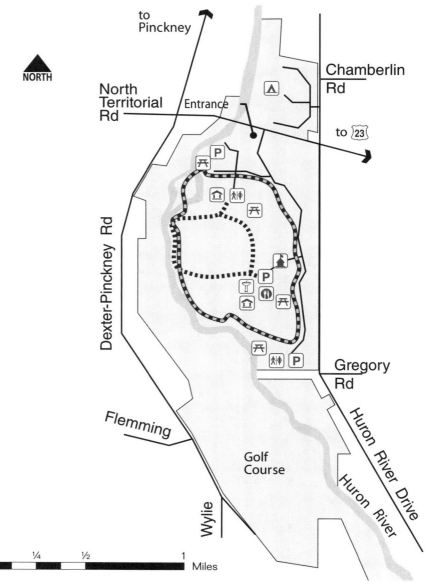

Huron Valley Trail

Trail Uses	🚴 🛼 🏃 ⛷️	**Setting**	Urban, open areas
Grid	I8 **Trail ID** 333	**Location**	Wixom, South Lyon
Length	25 miles	**Lat/Long**	Latitude 42-38 Longitude 83-39 South Lyon
Surface	Paved	**County**	Oakland
Difficulty	Easy	**Contact**	City of South Lyon 248-437-1735

Getting There   In addition to parking and access from the parks mentioned in the Trail Notes, there is also access from major road crossing such as Pontiac Trail, Grand River Avenue, Milford road, and Ten Mile Road.

Trail Notes   Built on former railroad corridor, connecting the cities of Wixom and South Lyon. It connects to numerous area parks including Lyon Oaks County Park Lyon Township Community Park, Kensington Metro Metro-Park and Island Lake State Recreation Area. The Trailway to South Lyon is relatively flat, while the section to Kensington/Island Lake provides some challenging hills.

Facilities   🅿️ 🚰 🚻 🛑

Indian Springs MetroPark

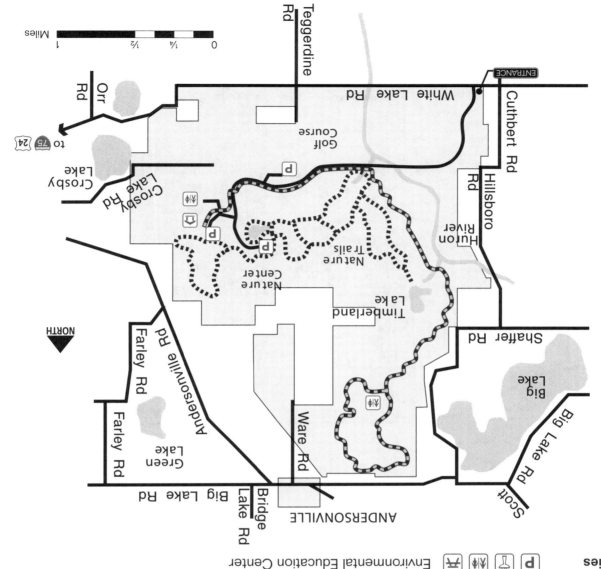

Trail Uses		**Setting**	Wooded, most flat with one big hill
Grid	H8 **Trail ID** 179	**Location**	White Lake
Difficulty	Easy	**Contact**	Indian Springs Metro Park 248-625-7280
Length	8 miles	**Lat/Long**	42-43 / 83-29 Nature Center parking
Surface	Paved	**County**	Oakland
Acres	2,232	**Fees**	Vehicle entry

Getting There From the intersection of I-24, Routes 59 and 75 in Pontiac, take I-24 northwest for 8 miles to Andersonville Road, then west 2 miles to While Lake Road. Continue west on West Lake Road to the park entrance a 1/2 mile west of the Huron River.

Trail Notes Indian Springs consists of 2,232-acres of parkland at the headwaters of the Huron River, 9 miles Northwest of Pontiac. Much of the park is dedicated to the preservation and interpretation of the natural setting. Facilities include toilets, water, concession and picnic shelters. Advance reservations are necessary for picnic areas. There is a separate nature trail and Nature Center.

Facilities [P] [picnic] [restroom] [shelter] Environmental Education Center

Island Lake Recreation Area

Trail Uses		**Setting**	Hardwood forest, open meadows
Grid	I8 **Trail ID** 182	**Location**	Brighton
Length	18 miles	**Lat/Long**	42-30 / 83-45 Parking area
Surface	Nature	**County**	Livingston
Difficulty	Easy to moderate	**Contact**	Island Lake Recreation Area 810-229-7067
Acres	4,000	**Fees**	Vehicle entry

Getting There The Park is about 4 miles east of Brighton. Exit I-96 south on Kensington Road (exit 151) for a half mile to the Park entrance on the east side of the road. Parking for the east trailhead is about .7 miles east of Kensington Road. Parking for the west trailhead is a little over a mile west of Kensington Road.

Trail Notes This is one of the most popular trails in southeast Michigan. Effort level is easy to moderate. The setting consists of meadows, rolling terrain, lake, wooded area, and farmland. The Huron River winds through the middle of the park and is open to canoeing. The East Loop (Yellow Loop) is over 5 miles and single track, and is the more difficult of the two with its steep descents and woods. The West loop is over 9 miles, single track, and more open. The trails are clearly marked and run counter-clockwise. Two-way short trails take you from the parking lot the East loop trailhead.

Facilities

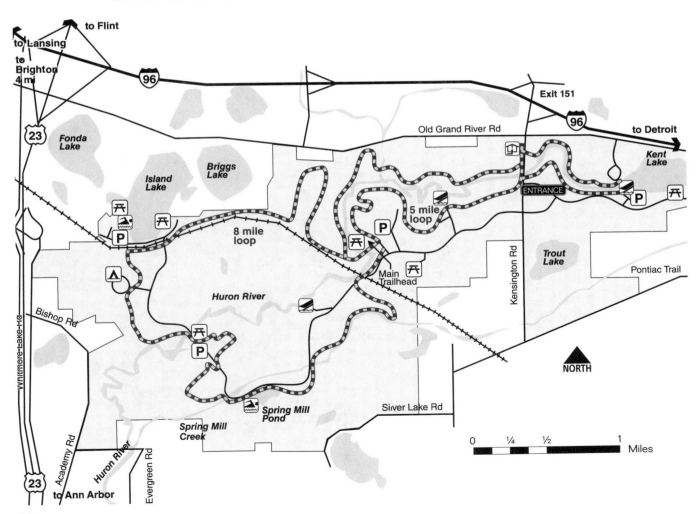

Ithaca Jailhouse Trail

Trail Uses	🚴 🏃 🚶	**Setting**	Flat, small hills, woods, farmland
Grid	G6 **Trail ID** 305	**Location**	Ithaca
Length	4 miles, loops	**Lat/Long**	43-17 / 84-37 Trailhead area
Surface	Natural, singletrack	**County**	Gratiot
Difficulty	Easy to moderate	**Contact**	City of Itaca 517-875-3200

Getting There Center Street in downtown Ithaca west to South River Road, then south past the main fairground area, across a parking area field to the west and the trailhead. Note: Center Street becomes Washington Road outside of town.

Trail Notes The trail is attached to the county fair grounds. It's wooded, consists of many loops, and was developed as a mountain bike trail. The trail is marked with large red arrows. Effort level is easy to moderate. Riding in dry conditions is recommended because of the heavy clay soil.

Facilities 🏕️ 🅿️

TRAIL LEGEND

▪▪▪▪▪ Trail
▪ ▪ ▪ ▪ Skiing only Trail
▪▪▪▪▪▪ Hiking only Trail
▪ ▪ ▪ ▪ Planned Trail
▪ ▪ ▪ ▪ Alternate Trail
—— Road
+++++ Railroad Tracks

SYMBOL LEGEND

🏊 Beach/Swimming
🚲 Bicycle Repair
🏛️ Cabin
🔺 Camping
🛶 Canoe Launch
➕ First Aid
🍴 Food
GC Golf Course
? Information
🛏️ Lodging
🔭 Overlook/Observation
🅿️ Parking
🏕️ Picnic
🗼 Ranger Station
🚻 Restrooms
🏠 Shelter
T Trailhead
🏢 Visitor Center
🚰 Water

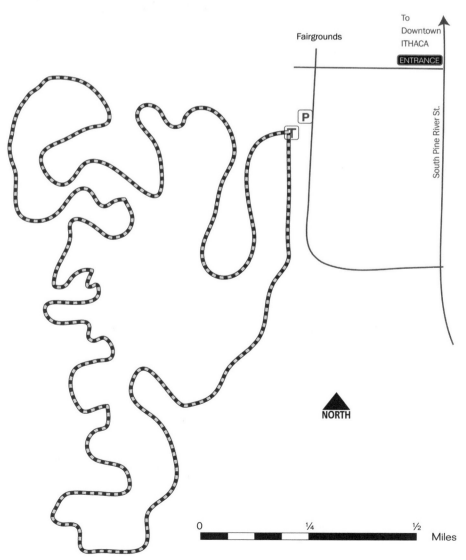

35

Kensington MetroPark

Trail Uses	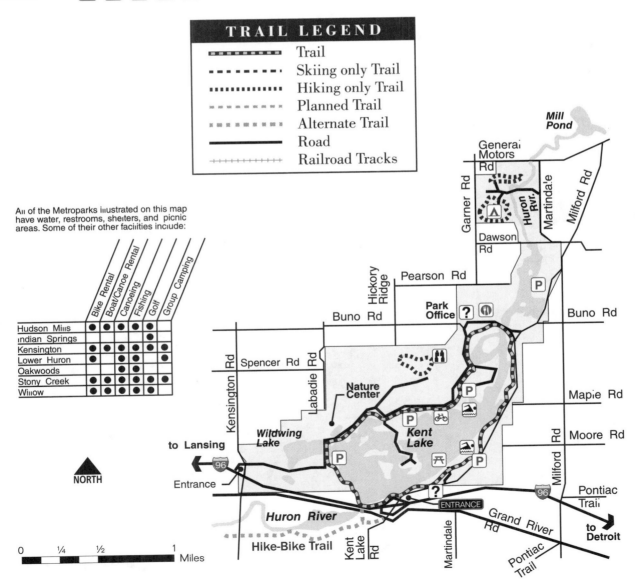	**Setting**	Woods, open
Grid	I8 **Trail ID** 184	**Hours**	Daylight to dusk
Length	8 miles	**Location**	Milford
Surface	Paved, gravel	**Lat/Long**	43-32 / 83-36 Kent Lake Beach parking
Difficulty	Easy to moderate	**Counties**	Oakland, Livingston
Acres	4,357	**Contact**	Kensington Metro Park 313-227-2757
		Fees	Vehicle entry

Getting There   Exit I-96 at Lake Road (exit 153) southwest of Milford, then north to the park.

Trail Notes   The trail system consists of 4 loops. The Tamarack Trail is a half mile long. It leads you through remnants of an ancient bog. The Dear Run Trail is 1.75 miles long (1.25 miles with the shortcut). Setting is field and forest habitats, with beautiful spring wildflowers. Aspen Trail is 1.3 miles long, and wanders through a variety of habitats. The Wildwing Trail is 2.5 miles long and encircles Wildwing Lake.

Facilities   Nature Center

TRAIL LEGEND

- Trail
- Skiing only Trail
- Hiking only Trail
- Planned Trail
- Alternate Trail
- Road
- Railroad Tracks

All of the Metroparks illustrated on this map have water, restrooms, shelters, and picnic areas. Some of their other facilities include:

	Bike Rental	Boat/Canoe Rental	Canoeing	Fishing	Golf	Group Camping
Hudson Mills	●	●	●	●		
Indian Springs					●	
Kensington	●	●	●	●		
Lower Huron	●		●	●		●
Oakwoods			●	●		
Stony Creek	●	●	●	●	●	●
Willow	●	●	●	●	●	

0   ¼   ½   1
Miles

Kiwanis Trail

Trail Uses		**Setting**	Old railroad right-of-way, open
Grid	J7 **Trail ID** 187	**Location**	Adrian
Length	7 miles	**Lat/Long**	41-54 / 84-03 Adrian-Michigan & Water St.
Surface	Asphalt	**County**	Lenawee
Difficulty	Easy	**Contact**	City of Adrian 517-263-2161

Getting There   The trail begins at Trestle Park in Adrian. The park entrance is north of the city off M-52. The southern trailhead is located off Route 223 just west of the Raisin River and east of Adrian College.

Trail Notes   The southern trailhead begins in downtown Adrian, and was developed on railroad right-of-way. The trail continues northeast, ending at Ives Road. A popular attraction in route is Trestle Park. The pathway is lighted.

Facilities   P 🚻 🪑 🏠   Amphitheater

SYMBOL LEGEND

- Beach/Swimming
- Bicycle Repair
- Cabin
- Camping
- Canoe Launch
- First Aid
- Food
- Golf Course
- Information
- Lodging
- Overlook/Observation
- Parking
- Picnic
- Ranger Station
- Restrooms
- Shelter
- Trailhead
- Visitor Center
- Water

Lakelands Trail State Park

Trail Uses			
Grid	I7 **Trail ID** 190	**Location**	Stockbridge, Pinckney
Length	13 miles, linear	**Lat/Long**	42-27 / 83-48 Hamburg trailhead at Hall Rd
Surface	Crushed stone	**Counties**	Ingham, Livingston, Washtenaw
Difficulty	Easy	**Contact**	Lakelands Trail State Park 734-426-4913
Setting	Open	**Fees**	Trail pass

Getting There   At the western trailhead in Stockbridge, parking is available at the park-and-ride lot on M-52/106, south of the Stockbridge Township Hall on the village square. The Pinckney trailhead is located a quarter mile north of M-36 on D-19.

Trail Notes   The Park was developed on abandoned railroad right-of-way, and runs from Stockbridge to Pinckney. The area is rural, with wooded areas, rolling farmland, and small communities.

Facilities

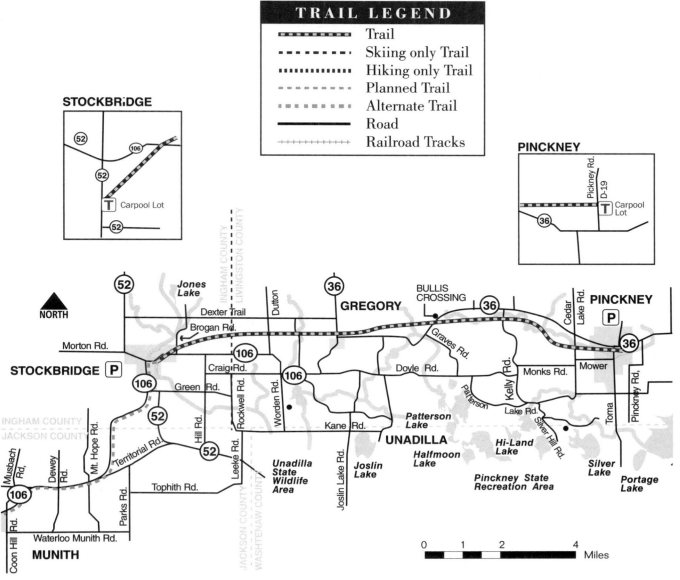

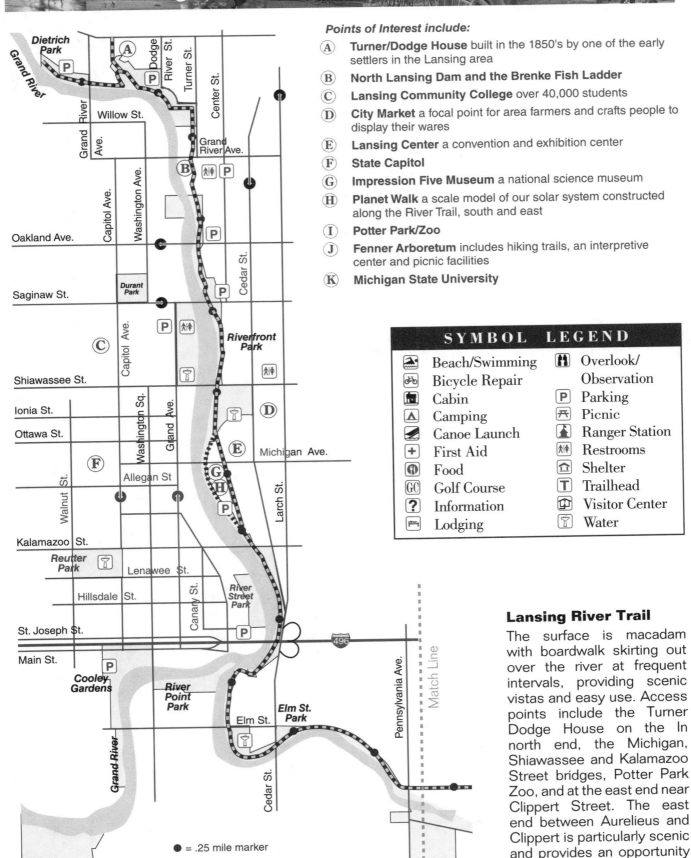

Points of Interest include:

Ⓐ **Turner/Dodge House** built in the 1850's by one of the early settlers in the Lansing area

Ⓑ **North Lansing Dam and the Brenke Fish Ladder**

Ⓒ **Lansing Community College** over 40,000 students

Ⓓ **City Market** a focal point for area farmers and crafts people to display their wares

Ⓔ **Lansing Center** a convention and exhibition center

Ⓕ **State Capitol**

Ⓖ **Impression Five Museum** a national science museum

Ⓗ **Planet Walk** a scale model of our solar system constructed along the River Trail, south and east

Ⓘ **Potter Park/Zoo**

Ⓙ **Fenner Arboretum** includes hiking trails, an interpretive center and picnic facilities

Ⓚ **Michigan State University**

SYMBOL LEGEND

	Beach/Swimming		Overlook/ Observation
	Bicycle Repair		
	Cabin	Ⓟ	Parking
Ⓐ	Camping		Picnic
	Canoe Launch		Ranger Station
+	First Aid		Restrooms
	Food		Shelter
GC	Golf Course	Ⓣ	Trailhead
?	Information		Visitor Center
	Lodging		Water

● = .25 mile marker

Lansing River Trail

The surface is macadam with boardwalk skirting out over the river at frequent intervals, providing scenic vistas and easy use. Access points include the Turner Dodge House on the In north end, the Michigan, Shiawassee and Kalamazoo Street bridges, Potter Park Zoo, and at the east end near Clippert Street. The east end between Aurelieus and Clippert is particularly scenic and provides an opportunity to experience wetlands, woods and native wildlife.

Lansing River Trail

Lansing River Trail

Trail Uses	🚴 ⛸ 🏃 🚶	**Setting**	Riverfront park land, urban
Grid	H6 **Trail ID** 253	**Location**	Lansing
Length	6 miles	**Lat/Long**	42-43 / 84-30 Potter Park Zoo
Surface	Asphalt	**County**	Ingham
Difficulty	Easy	**Contact**	Lansing City Hall 517-483-4277

Getting There   The eastern trailhead is located at the south end of Clippert Street just west of the Michigan State University campus. The western trailhead is located at Grand River Avenue at the Grand River.

Trail Notes   The River Trail parallels the Grand and Red Cedar River in Lansing. Points of interest along the route include the Turner/Dodge House, North Lansing Dam, Lansing Community College, State Capitol, Impression Five Museum, Planet Walk, Potter Park/Zoo, Fenner Arboretum, and Michigan State University. The east end between Aurelieus and Clippert is particularly scenic and provides an opportunity to experience wetlands, woods, and native wildlife.

Facilities   P ⛲ 🚻

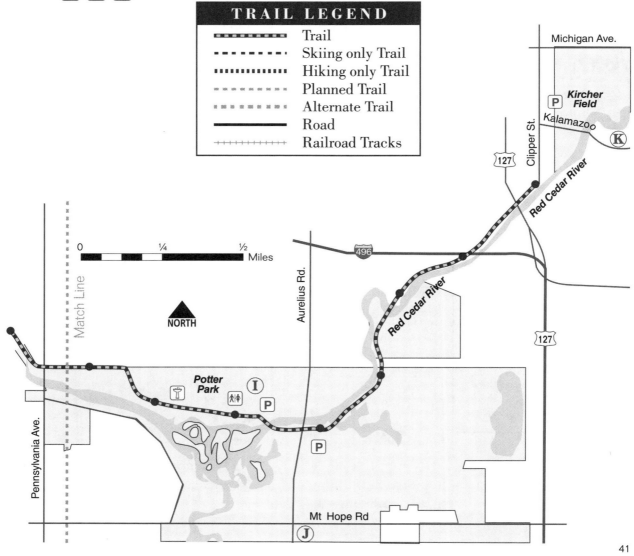

TRAIL LEGEND

▪▪▪▪▪▪▪▪	Trail
▪ ▪ ▪ ▪ ▪ ▪	Skiing only Trail
▪▪▪▪▪▪▪▪▪▪	Hiking only Trail
▪ ▪ ▪ ▪ ▪ ▪	Planned Trail
▪ ▪ ▪ ▪ ▪ ▪	Alternate Trail
─────	Road
+++++++++++	Railroad Tracks

Lower Huron MetroPark

Trail Uses	
Grid	I9 **Trail ID** 196
Length	5 miles, linear
Surface	Asphalt
Difficulty	Easy
Acres	1,258

Hours	6 am to 10 pm
Setting	Woods, Huron River
Location	New Boston, Romulus
Lat/Long	42-09 / 83-24 Trailhead at Waltz Rd
County	Wayne
Contact	Lower Huron Metro Park 734-697-9181
Fees	Vehicle entry

Getting There   From the I-94/275 interchange, take I-94 west 1 mile to the Haggerty Rd exit. Proceed south .6 mile to Huron River Dr, then west .4 mile where you pick up Haggerty Road again southbound. About 2 miles further is Bemis Road and the park entrance to the left.

Trail Notes   A 1,258-acre park straddling the Huron River just southwest of I-94 and I-275 interchange. The scenic Huron River and mature trees provide the perfect setting for any activity.

Facilities

Guided nature tours

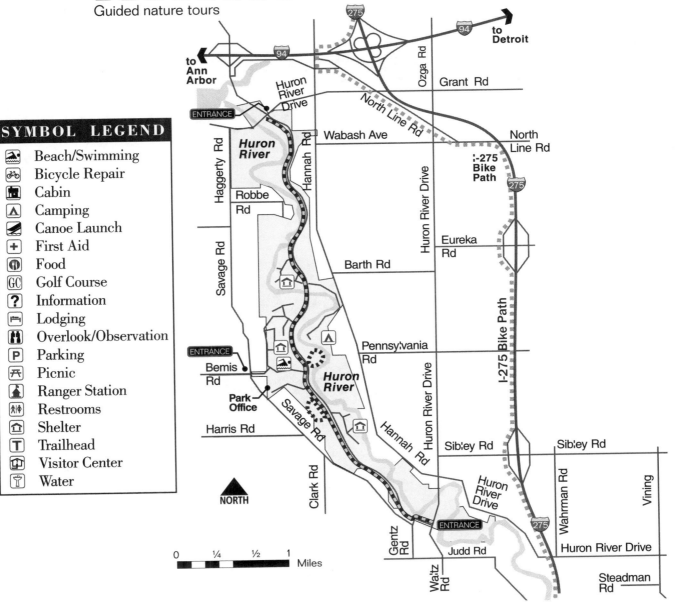

SYMBOL LEGEND

	Beach/Swimming
	Bicycle Repair
	Cabin
	Camping
	Canoe Launch
	First Aid
	Food
GC	Golf Course
?	Information
	Lodging
	Overlook/Observation
P	Parking
	Picnic
	Ranger Station
	Restrooms
	Shelter
T	Trailhead
	Visitor Center
	Water

Maybury State Park

Trail Uses		**Setting**	Forest, meadows, rolling hills
Grid	I8 **Trail ID** 206	**Location**	Northville
Length	19 miles	**Lat/Long**	42-26 / 83-32 Maybury Living Farm
Surface	Paved, natural	**Counties**	Oakland, Wayne
Difficulty	Easy to moderate	**Contact**	Maybury State Park 248-349-8390
Acres	1,000	**Fees**	Vehicle entry

Getting There From I-96 take Beck Road (exit 159) south for about 4 miles and past 8 Mile Road. The entrance is on the right side of the road. Follow the entrance road past the park headquarters to parking and a staging area for both mountain bikers and horses. The trailhead is .4 miles further west by way of a two-track trail.

Trail Notes Maybury consists of 1,000-acres of gently rolling terrain, open meadow, mature forest with a variety of wildlife and wildflowers. The mountain biking trails takes advantage of its dense woods, with sudden, short climbs and winding singletrack, and are maintained in part by the Michigan Mountain Biking Association. The mountain biking trails are closed from December 15 to April 15.

Facilities P ⛲ 🚻 🎧 🎋 🏠 ⛺

TRAIL LEGEND

▬ ▬ ▬ ▬	Trail
- - - - -	Skiing only Trail
▪▪▪▪▪▪▪▪	Hiking only Trail
━ ━ ━	Planned Trail
▪ ▫ ▪ ▫ ▪	Alternate Trail
━━━━	Road
++++++++++	Railroad Tracks

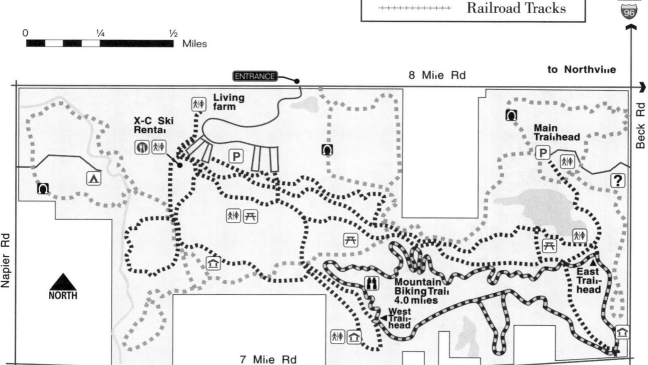

Middle Rouge Parkway

Trail Uses		**Setting**	Parkland, woods, urban
Grid	I8-9 **Trail ID** 208	**Location**	Dearborn Heights, Dearborn, Plymouth
Length	9 miles	**Lat/Long**	42-25 / 83-29 Northville Arboretum
Surface	Asphalt	**County**	Wayne
Difficulty	Easy	**Contact**	Wayne County Division of Parks 313-261-1990

Getting There From the intersection of Route 24 and Michigan Avenue, proceed north on Route 24 to Ford Street, then east to Edward H. Hines Drive and the trailhead.

Trail Notes Located in Wayne County, the trail runs from west of Dearborn Heights to Northville. The setting is open parkway and wooded areas along the Middle Rouge River. There are 4 lakes along the parkway, and the J.M. Bennett Arboretum.

Facilities P

TRAIL LEGEND

- Trail
- Skiing only Trail
- Hiking only Trail
- Planned Trail
- Alternate Trail
- Road
- Railroad Tracks

SYMBOL LEGEND

Beach/Swimming · Bicycle Repair · Cabin · Camping · Canoe Launch · First Aid · Food · Golf Course · Information · Lodging · Overlook/Observation · Parking · Picnic · Ranger Station · Restrooms · Shelter · Trailhead · Visitor Center · Water

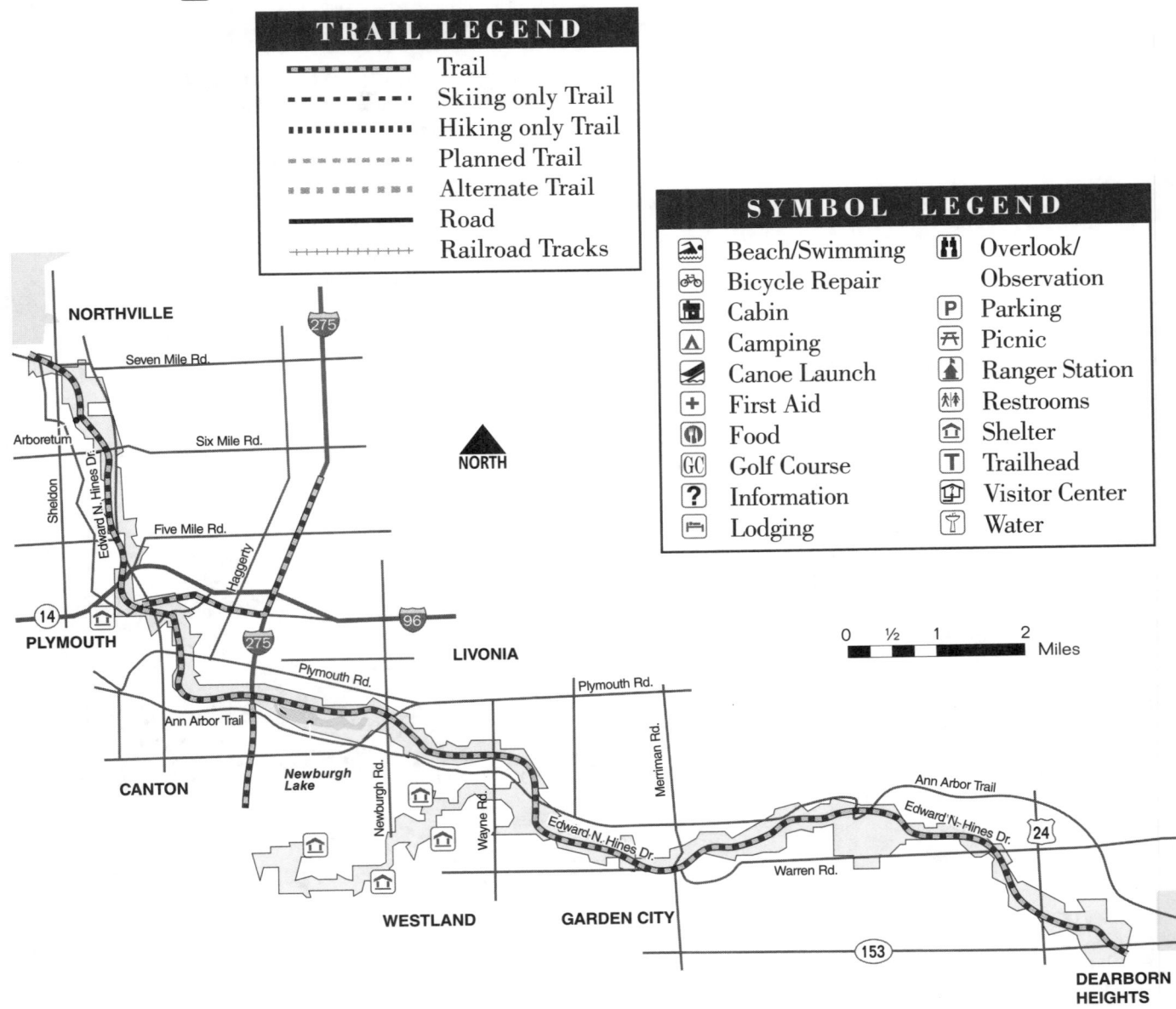

Novi North Park

Trail Uses	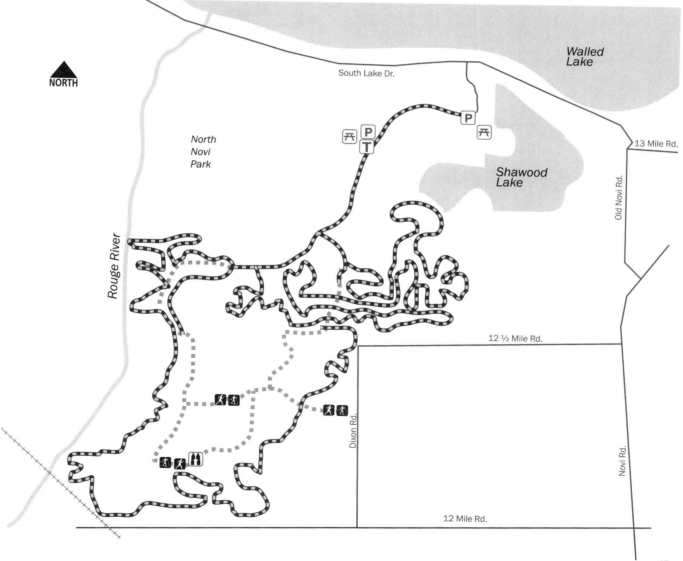	**Setting**	Flat, rolling hills
Grid	I8 **Trail ID** 334	**Location**	Novi
Length	12 miles	**Lat/Long**	42-30 / 83-30 Novi Park
Surface	Natural	**County**	Oakland
Difficulty	Easy to moderate	**Contact**	Friends of Novi Parks 248-374-1888
Acres	500	**Fees**	Vehicle entry for non-residents

Getting There North on Novi Road for 1 mile from its intersection with I-96, then north on Old Novi Road for a half mile to South Lake Drive. West on South Lake Drive for another half mile, then south into the Lakeshore Park entrance. Park at the end of the road.

Trail Notes The Michigan Mountain Biking Association has developed the trail system in this park into a pleasant, fairly easy experience. The singletrack wanders through a Christmas tree farm and an old fruit orchard. It is marked with black arrows on yellow diamonds and white mountain bike signs.

Facilities P ⛱

Oakwood MetroPark

Trail Uses		**Setting**	Woods
Grid	I9 **Trail ID** 227	**Hours**	Daylight to dusk
Length	3 miles	**Location**	Flatrock, Taylor
Surface	Paved	**Lat/Long**	42-06 / 83-19 Nature Center parking
Difficulty	Easy	**County**	Wayne
Acres	400	**Contact**	Oakwoods Metro Parks 734-782-3956
		Fees	Vehicle entry

Getting There From the I-94/275 interchange, take I-275 south 9 miles to Will Carleton Road, east .7 miles to Romine Road, then north 1.5 miles to Willow Road. East on Willow a short distance to the park entrance.

Trail Notes The Oakwood Metropark bike trail connects to Willow Metropark trail to the northwest. There are self-guiding interpretive trails and a Nature Center

Facilities P ⛲ 🚻 ♿ Nature Center

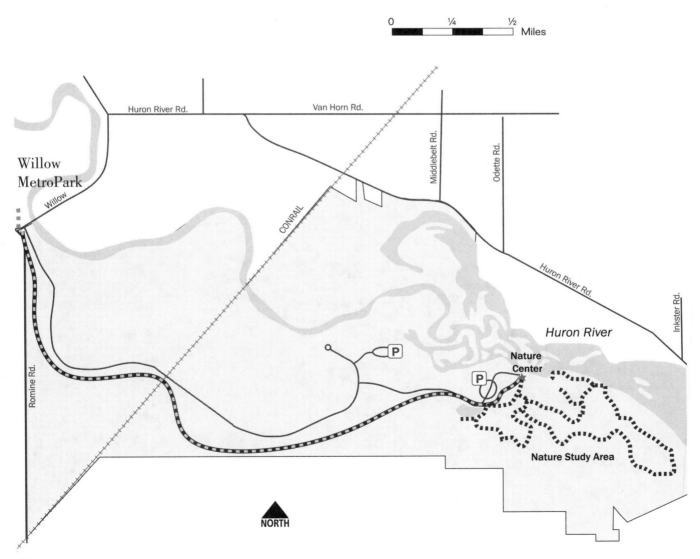

Ortonville State Recreation Trail

Trail Uses		**Setting**	Hilly, sandy areas
Grid	H9 **Trail ID** 230	**Location**	Ortonville
Length	3.5 miles, loops	**Lat/Long**	42-53 / 83-24 Big Fish Lake parking area
Surface	Natural	**County**	Oakland
Difficulty	Easy to moderate	**Contact**	Ortonville State Recreation Area 810-797-4439
Acres	5,400	**Fees**	Vehicle entry fee

Getting There Located in Oakland County, just north of Ortonville. Exit I-75 north on M-15 (exit 91) for 8 miles to Oakwood Road. Go east on Oakwood Road for 1 mile and then north on Sands Road for .8 miles to State Park Road. Proceed east on State Park Road to the entrance and parking area. You should see a "Ortonville Recreation Area" sign.

Trail Notes The terrain varies from hilly, to moderate and flat, with a few steep descents. You'll experience woodlands and open fields, with challenges of occasional roots and sand along the route. Effort level is easy to moderate. The outside loop is two track, with the inside loop initially single track and a couple of single spurs. The trail is not well marked.

Facilities P ⊼ ⌂

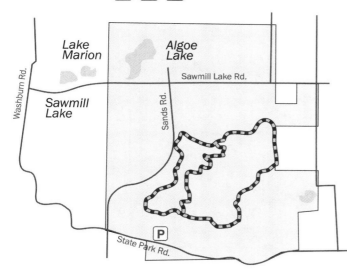

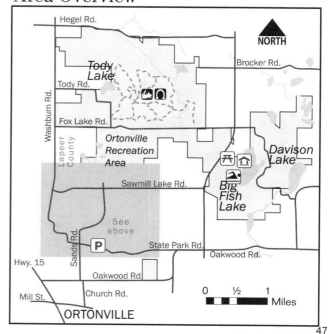

Ortonville Recreation Area Overview

TRAIL LEGEND

▪▪▪▪▪▪▪▪	Trail
▪ ▪ ▪ ▪ ▪ ▪	Skiing only Trail
▪▪▪▪▪▪▪▪▪▪	Hiking only Trail
▫ ▫ ▫ ▫ ▫	Planned Trail
▪ ▪ ▪ ▪ ▪	Alternate Trail
━━━━━	Road
+++++++++	Railroad Tracks

Paint Creek & Polly Ann Trails

Trail Uses 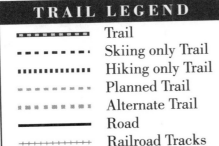 Polly Ann

Grid H9 **Trail ID** 231

Length Paint Creek – 10.5 miles
Polly Ann – 12.2 miles

Surface Paint Creek – Limestone screenings
Polly Ann – Gravel, ballast, grass

Difficulty Easy

Setting Urban, small communities, woods, open areas

Location Rochester Hills, Addison, Oxford, Auburn Hills

Lat/Long 42-46 / 83-13   Parking off Clarkston Rd

County Oakland

Contact Oakland County Parks   248-651-9260

Getting There Paint Creek Trail - The Rochester Municipal Park entrance is located off Ludlow Road between University and Woodard.

Polly Ann Trail – It begins in Orion Township on Joslyn and Indianwood Road and continues northeast through Oxford and Leonard to the Oakland/Lapeer County line at Bordman Road.

Trail Notes Paint Creek is located in Oakland County and runs between Rochester and Lake Orion. The trail begins at the south end of Rochester Municipal Park. Parking is nearby. Turn left at the north edge of the park trail system. There are many scenic bridge crossings. Dinosaur Hill Nature Preserve is located across Ludlow Road, and offers self-guided tours.

The Polly Ann Trail uses the abandoned railroad corridor through some of the most scenic and untouched landscape in northern Oakland County.

Facilities P

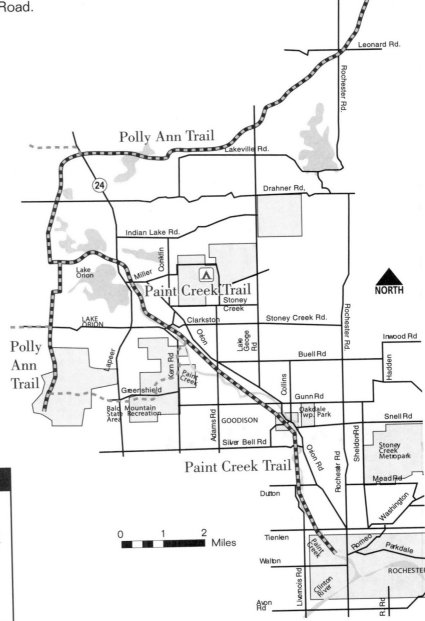

TRAIL LEGEND

▪▪▪▪▪▪	Trail
– – – – –	Skiing only Trail
▪▪▪▪▪▪▪	Hiking only Trail
┄┄┄┄┄	Planned Trail
▪▫▪▫▪▫	Alternate Trail
─────	Road
+++++++	Railroad Tracks

48

Pinckney State Recreation Trail

Trail Uses	(icons)	**Setting**	Rolling & hilly
Grid	I7 **Trail ID** 238	**Location**	Pinckney
Length	17.5 miles, singletrack	**Lat/Long**	42-25 / 83-58 Silver Lake Parking area
Surface	Natural & geoweb	**Counties**	Livingston, Washtenaw
Difficulty	Easy to difficult	**Contact**	Pinckney Recreation Area 734-426-4913
Acres	11,000	**Fees**	Vehicle entry fee

Getting There Located 3 miles south of Pinckney and 14 miles northwest of Ann Arbor. From the Hwy 23 and Hwy 14 intersection north of Ann Arbor, proceed north on Hwy 23 for 4 miles to North Territorial Road. West on North Territorial Rd 10 miles to Dexter/Townhall Road, and then north a mile to Silver Lake Road.

Trail Notes The Pinckney Recreation Area is the most popular biking destination in Michigan with over 120,000 riders annually. The three trails all begin from a common trailhead at the Silver Lake day use area. Silver Lake is 1.9 miles, Crooked Lake is 5.1 miles, and Potawatomi is 17.5 miles. Effort level is easy to difficult. The trails are single track and run clockwise. There are many hills and ridges, with climbs and descents ranging from 30' to 100' with most in the 30' range. The trails skirt the shorelines of ponds, marshes and several lakes.

Facilities (icons)

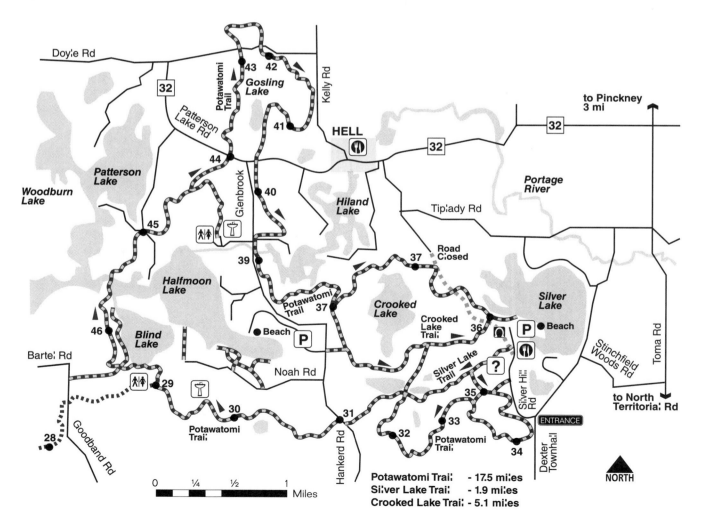

Potawatomi Trail - 17.5 miles
Silver Lake Trail - 1.9 miles
Crooked Lake Trail - 5.1 miles

Pointe Mouillee Game Area

Trail Uses	🚵 🏃	**Acres**	3,600
Grid	J9 **Trail ID** 244	**Setting**	Natural, marshland
Length	7 miles	**Location**	Monroe
Surface	Diked marshlands and ponds	**Lat/Long**	42-01 / 83-13 Park Headquarters
		County	Rockland, Wayne
Difficulty	Easy	**Contact**	Pointe Mouillee Field Office 734-379-9692

Getting There From I-75, exit 27 and proceed east on North Huron River Road for 2 miles, then south on Jefferson Rd for 1.5 miles. Turn east on Campau Road to the headquarters, then continue south, crossing the Huron River. Turn right on Sigler Road, and proceed to the end where there is parking and a locked gate.

Trail Notes This state game area consists of marshes, pools, and disked ponds surrounding the mouth of the Huron River and Lake Erie's shoreline. It's known for it's birding area. The ride itself is flat.

Facilities P

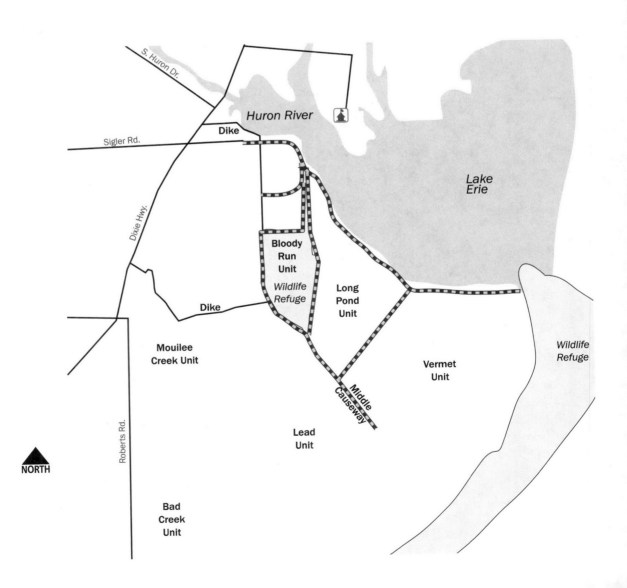

Pontiac Lake Recreation Area

Trail Uses	(icons)	**Setting**	Rolling, wooded, fields	
Grid	H8 Trail ID 246	**Location**	Oxbow, Pontiac	
Length	11.5	**Lat/Long**	42-40 / 83-27	Beach area
Surface	Crushed stone, natural	**County**	Oakland	
Difficulty	Moderate to difficult	**Contact**	Pontiac Lake Recreation Area	248-666-1020
Acres	3,800	**Fees**	Vehicle entry	

Getting There From I-24, go 7 miles west on M-59 to Williams Lake Road. Continue north about a mile to Gale Road and then west to the beach parking lot. From the parking lot, the trail immediately crosses Gale Road.

Trail Notes The trail is single track and runs clockwise. The Park provides a wide variety of terrain with a setting of rolling hills and both steep and flat areas. Heavily wooded with open areas, lake, and marshes. The area is noted for its rocks and roots. Elevations range from 50 to 90-feet. Mountain bikers should use caution in the challenging areas, as the climbs can be steep and loose. The Park has over 3,700-acres, with separate hiking and horseback trails. Facilities include a 1/3 mile beach, concession stand, boat launch, bathhouse, and picnic area.

Facilities (icons)

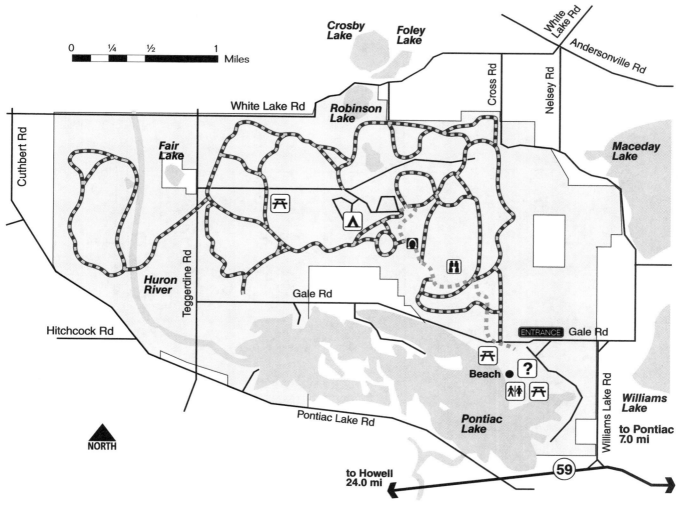

Proud Lake Recreation Area

Trail Uses	(icons)		**Setting**	Woods, open area
Grid	H8 **Trail ID** 247		**Location**	Farmington Hills, Milford
Length	10 miles		**Lat/Long**	42-34 / 83-34 Parking off Wixom Rd
Surface	Natural, groomed		**County**	Oakland
Difficulty	Easy		**Contact**	Proud Lake Recreation Area 248-685-2433
Acres	4,700		**Fees**	Vehicle entry fee

Getting There Proud Lake is located about 10 miles west of Farmington Hills and 2 miles southeast of Milford. From I-96 take Wisom Road for 6 miles north to Garden Road to the entrance. There you will find parking, information facilities and access to the trails.

Trail Notes The existing trail system is located at the west side of the Recreation Area, and consists of several connecting loops and a connector trail. Effort level is easy with terrain that is largely flat and rolling with only moderate elevation. There is a planned 5 mile single loop trail to be located in the eastern half of the Recreation Area, north of Proud Lake. It will be designed as a beginners trail and will accommodate the physically challenged, three wheel bikes, and tandems.

Facilities (icons)

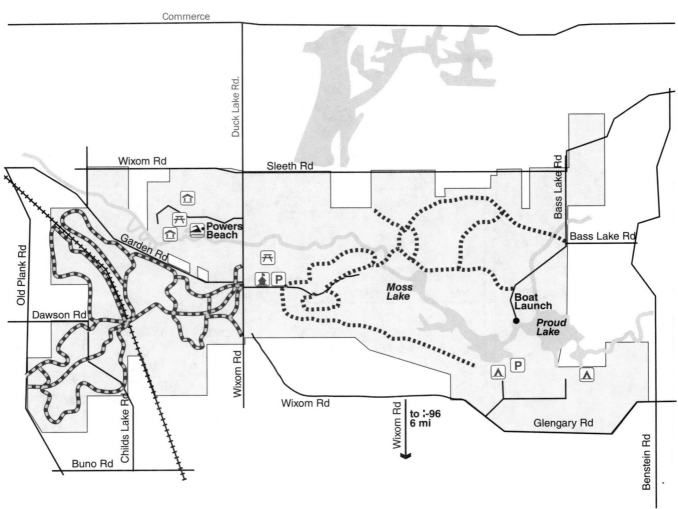

Rose Lake Wildlife Area

Trail Uses

Grid	H6 **Trail ID** 255	**Setting**	Rolling farmland, fields, lowland woods, marsh
Length	10 miles	**Location**	Lansing
Surface	Natural	**Lat/Long**	42-48 / 84-24 Parking off Stoll Rd
Difficulty	Easy to moderate	**County**	Clinton
Acres	4,140	**Contact**	Rose Lake Wildlife Area 517-373-9358

Getting There   Located twelve miles northeast of Lansing. Take I-69 9 miles northeast from its junction with I-496 between Lansing and East Lansing. Exit north on Upton, Peacock, or Woodbury Road to the parking areas.

Trail Notes   The Rose Lake Wildlife Area is divided into 7 color-designated areas, each with appropriate signs for research purposes. The terrain is largely flat and moderately hilly, with lowland woods, marsh and farmland. The area west of Peacock Road is flat and open. The area east of Peacock Road is hilly and wooded, providing the best terrain for biking. Effort level is easy to moderate. The trails are popular with local residents. Be aware that hunting season is from September 15 to March 31.

Facilities   P

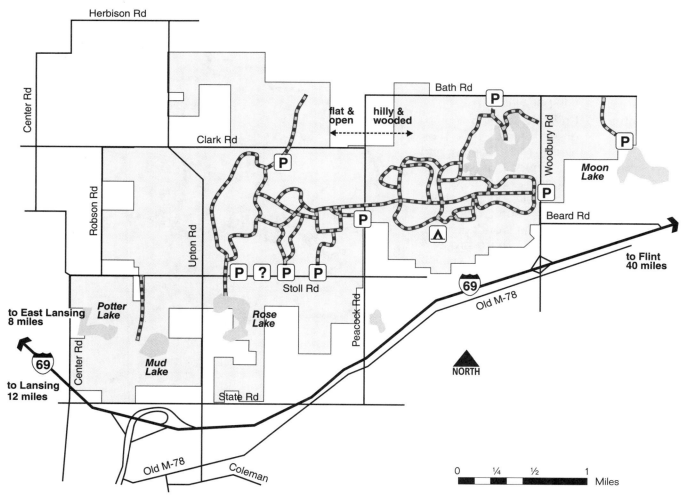

Ruby Campground

Trail Uses	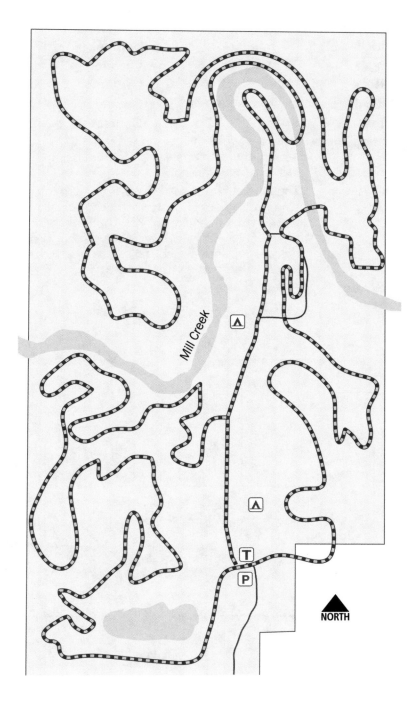
Grid	G10 Trail ID 256
Length	5 miles
Surface	Natural
Difficulty	Moderate to difficult
Setting	Woods and open areas
Location	Avoca
Lat/Long	Latitude 43-03 Longitude 82-37 Campground area
County	St. Clair
Contact	Ruby Campground 810-324-2766
Fees	Trail fee
Getting There	From I-69 east, take exit 189 (Wales Center Road), and go left for 1 mile to Lapeer Road. Turn right and go 2 miles to Cribbens Road. Turn left and go for 3 miles to Imlay City Road, then left a ¼ mile to the campground.
Trail Notes	Privately owned campground area. Trail runs along Mill Creek, and a former gravel pit. Rugged singletrack, with a couple long, steep climbs and descents. Setting is wooded open, and hilly. There are two water crossings, which are rideable. Effort level is moderate to difficult.
Facilities	

Saginaw Valley Trail

Trail Uses

Grid   G7 **Trail ID** 335

Length   10 miles

Surface   Paved

Difficulty   Easy

Getting There   St. Charles is located at M-52 southeast of Saginaw.

Trail Notes   The trail is currently paved for 6 of its 10 miles. It runs north from the trailhead in St. Charles at Lumberjack Park to Saginaw City. Most of the trail is shaded as it runs between farms and rural homes. Much of the trail is adjacent to the lightly used Teft and Martine Roads, but it does pass near M-52.

Facilities

Setting   Woods, farmland, open, urban

Location   Saginaw, St. Charles

Lat/Long   43-01 / 83-18   St. Charles trailhead

County   Saginaw

Contact   Saginaw County Parks   989-790-5280

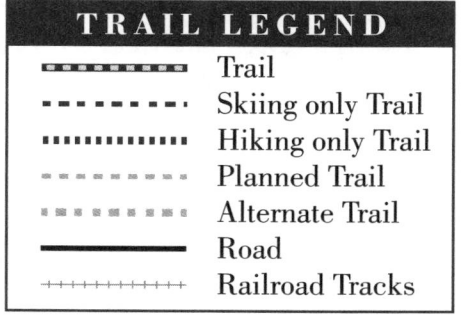

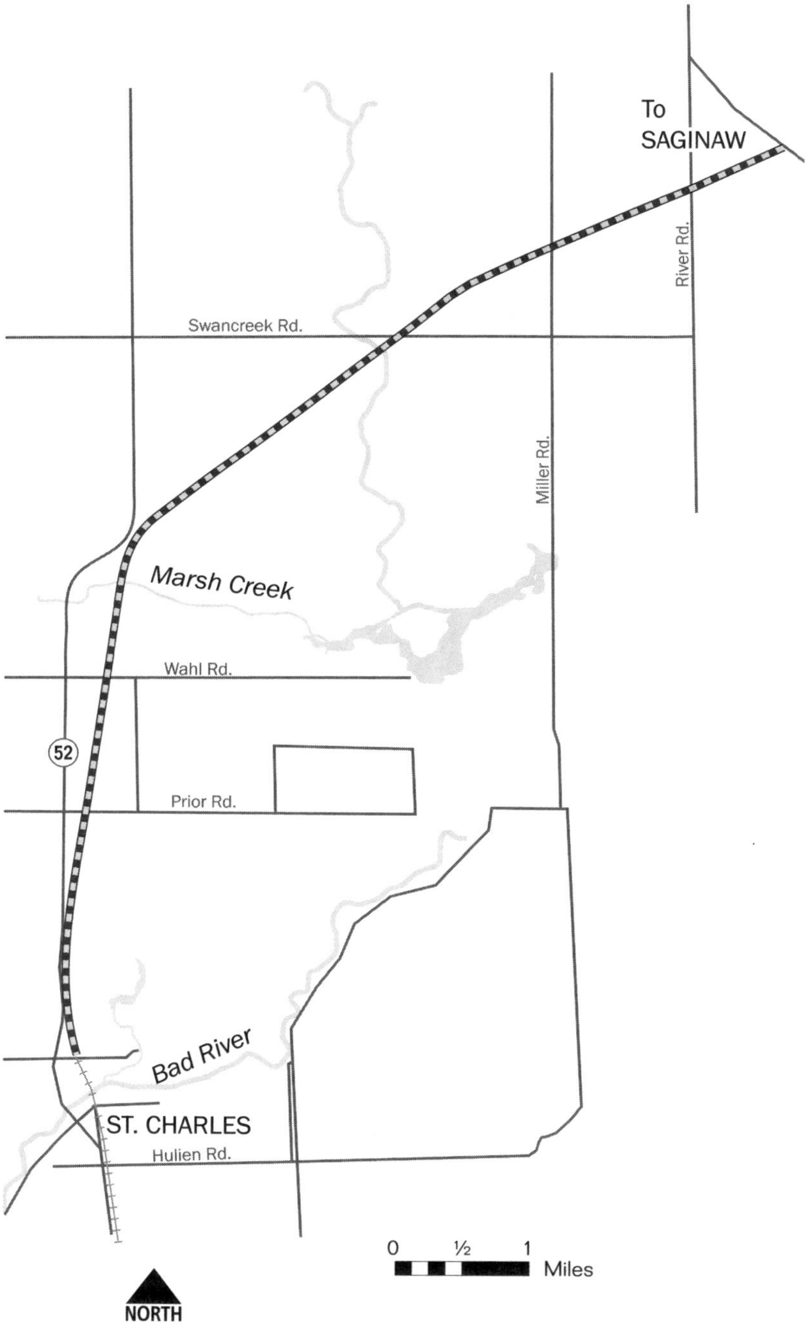

TRAIL LEGEND

▪▪▪▪▪▪▪▪▪▪	Trail
▪ ▪ ▪ ▪ ▪ ▪	Skiing only Trail
▪▪▪▪▪▪▪▪▪▪▪	Hiking only Trail
▪ ▪ ▪ ▪ ▪	Planned Trail
▪ ▪ ▪ ▪ ▪	Alternate Trail
──────	Road
++++++++++	Railroad Tracks

To SAGINAW

River Rd.

Swancreek Rd.

Miller Rd.

Marsh Creek

Wahl Rd.

52

Prior Rd.

Bad River

ST. CHARLES

Hulien Rd.

0   ½   1 Miles

NORTH

Seven Lakes State Park

Trail Uses	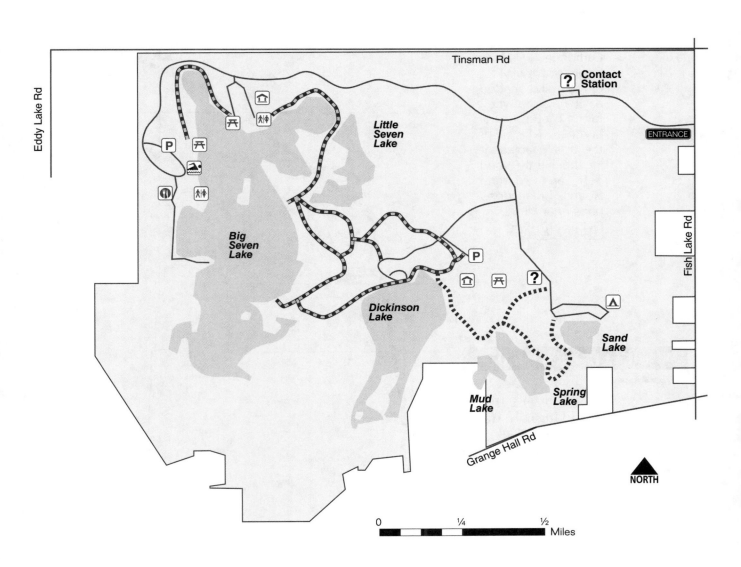	**Setting**	Rolling hills, woods, lakes, fields
		Location	Holly
Grid	H8 **Trail ID** 259	**Lat/Long**	43-49 / 83-41 Beach area
Length	5 miles	**County**	Oakland
Surface	Natural	**Contact**	Seven Lakes State Park 248-634-7271
Difficulty	Moderate	**Fees**	Vehicle entry

Getting There   The park is located north of Fenton between US-23 and I-75. Take Grange Hall Road to Fish Lake Road, then north for 1 mile to the park entrance.

Trail Notes   Single track. Effort level is easy to moderate. Setting is rolling hills, fields and lakes. The terrain includes a stream, swamps and low swales.

Facilities   Boat launches

Sleepy Hollow State Park

Trail Uses

Grid	H6 **Trail ID** 269
Length	16 miles
Surface	Natural
Difficulty	Easy to moderate
Acres	2,678

Setting	Mature hardwood, meadows, brush lands
Location	Lainsburg, Lansing
Lat/Long	42-56 / 84-25 Entrance off Price Rd
County	Clinton
Contact	Sleepy Hollow State Park 517-651-6217
Fees	Vehicle entry

Getting There The Park is located 18 miles northeast of Lansing. From the Hwy 27/69 interchange, north of Lansing, proceed north on Hwy 27 for .5 mile to Price Road, then go east 6 miles to the park entrance.

Trail Notes Effort level is easy. The setting is mostly flat with a few hills. The trail circles Lake Ovid, and is approximately 40% wooded and 60% open. The route can be muddy.

Facilities

SYMBOL LEGEND

🏊	Beach/Swimming
🚲	Bicycle Repair
🏠	Cabin
⛺	Camping
🛶	Canoe Launch
➕	First Aid
🍴	Food
GC	Golf Course
❓	Information
🛏	Lodging
🔭	Overlook/Observation
P	Parking
🪑	Picnic
🗼	Ranger Station
♨	Restrooms
🏚	Shelter
T	Trailhead
🏛	Visitor Center
🚰	Water

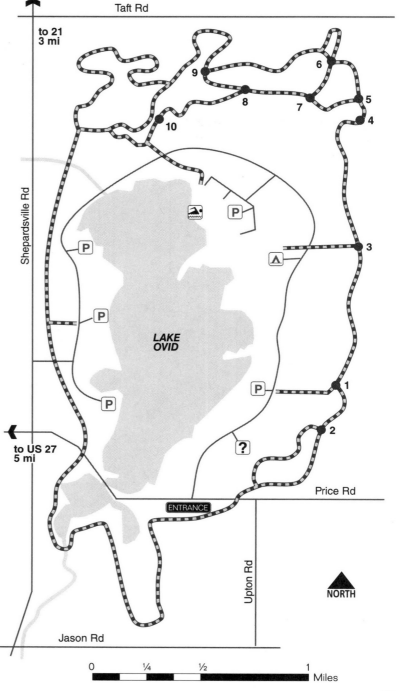

Sterling State Park

Trail Uses		Setting	Flat
Grid	J9 **Trail ID** 276	Location	Monroe
Length	6 miles	Lat/Long	41-55 / 83-20 Park Headquarters
Surface	Paved	County	Monroe
Difficulty	Easy	Contact	Sterling State Park 734-289-2715
Acres	1,000	Fees	Vehicle entry fee

Getting There From Monroe, east on Dixie Hwy from I-75 exit about 1 mile to the park entrance.

Trail Notes Located along the backwater marsh of Lake Erie. Surface is asphalt. Setting is semi-wooded and marshland, small inclines. There is an observation tower to over look the marsh area. Facilities include toilets, a beach house, swimming beaches and a boat launch.

Facilities

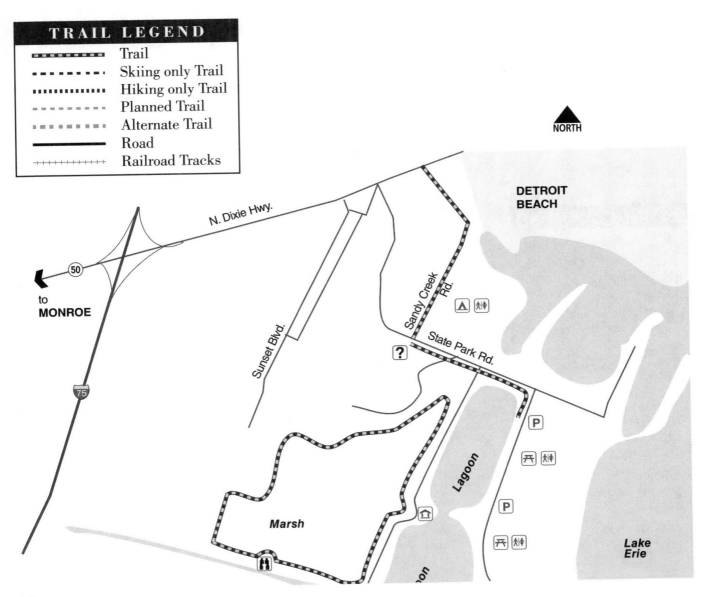

```
TRAIL LEGEND
▪▪▪▪▪▪▪▪▪▪   Trail
- - - - - -   Skiing only Trail
▪▪▪▪▪▪▪▪▪▪   Hiking only Trail
- - - - - -   Planned Trail
▪ ▪ ▪ ▪ ▪   Alternate Trail
──────   Road
+++++++++   Railroad Tracks
```

NORTH

N. Dixie Hwy.

50

to MONROE

75

Sunset Blvd.

Sandy Creek Rd.

State Park Rd.

?

DETROIT BEACH

Lagoon

Marsh

Lake Erie

Stoney Creek MetroPark

Trail Uses

Grid H9 **Trail ID** 277

Length 6.2 miles

Surface Asphalt

Difficulty Easy

Acres 4,161

Fees Vehicle entry

Getting There From the M-59 and M-53 interchange just north of Sterling Heights, take M-53 north 6 miles to 26 Mile Road, then west 2 miles to the park entrance.

Trail Notes Stony Creek consists of 4,461-acres and is located in Oakland and Macomb Counties. The terrain is hilly. The Nature Center is open year round. The terrain is hilly, and the trail surrounds its 500-acre Stony Creek Lake. Bicycle rental at the Bay Point and Eastwood Beaches:

Facilities 🅿 🚰 🚻 🏕 ⛺ 🚲
Nature Center

Hours 6am to 10pm May through September; 8am to 8pm October through April

Setting Hilly, woods, open

Location Washington

Lat/Long 42-43 / 83-04   Entrance off 26 Mile RdL

County Oaklank, Macomb

Contact Stony Creek Metro Park   586-781-4242

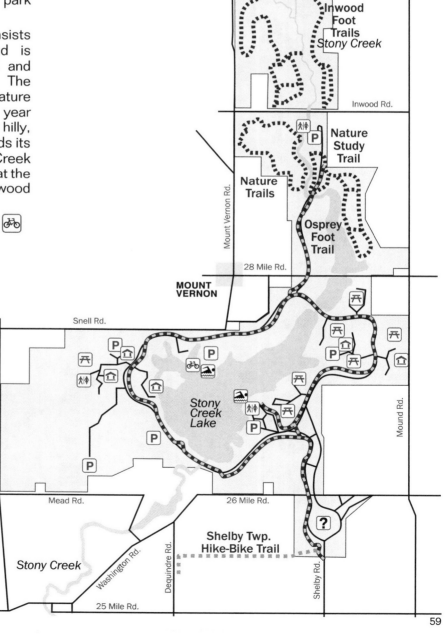

TRAIL LEGEND

- ▪▪▪▪▪ Trail
- - - - - Skiing only Trail
- ▪▪▪▪▪▪▪ Hiking only Trail
- - - - - Planned Trail
- ▪ ▪ ▪ ▪ Alternate Trail
- —— Road
- ┼┼┼┼┼ Railroad Tracks

Wadhams to Avoca Trail

Trail Uses	[icons]	**Setting**	Woods, open
Grid	G10 **Trail ID** 336	**Location**	Wadhams, Avoca
Length	10 miles	**Lat/Long**	42-59 / 82-32 Wadhams
Surface	Crushed stone	**County**	St. Clair
Difficulty	Easy	**Contact**	St. Clair County Parks 810-325-9022

Getting There From Fort Port Huron take Lapeer Road west about 5 miles to the small community of Wadhams and the east trailhead.

Trail Notes The trail surface is crushed stone, except for a 1.2 mile paved section from Lapeer Road southeast to Bartlett Road. The centerpiece of the trail is the 60-foot high, 640-foot long Mill Creek Trestle built in the 1800's. Parking and vault toilets are available where the trail intersects at Avoca Road and Imlay City Road.

Facilities [P] [restroom icon]

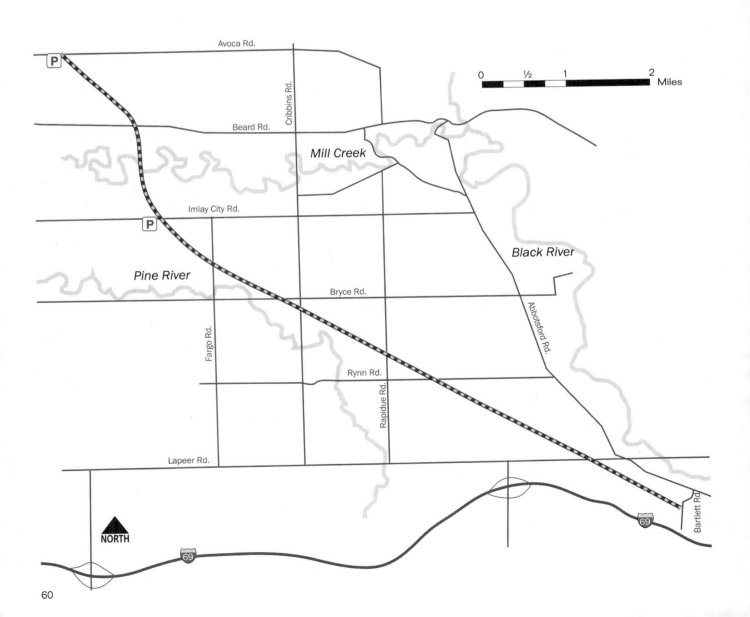

West Bloomfield Trail Network

Trail Uses

Grid H9 **Trail ID** 295

Length 8 miles (plus the 4 mile Multi-Jurisdictional Trail)

Surface Crushed limestone

Difficulty Easy

Setting Flat, urban

Location West Bloomfield

Lat/Long 42-34 / 83-24   Trailhead at Arrowhead Rd

County Oakland

Contact West Bloomfield Parks & Recreation
248-592-9142

Getting There From Route 24, take Lonepine Road west 5 miles to Orchard Lake Road, north a 1/2 mile to Pontiac Trail, then west about 2 miles to Arrowhead Road. Go south a short distance is the trailhead and parking.

Trail Notes The West Bloomfield Trail Network, located in Oakland County, is designated an Urban Wildlife Sanctuary. Interspersed among the wetland lakes is an urban setting, with homes and shopping centers. The trail begins at Arrowhead Road, just north of the West Bloomfield Nature Preserve, where it also connects with the Multi-Jurisdictional Trail. Parking and restrooms are available here.

Facilities

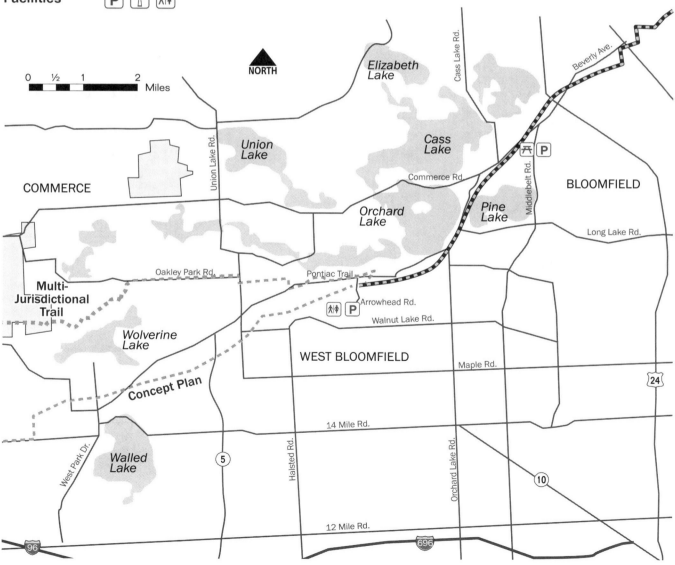

Willow MetroPark

Trail Uses	
Grid	I9 **Trail ID** 301
Length	4.5 miles
Surface	Paved

Difficulty	Easy
Hours	6am to 10pm
Setting	Wooded
Location	New Boston
Lat/Long	42-07 / 83-22 Park area
County	Wayne
Contact	Willow Metro Park 734-697-9181
Fees	Vehicle entry
Getting There	From the I-94/275 interchange, take I-275 south 6 miles to South Huron Road. Proceed east a short distance to the park entrance.
Trail Notes	Located south of the Lower Huron Metro Park and just east of I-275. This paved trail circles the park and connects to Oakwoods at Huron Metro Parks. The park offers bike, ski and boat rentals.
Facilities	

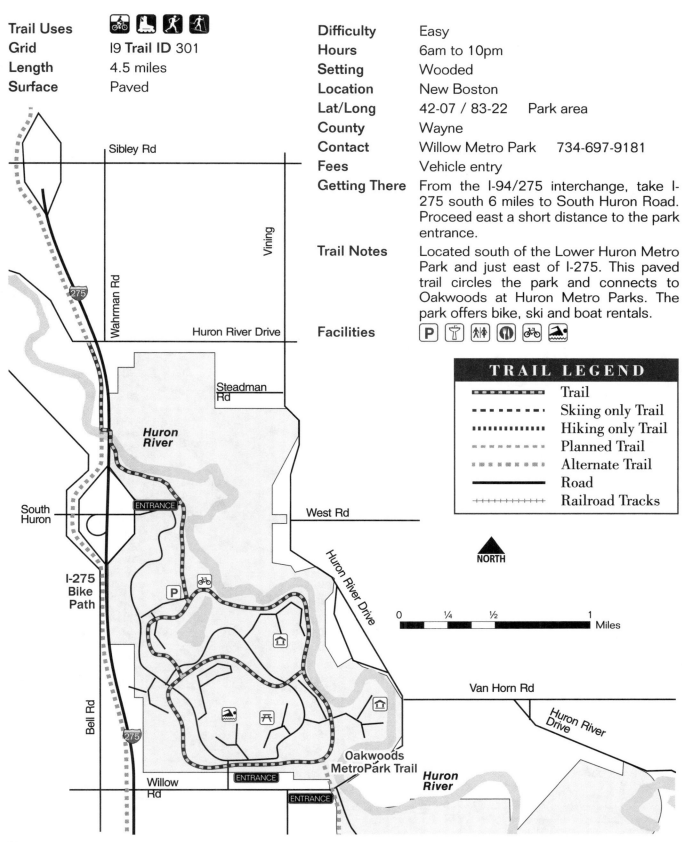

TRAIL LEGEND

▪▪▪▪▪▪▪	Trail
– – – – –	Skiing only Trail
▪▪▪▪▪▪▪▪	Hiking only Trail
– – – – –	Planned Trail
▪ ▪ ▪ ▪ ▪	Alternate Trail
——————	Road
+++++++++	Railroad Tracks

NORTH

0   ¼   ½   1
Miles

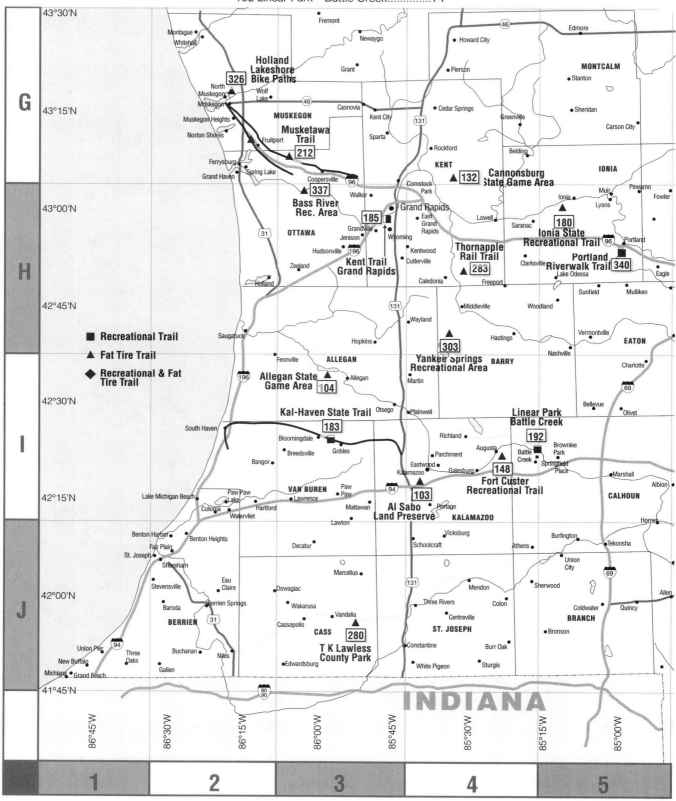

Al Sabo Land Preserve

Trail Uses

Grid	I4 **Trail ID** 103	**Setting**	Open, marshland
Length	6 miles	**Location**	Kalamazoo
Surface	Natural, gravel road	**Lat/Long**	42-13 / 85-40 Entrance
Difficulty	Easy to moderate	**County**	Kalamazoo
Acres	750	**Contact**	Kalamazoo City Parks Dept. 269-337-3191

Getting There From I-94 west of Kalamazoo, exit 92 (9th Street) past Kalamazoo Valley Community College to Texas Drive. Turn left and continue about a mile to the park area for the preserve.

Trail Notes Single, double track, gravel road, counter clockwise. There is a trail display area at trailhead. Trailhead is at north side of parking lot. There are a few downhills and climbs where the trail moves off the ridges into the Portage Creek drainage area.

Facilities P

SYMBOL LEGEND

- 🏊 Beach/Swimming
- 🚲 Bicycle Repair
- 🏚 Cabin
- Ⓐ Camping
- 🛶 Canoe Launch
- ➕ First Aid
- 🍴 Food
- GC Golf Course
- ❓ Information
- 🛏 Lodging
- 🔭 Overlook/Observation
- P Parking
- 🏕 Picnic
- 🌲 Ranger Station
- 🚻 Restrooms
- 🏠 Shelter
- T Trailhead
- 🏛 Visitor Center
- 🚰 Water

TRAIL LEGEND

- Trail
- Skiing only Trail
- Hiking only Trail
- Planned Trail
- Alternate Trail
- Road
- Railroad Tracks

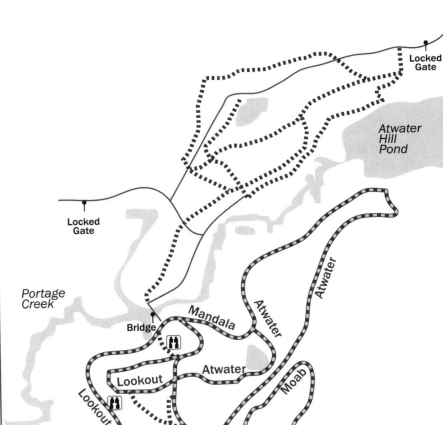

Allegan State Game Area

Trail Uses

Grid I3 **Trail ID** 104

Length 21 miles

Surface Natural

Difficulty Moderate

Acres 45,000

Setting Hardwood forests, marsh

Location Allegan

Lat/Long 42-33 / 85-60
118th & 46 St.

County Allegan

Contact Allegan State Game Area
269-613-2430

Getting There From Allegan, take M-89 north to Monroe Road. Follow Monroe Road (118th Avenue) about 7 miles around Lake Allegan, and across Swan Creek Dam another 1/4 mile to refuge headquarters. Trailhead is off 46th Street.

Trail Notes Moderate. Hardwood forest and flooded wildlife area. Single & double-track, clockwise, lightly posted. Very sandy in places. Insects can be bad during the early summer months.

Facilities [P] [🔭] [🚻]

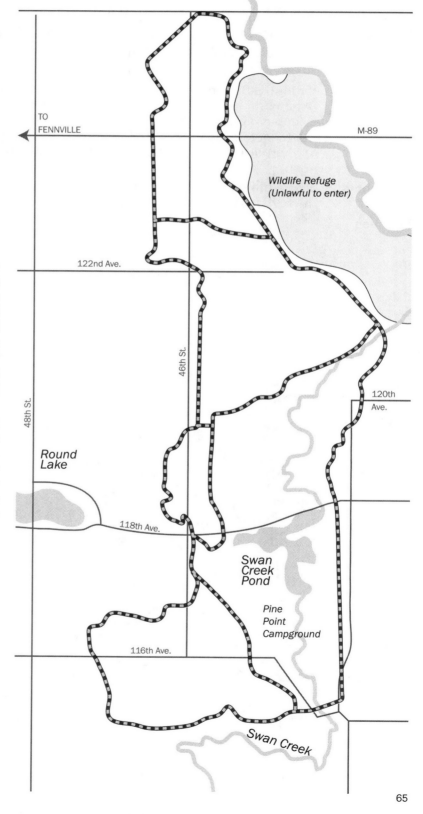

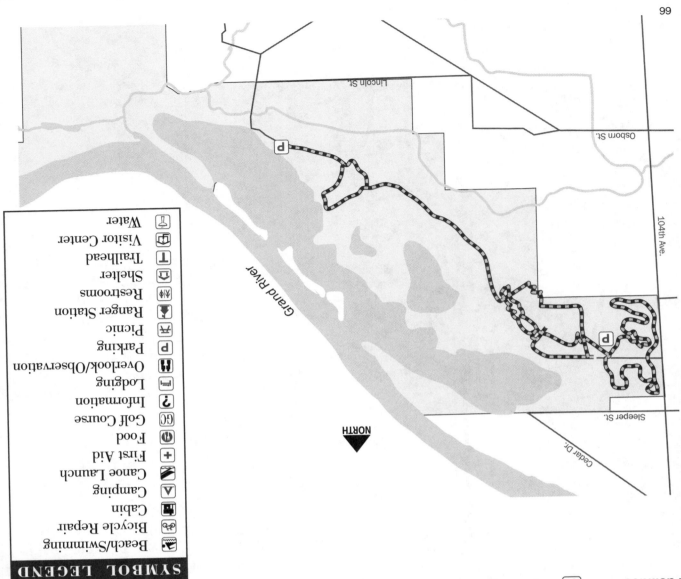

Bass River Recreation Area

Trail Uses			
Grid	H3 **Trail ID** 337	**Setting**	Dense woods, open areas
Length	8 miles	**Location**	Grand Haven
Surface	Natural	**Lat/Long**	43-00 / 86-02 Recreation area
Difficulty	Easy to moderate	**County**	Ottawa
Acres	1,100	**Contact**	Bass River Recreation Area 231-798-3711

Getting There From US-31, proceed east on M-45 (Lake Michigan Drive) for 7 miles to 104th Avenue, then north for 3.4 miles to a gravel road on the east side of 104th. Pull up to the sign 'No Motor Vehicles Beyond this point', and park off to the side of the road to the west. The north loop is also about 4 miles long, and mostly single track except for double track for a short distance at the beginning of the ride. Dense woods, but straighter than the south loop.

Trail Notes There are occasional sand mounds and loose sand. This whole area is dense woods, with narrow gaps between trees and tight turns.

Facilities 🅿

SYMBOL LEGEND

🏊	Beach/Swimming
🚲	Bicycle Repair
🏠	Cabin
⛺	Camping
🛶	Canoe Launch
✚	First Aid
🍴	Food
⛳	Golf Course
ℹ	Information
🛏	Lodging
👀	Overlook/Observation
🅿	Parking
🍴	Picnic
🔦	Ranger Station
🚻	Restrooms
🏚	Shelter
🚩	Trailhead
🏛	Visitor Center
🚰	Water

NORTH

Grand River

Lincoln St.

Osborn St.

104th Ave.

Sleeper St.

Cedar Dr.

Fort Custer Recreation Area

Trail Uses	🚶 🚲 🥾 🎿 �︎	**Setting**	Open fields, woods	
Grid	I4 Trail ID 148	**Location**	Augusta	
Length	20 miles	**Lat/Long**	42-21 / 85-20	Park entrance
Surface	Paved, gravel, natural	**County**	Kalamazoo	
Difficulty	Easy to difficult	**Contact**	Fort Custer Recreation Area	269-731-4200
Acres	3,000	**Fees**	Vehicle entry	

Getting There From Battle Creek, 8 miles west on M-96, just across the Kalamazoo River from Augusta.

Trail Notes The setting consists of woods, hills, open fields and some double track roads. Effort level is easy to difficult. Trails are single and two-track, and counter clockwise. Open year round, but the surface can be soft in poor weather. There is a 6.6 mile Green loop, a 7.7 mile Red loop, a yellow loop and a blue loop. Hardwood forest and flooded wildlife area. Lightly posted. Very sandy in places. Insects can be bad during the early summer months.

Facilities P ⛐

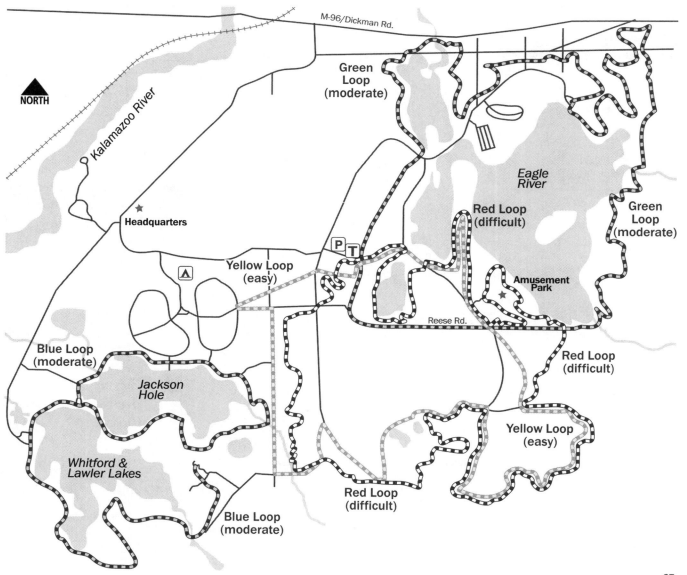

Fred Meijer Heartland Trail

Trail Uses	🚲 🛼 🏃	**Setting**	Woods, open, farmland
Grid	G4-5 **Trail ID** 166	**Location**	Cedar Lake, Edmore, Elwell, Greenville
Length	35 miles	**Lat/Long**	43-35 / 85-13 Elwell
Surface	Paved	**Counties**	Gratiot, Montcalm
Difficulty	Easy	**Contact**	Friend of the Heartland Trail 989-427-5555

Getting There West trailhead - From M-91 in Greenville, go north about 2 miles to Peck Road, then east to Lake Road, then north to trailhead.

East trailhead - Pingree Road, N of CR 540 in Elwell.

Trail Notes This trail is an old railroad bed connecting the towns of Greenville and Elwell. Open, farmland.

Facilities P T 🚻 🍴 🛏

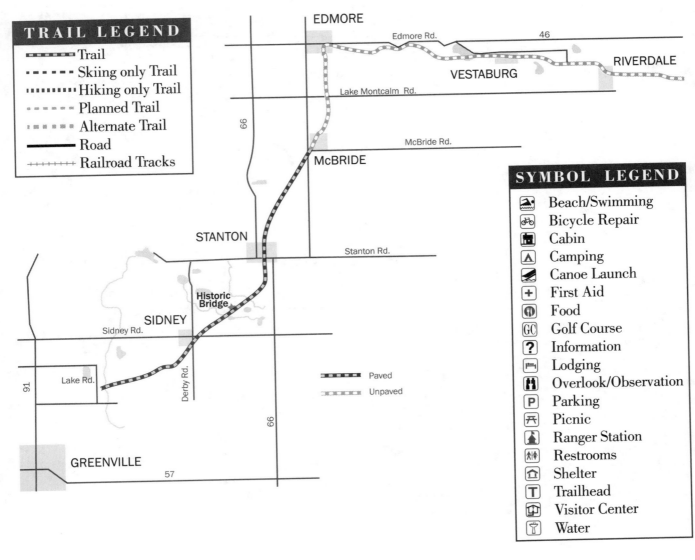

TRAIL LEGEND
- Trail
- Skiing only Trail
- Hiking only Trail
- Planned Trail
- Alternate Trail
- Road
- ++++++ Railroad Tracks

Paved
Unpaved

SYMBOL LEGEND
- 🏊 Beach/Swimming
- 🚲 Bicycle Repair
- 🏠 Cabin
- △ Camping
- 🛶 Canoe Launch
- + First Aid
- 🍴 Food
- GC Golf Course
- ? Information
- 🛏 Lodging
- 👀 Overlook/Observation
- P Parking
- 🪑 Picnic
- 🏠 Ranger Station
- 🚻 Restrooms
- 🏠 Shelter
- T Trailhead
- 🏛 Visitor Center
- 🚰 Water

Hofma Preserve (Grand Haven Township)

Trail Uses

Grid   H2 **Trail ID** 171   **Setting**   Woods, open areas

Length   4.5 miles   **Location**   Grand Haven

Surface   Natural   **Lat/Long**   Latitude 43-01 / 86-11   Trailhead area

Difficulty   Easy to difficult   **County**   Ottawa

Acres   407   **Contact**   Grand Haven Township   616-842-5988

Getting There   Exit Hwy 31 three miles south of Grand Haven at Ferris Street, proceed east 1 mile to a gravel road and then north .5 mile to the park entrance.

Trail Notes   Trails are ungroomed, wide, and well marked with a counter clockwise direction. The terrain is relatively flat. There are multiple intersecting loops.

Facilities   P   T   ☖   ⚭ (except winter)

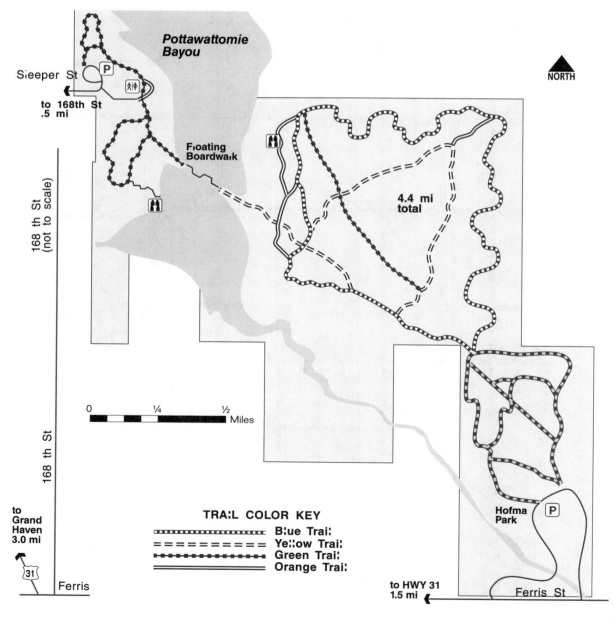

Pottawattomie Bayou

Sleeper St

P

to 168th St
.5 mi

NORTH

168 th St
(not to scale)

Floating
Boardwalk

4.4 mi
total

0   ¼   ½
Miles

168 th St

to
Grand
Haven
3.0 mi

31

Ferris

TRAIL COLOR KEY

Blue Trail

Yellow Trail

Green Trail

Orange Trail

Hofma
Park

P

to HWY 31
1.5 mi

Ferris St

Holland Lakeshore Bike Paths
(Park Township Bike Paths)

Trail Uses		**Setting**	Urban
Grid	H2 **Trail ID** 326	**Location**	Holland
Length	50 miles	**Lat/Long**	42-45 / 86-11 Parking off James St.
Surface	Paved	**County**	Ottawa
Difficulty	Easy	**Contact**	Park Township 313-339-4520

Getting There Accesses from James Street or Riley Street in Holland.

Trail Notes Urban and park setting. Surface is paved except for the Riley Trail, which is natural.

Facilities

Ionia Recreation Area

Trail Uses	🚲 🎿 🏃 🎠	**Setting**	Woods, meadows, wetland
Grid	H5 **Trail ID** 180	**Location**	Ionia, Saranac
Length	9 miles	**Lat/Long**	42-57 / 85-08 Sessions Lake parking
Surface	Natural	**County**	Ionia
Difficulty	Easy to moderate	**Contact**	Ionia Recreation Area 616-527-3750
Acres	4,500	**Fees**	Vehicle entry

Getting There From Ionia, go 3.5 miles south on M-66 to David Highway, then 3 miles west to the park entrance; or 3.5 miles east of Saranac on David Hwy.

Trail Notes Ionia Recreation Area is a mixture of open fields, mature hardwood forest, and pine plantations. The park's Sessions Lake, is 140-acres and reaches depths of 60 feet. The trail is mostly single track, counter clockwise. Four miles of the Grand River flows along the north border of the park.

Facilities P 🍴 🚻 🎪 ⛺

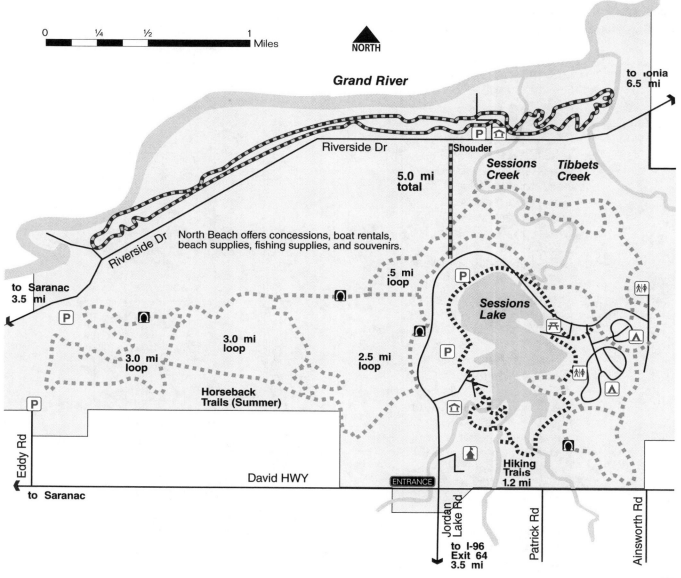

Kal-Haven Trail State Park

Trail Uses

Grid I2-3 **Trail ID** 183

Length 34 miles

Surface Crushed limestone

Difficulty Easy

Setting Farmland, wooded areas, meadows

Location South Haven, Kalamazoo

Lat/Long 42-25 / 86-48 Trailhead at Blue Star Memorial

Counties Van Buren, Kalamazoo

Contact Kal-Haven State Park 269-637-2788

Fees Trail pass

Getting There Kalamazoo Trailhead: Take US-31 west of Kalamazoo to M-43, then on M-43 a ¼ mile to 10th Street. North on 10th Street for 2 miles to the entrance.

South Haven Trailhead: Take I-296 to North Shore Drive (exit 22), and go west to A2 (Blue Star). Continue south on A2 for about a mile, then right (west) on Wells Street for a ¼ mile. Turn right (north) on Baily Street to the park entrance.

Trail Notes The trail was built on abandoned railroad right-of-way, and is 10 feet wide. There are some steep slopes alongside the grade as you head initially north through woods from the east trailhead. After about 4 miles, the trail curves to the left in a more westerly direction and the landscape becomes flat and open. This was the first rail trail in Michigan. Trail highlights include a camelback bridge and a covered bridge.

Facilities

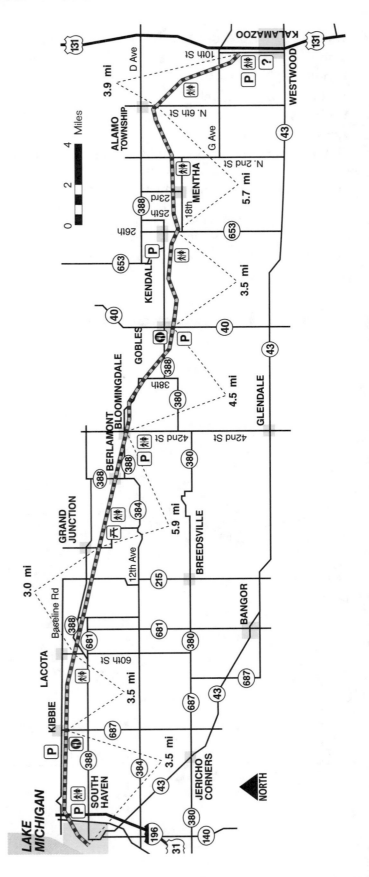

Kent Trail – Grand Rapids

Trail Uses

Grid   H3 **Trail ID** 185

Length   15 miles

Surface   Asphalt, road

Difficulty   Easy

Setting   Urban, rural countryside, river front park land

Location   Grand Rapids

Lat/Long   42-49/ 85-44 Trailhead at Byron Center at 84th St.

County   Kent

Contact   Kent County Parks Dept. 616-336-7275

Getting There   From John Ball Park at the northern end, with its zoo and parking, proceed south by road to the trailhead, across the street from the Coca-Cola bottling plant. The southern trailhead ends at Byron Center on 84th St, or via a spur to Douglas Walker Park.

Trail Notes   Most of the trail follows abandoned railroad line. The terrain is flat with no sharp turns. It travels through six government jurisdictions – Grand Rapids, Grandville, Walker, Wyoming and Byron Township. The four main access points are located at Johnson Park, John Ball Park, Douglas Walker Park and the Byron Center at 84th Street.

Facilities

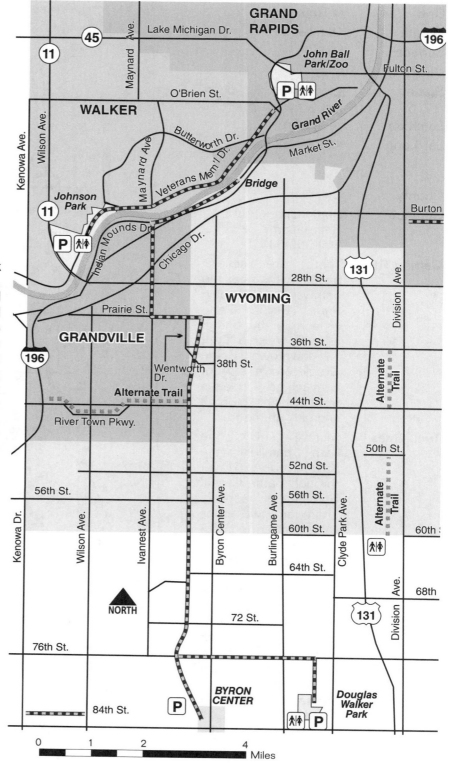

Linear Park – Battle Creek

Trail Uses	
Grid	I4 **Trail ID** 192
Length	18 miles
Surface	Paved
Difficulty	Easy
Setting	Wooded areas, open fields, parks, urban
Location	Battle Creek
Lat/Long	42-19 / 83-48 Parking at Capitol Ave.
County	Calhoun
Contact	Battle Creek Parks & Recreation 269-966-3431

Getting There There are several parking sites near the pathway. Riverview Park, Bailey Park, or across the bridge near Friendship Park in downtown Battle Creek are a few of convenient places from which to park and pick up the trail.

Trail Notes Much of the path parallels the Kalamazoo River through Battle Creek. Surface is asphalt. There are two loops - the East Loop is 6.7 miles and the West Loop 7.1 miles. Points of interest along the route include: Kellogg World Headquarters, Horseshoe Bend/Boardwalk, Verona Dam, Kellogg Community College, Stouffer/McCamly Arena, Takasaki Gardens, Leila Arboretum and Kingman Museum.

Facilities

Roller-blade rental

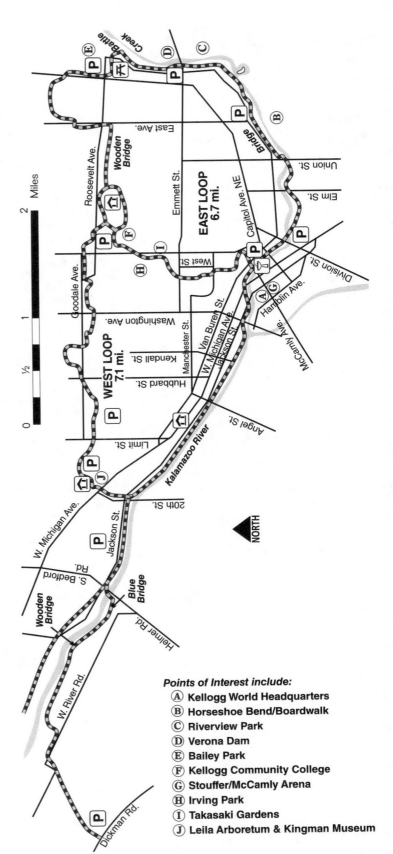

Points of Interest include:
- **A** Kellogg World Headquarters
- **B** Horseshoe Bend/Boardwalk
- **C** Riverview Park
- **D** Verona Dam
- **E** Bailey Park
- **F** Kellogg Community College
- **G** Stouffer/McCamly Arena
- **H** Irving Park
- **I** Takasaki Gardens
- **J** Leila Arboretum & Kingman Museum

Musketawa Trail

Trail Uses		**Setting**	Small villages, farmland, wetlands, creek crossings
Grid	G3 **Trail ID** 212	**Location**	Marne, Muskegon
Length	26 miles	**Lat/Long**	43-14 / 86-15 Muskegon at 1st St.
Surface	Paved	**Counties**	Ottawa, Muskegon
Difficulty	Easy	**Contact**	Trail Manager 231-853-5476

Getting There North of B-72 and east of US-31 & I-96 on the east side of Muskegon Heights. To get to the Ravenna trailhead, take M-46 to Ravenna Road, then south to the trailhead on the left

Trail Notes The Musketawa Trail is built on old railroad right-of-way and runs between Muskegon and Marne. It passes through Conklin and Ravenna. The terrain is flat and generally open. The east end of the trail is located just west of Grand Rapids.

Facilities

SYMBOL LEGEND

- Beach/Swimming
- Bicycle Repair
- Cabin
- Camping
- Canoe Launch
- First Aid
- Food
- GC Golf Course
- ? Information
- Lodging
- Overlook/ Observation
- P Parking
- Picnic
- Ranger Station
- Restrooms
- Shelter
- T Trailhead
- Visitor Center
- Water

TRAIL LEGEND

- Trail
- Skiing only Trail
- Hiking only Trail
- Planned Trail
- Alternate Trail
- Road
- ++++++++ Railroad Tracks

Portland Riverwalk Trail

Trail Uses	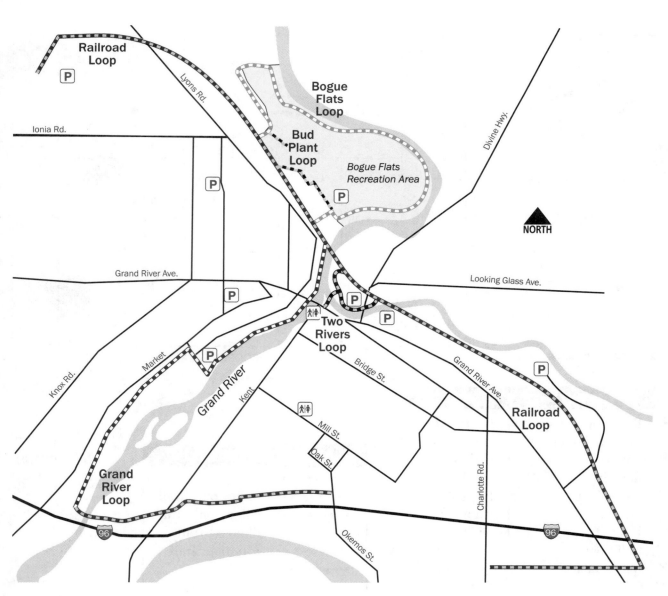	**Setting**	Urban, parks
Grid	H5 **Trail ID** 340	**Location**	Portland
Length	8 miles	**Lat/Long**	45-52 / 84-50 Portland area
Surface	Paved	**County**	Ionia
Difficulty	Easy	**Contact**	Portland Parks & Recreation 517-647-7985

Getting There Portland is located northwest of Lansing via I-96. The trailhead at the west end of town is located at the Portland High School parking lot.

Trail Notes The Portland River Walk bisects the City of Portland with a quiet and scenic linear park connecting a number of municipal parks. The trail is paved & 10-foot wide. Most of the trailheads around the City have parking lots.

Facilities

T. K. Lawless County Park

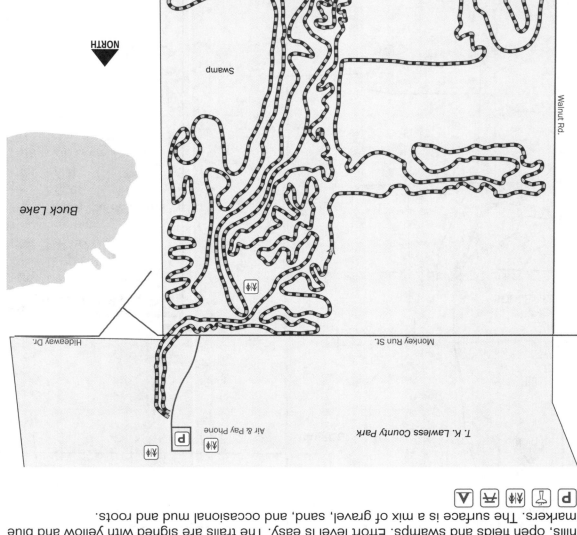

Trail Uses			
Grid	J3 **Trail ID** 280	**Location**	Vandalia
Length	10.5 miles	**Lat/Long**	41-54 / 85-52 **Parking area**
Surface	Natural	**County**	Cass
Difficulty	Easy to moderate	**Contact**	Cass County Parks & Recreation
Setting	Woods, fields, marsh		616-445-8611
		Fees	Park entry

Getting There The park is located about 30 miles southwest of Kalamazoo. Go east of Vandalia on M-60 to Lewis Lake Road. Turn left on Monkey Run Road for about a mile to the park entrance.

Trail Notes Single track, counter clockwise, loops with many intersections. Setting is woods, rolling hills, open fields and swamps. Effort level is easy. The trails are signed with yellow and blue markers. The surface is a mix of gravel, sand, and occasional mud and roots.

Facilities P   ⛺

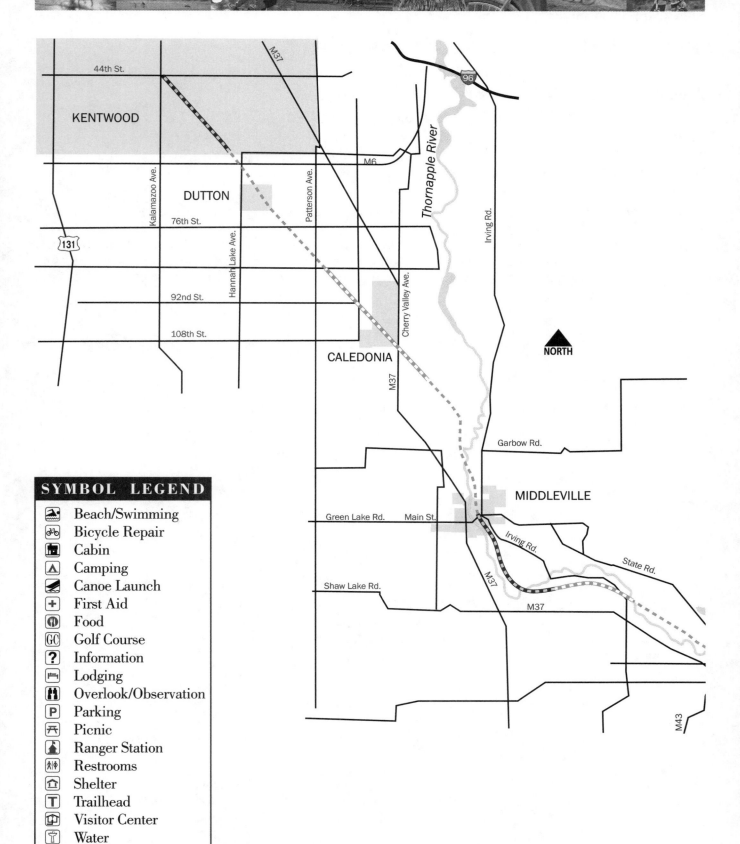

KENTWOOD

44th St.

M37

I96

DUTTON

Kalamazoo Ave.

Patterson Ave.

M6

Thornapple River

Irving Rd.

131

76th St.

Hannah Lake Ave.

92nd St.

Cherry Valley Ave.

108th St.

CALEDONIA

M37

NORTH

Garbow Rd.

MIDDLEVILLE

Green Lake Rd.

Main St.

Irving Rd.

State Rd.

M37

Shaw Lake Rd.

M37

M43

SYMBOL LEGEND

- Beach/Swimming
- Bicycle Repair
- Cabin
- Camping
- Canoe Launch
- First Aid
- Food
- GC Golf Course
- ? Information
- Lodging
- Overlook/Observation
- P Parking
- Picnic
- Ranger Station
- Restrooms
- Shelter
- T Trailhead
- Visitor Center
- Water

Thornapple Trail

Trail Uses	
Grid	H4 **Trail ID** 283
Length	6 miles – 2.5 miles in Kentwood & 3.5 miles between Middleville & Irving (42 miles when complete)

Surface	Asphalt, crushed stone
Difficulty	Easy
Setting	Small towns, farmland, woodlands
Location	Grand Rapids, Wyoming, Dutton
Lat/Long	42-40 / 83-23 Fairgrounds in Irving
Counties	Kent, Barry, Eaton
Contact	Kent County Parks 616-386-7275

Getting There Southeast trailhead - From Hastings, about 5 miles west to Irving Road, then north 1 mile to the trailhead by a private campground. Northwest trailhead - From Kentwood, 2 miles west of M-37 at 60th Street and Patterson Road.

Trail Notes When complete this 42 miles multi-use trail will run from Grand Rapids to Vermontville. It is being developed on former railroad corridor. The scenic highlight of the trial is its proximity to the Thornapple River.

Facilities P T ♦♦ ◑ ⊨

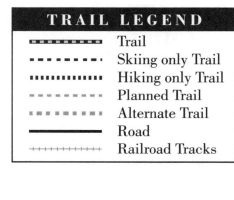

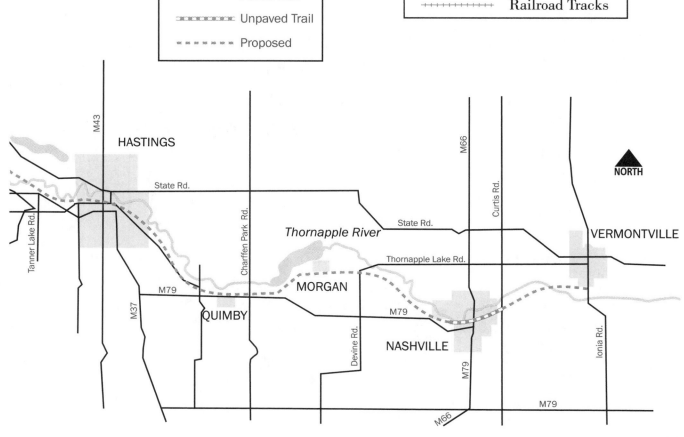

Yankee Springs Recreation Area

Trail Uses		**Setting**	Rugged terrain, bogs, marshes, lakes and streams, sand, pines
Grid	H4 **Trail ID** 303	**Location**	Middleville
Length	13 miles	**Lat/Long**	42-37 / 85-27 Trailhead area
Surface	Natural	**County**	Barry
Difficulty	Easy to difficult	**Contact**	Yankee Springs Recreation Area 269-795-9081
Acres	5,200	**Fees**	Vehicle entry fees

Getting There Located off US 131 approximately 20 miles south of Grand Rapids and 3 miles west of Wayland. Exit at 129th Avenue and proceed east for 8 miles to the park entrance at Briggs Road.

Trail Notes Yankee Springs Recreation Area consists of 5,200-acres and offers campgrounds, cabins, fishing, and trails for various uses. The setting is mostly wooded hills. It is the most popular trail in western Michigan. Be aware of some muddy conditions in wet weather.

Facilities

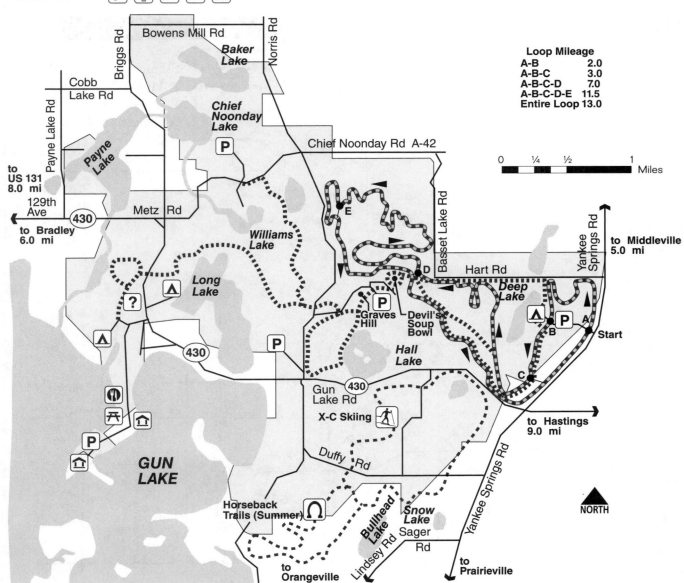

Loop Mileage

A-B	2.0
A-B-C	3.0
A-B-C-D	7.0
A-B-C-D-E	11.5
Entire Loop	13.0

Central East Michigan's Trails Overview

Legend:
- ■ Recreational Trail
- ▲ Fat Tire Trail
- ◆ Recreational & Fat Tire Trail

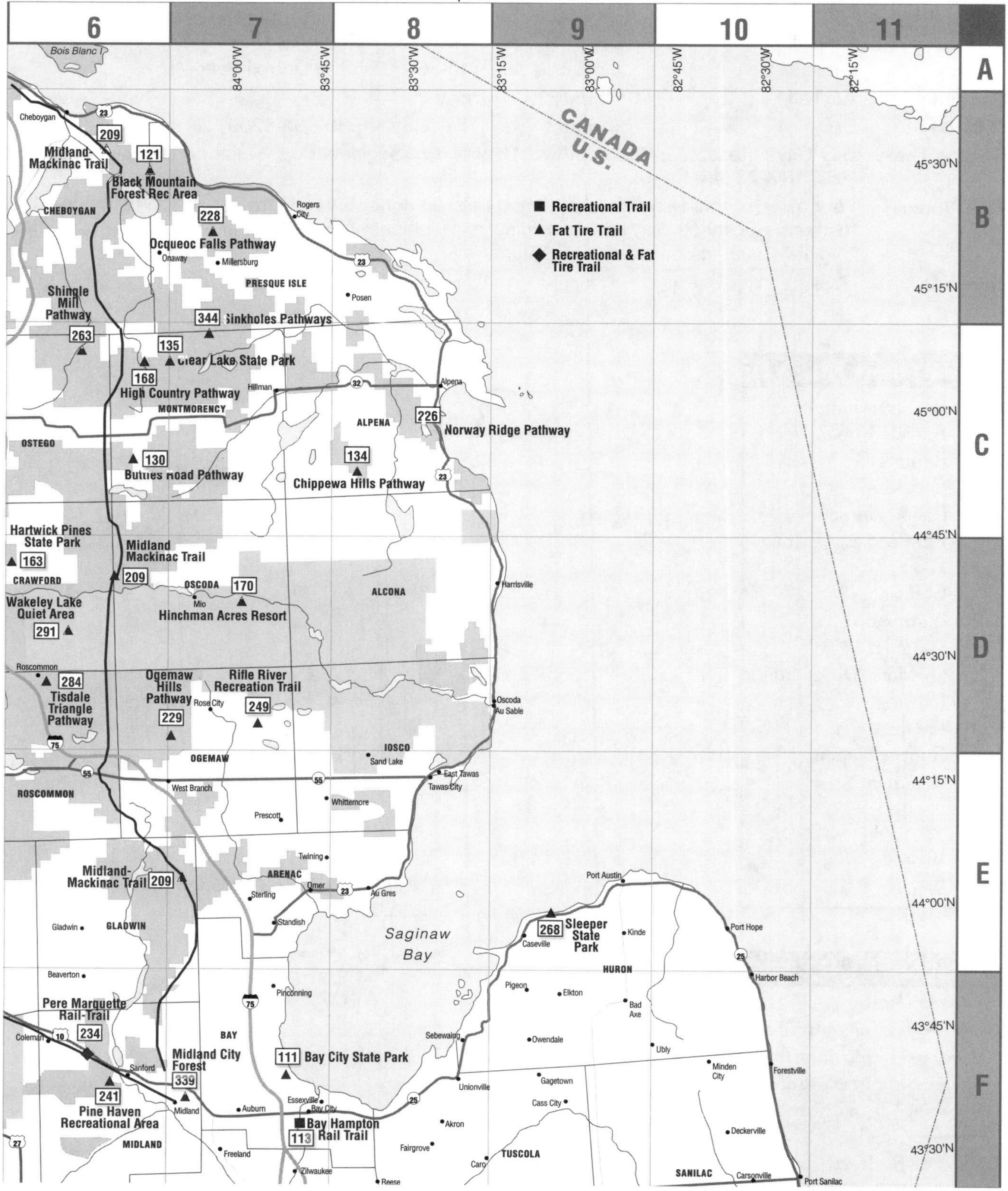

Bay Hampton Rail-Trail

Trail Uses		**Setting**	Open, urban
Grid	F7 **Trail ID** 113	**Location**	Bay City, Hampton
Length	6 miles	**Lat/Long**	43-36 / 83-52 Carroll Park
Surface	Asphalt	**County**	Bay
Difficulty	Easy	**Contact**	Bay City 989-894-8200

Getting There Bay City is located in the southwest section of Saginaw Bay. Major access highways are US-75/M-23 and M-10.

Trail Notes Four miles of the trail is on abandoned railroad right-of-way. Surface is asphalt. It connects to the Bay City River Walk, providing an additional four mile of trail that runs along the Saginaw River in downtown Bay City.

Facilities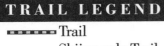

SYMBOL LEGEND

- Beach/Swimming
- Bicycle Repair
- Cabin
- Camping
- Canoe Launch
- First Aid
- Food
- GC Golf Course
- Information
- Lodging
- Overlook/Observation
- Parking
- Picnic
- Ranger Station
- Restrooms
- Shelter
- Trailhead
- Visitor Center
- Water

TRAIL LEGEND

- Trail
- Skiing only Trail
- Hiking only Trail
- Planned Trail
- Alternate Trail
- Road
- Railroad Tracks

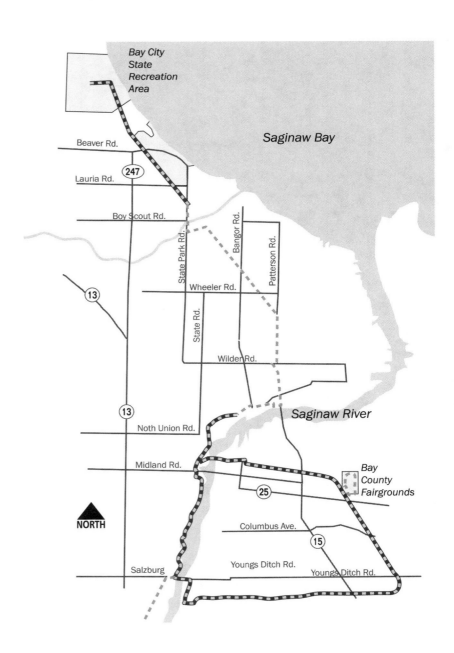

Black Mountain Forest

Trail Uses

Grid B6 **Trail ID** 121

Length 32 miles

Surface Natural

Difficulty Moderate to difficult

Setting Heavily wooded, some open areas

Location Cheboygan, Rogers City, Onaway

Lat/Long 47-28 / 84-12   Black Mountain Rd & CR-489

Counties Cheboygan, Presque Isle

Contact Atlanta Forest Area   517-786-4251

Getting There From Onaway, north on M-211 to County Road 489, then on to the trailhead.

Trail Notes Effort level ranges from moderate to difficult. Portions of the terrain are steep and hilly. Double track and forest roads, clockwise direction. Heavily wooded. There is also a short 1.2 mile asphalt handicapper trail available.

Facilities

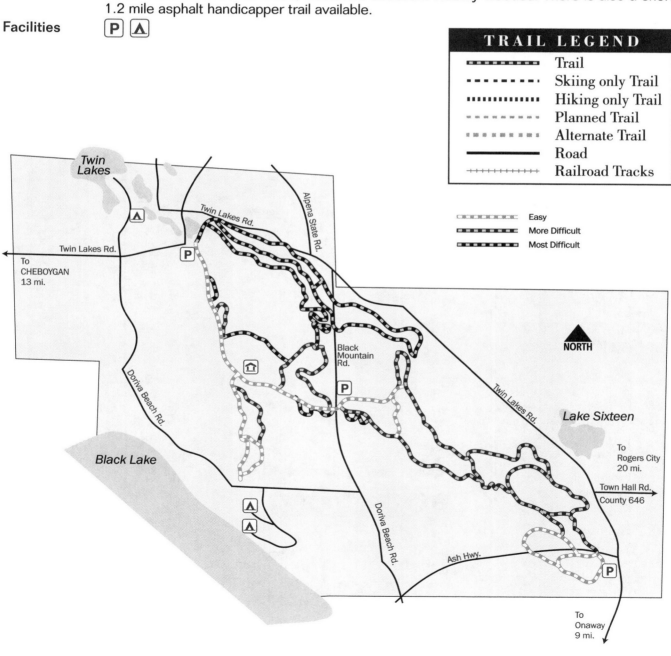

TRAIL LEGEND	
▪▪▪▪▪▪▪▪	Trail
▪ ▪ ▪ ▪ ▪ ▪	Skiing only Trail
▪▪▪▪▪▪▪▪▪▪	Hiking only Trail
▪ ▪ ▪ ▪ ▪	Planned Trail
▪ ▪ ▪ ▪ ▪	Alternate Trail
▬▬▬▬	Road
+++++++++	Railroad Tracks

Easy — More Difficult — Most Difficult

Twin Lakes

Twin Lakes Rd.

Alpena State Rd.

Twin Lakes Rd.

To CHEBOYGAN 13 mi.

Doriva Beach Rd.

Black Lake

Black Mountain Rd.

NORTH

Twin Lakes Rd.

Lake Sixteen

To Rogers City 20 mi.

Town Hall Rd. County 646

Doriva Beach Rd.

Ash Hwy.

To Onaway 9 mi.

Buttles Road Pathway

Trail Uses		**Setting**	Mostly open terrain
Grid	C6 **Trail ID** 130	**Location**	Lewiston
Length	7 miles	**Lat/Long**	44-55 / 84-19 Entrance off Buttles Rd
Surface	Natural	**County**	Montmorency
Difficulty	Easy	**Contact**	Atlanta DBR 517-785-4251

Getting There   Located between Lewiston and M32 on Buttles Road. From Lewiston, take Buttes Road north for 3 miles to a parking lot at the trailhead.

Trail Notes   Single track, clockwise direction. Effort level is easy. Terrain is mostly flat and open.

Facilities   P

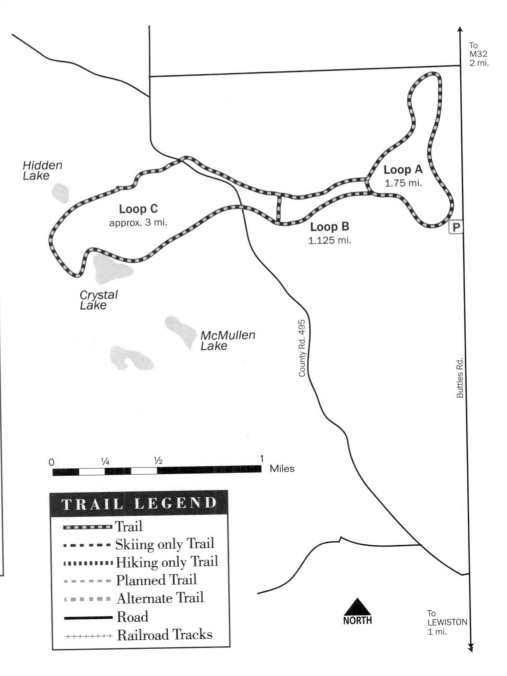

SYMBOL LEGEND

- Beach/Swimming
- Bicycle Repair
- Cabin
- Camping
- Canoe Launch
- First Aid
- Food
- GC Golf Course
- ? Information
- Lodging
- Overlook/Observation
- P Parking
- Picnic
- Ranger Station
- Restrooms
- Shelter
- T Trailhead
- Visitor Center
- Water

TRAIL LEGEND

- Trail
- Skiing only Trail
- Hiking only Trail
- Planned Trail
- Alternate Trail
- Road
- Railroad Tracks

Hidden Lake

Loop C
approx. 3 mi.

Crystal Lake

McMullen Lake

Loop A
1.75 mi.

Loop B
1.125 mi.

County Rd. 495

Buttles Rd.

To M32 2 mi.

To LEWISTON 1 mi.

NORTH

0   ¼   ½   1 Miles

Chippewa Hills Pathway

Trail Uses	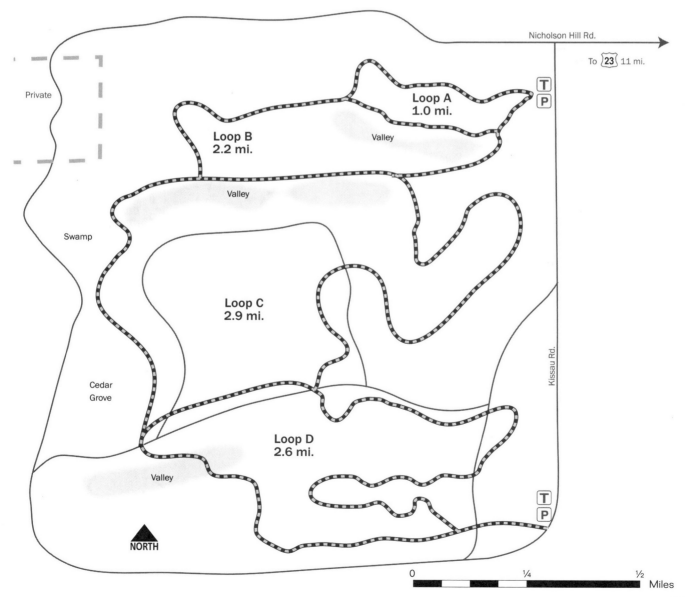		**Setting**	Woods and open areas
Grid	C8 **Trail ID** 134		**Location**	Alpena, Ossineke
Length	8 miles		**Lat/Long**	44-54 / 83-40 Parking off Nickolson Road
Surface	Natural		**County**	Alpena
Difficulty	Easy to moderate		**Contact**	Chippewa Hills 989-785-4251

Getting There   Located between Alpena and Harrisville. From Ossineke (US23) 11 miles west on Nicholson Hill Road to Kissau Road, then south to the entrance and trailhead.

Trail Notes   Effort level is easy to moderate. There are 4 loops. Single track, counter clockwise. Setting is open and woods.

Facilities   P

Clear Lake-Jackson Lake Pathway

Trail Uses	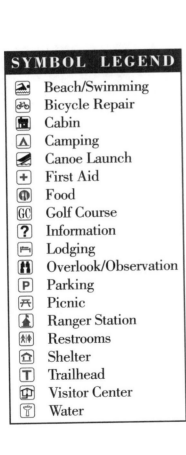		
Grid	C6 **Trail ID** 135	**Location**	Atlanta
Length	7.5 miles	**Lat/Long**	45-08 / 84-11 Entrance off Milbur Road
Surface	Natural	**County**	Montmorency, Presque Isle
Difficulty	Easy to moderate	**Contact**	Clear Lake State Park 989-785-4251
Setting	Open, Lake	**Fees**	Vehicle entry permit

Getting There From Atlanta N on M33 for 10 miles to Clear Lake State Park.

Trail Notes Three loops make us this pathway. There is a campground at the Jackson Lake State Forest and another near the north trailhead at Clear Lake State Park.

Facilities P A

SYMBOL LEGEND

- Beach/Swimming
- Bicycle Repair
- Cabin
- Camping
- Canoe Launch
- First Aid
- Food
- GC Golf Course
- ? Information
- Lodging
- Overlook/Observation
- P Parking
- Picnic
- Ranger Station
- Restrooms
- Shelter
- T Trailhead
- Visitor Center
- Water

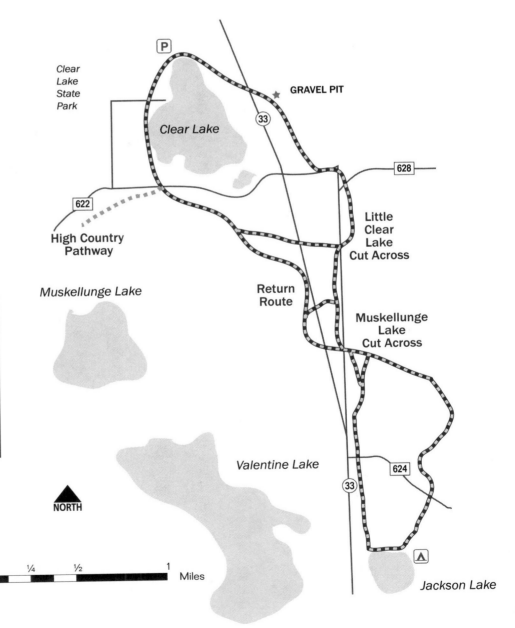

Hartwick Pines State Park

Trail Uses		**Setting**	Rolling hills, open, a 49 acre forest of Old Growth Pines
Grid	D6 **Trail ID** 163	**Location**	Grayling
Length	18 miles	**Lat/Long**	44-44 / 84-40 Park area
Surface	Natural	**County**	Crawford
Difficulty	Easy to moderate	**Contact**	Hartwick Pines State Park 989-348-7068
Acres	9,672	**Fees**	Vehicle entry

Getting There From Grayling, 7.5 mile northeast on M-93, or east off I-75 (exit 259) for 3 miles..

Trail Notes Effort level is easy to moderate. Single track, counter clockwise. There are three main loops: Weary Legs Trail – 7.5 miles; Deer Run Trail – 5 miles; Aspen Trail – 3 miles. The park contains a logging museum and interpretive center. The museum is open from 9 am to 4 pm Labor Day through October and May 1st through Memorial Day.

Facilities P ⛱ 🏠 ⛺

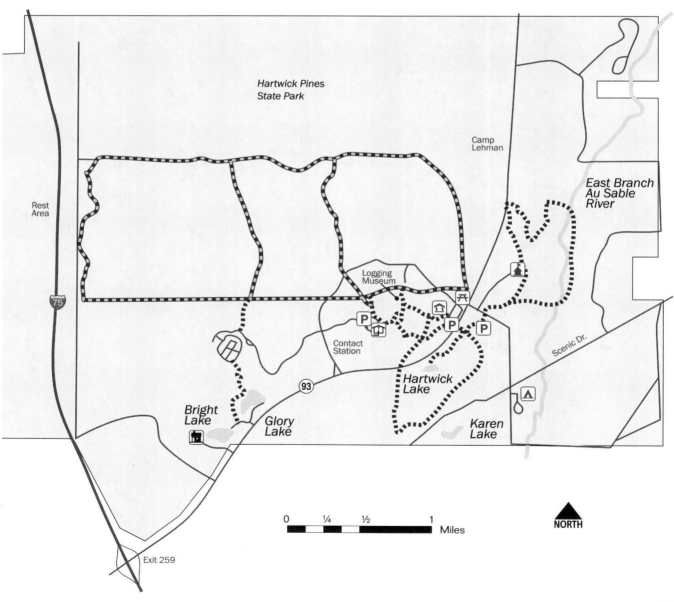

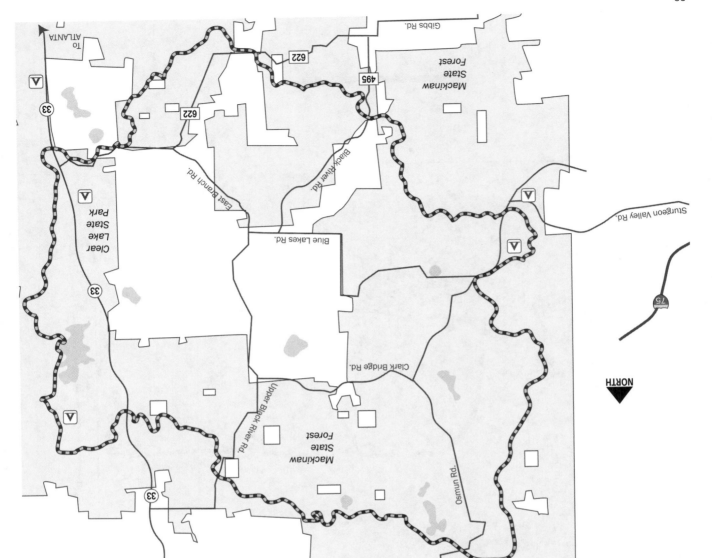

High Country Pathway

Trail Uses		**Setting**	Woods, open
Grid	C6 Trail ID 168	**Location**	Gaylord, Onaway, Vanderbilt, Wolverine
Length	77	**Lat/Long**	45-12 / 84-12 Hwy 33 & Tomahawk Rd.
Surface	Natural	**County**	Cheboygan, Otsego, Montmorency
Difficulty	Moderate	**Contact**	Pigeon River Country Association PO Box 122, Gaylord, MI 49734

Getting There From Vanderbilt, east on Sturgeon Valley Road for 11 miles to Tin Shanty Bridge Road, then right 1.5 miles to where the pathway crosses. There is parking in a clearing just off the road.

Trail Notes Effort level is moderate. Forest and open areas. Over looks Black River Valley. Counter clockwise.

Facilities P A (other towns near the pathway)

Hinchman Acres Resort

Trail Uses	(icons)	**Setting**	Woods, open	
Grid	D7 **Trail ID** 170	**Location**	Mio	
Length	20 miles	**Lat/Long**	44-40 / 84-07	Parking area
Surface	Natural	**County**	Oscoda	
Difficulty	Easy	**Contact**	Hinchman Acres Resort	989-826-3267

Getting There From the Detroit area, take I-75 north to M-33 (Rose City - exit 202). Take M-33 north 36 miles to Mio, then 4 blocks north of the traffic light on M-33 to the resort entrance. The resort is about 32 miles east of Grayling on M-72.

Trail Notes Effort level is easy. Terrain is mostly flat. Wooded and open areas. No trail fees when staying at the resort. Views of the Au Sable River.

Facilities P O bed

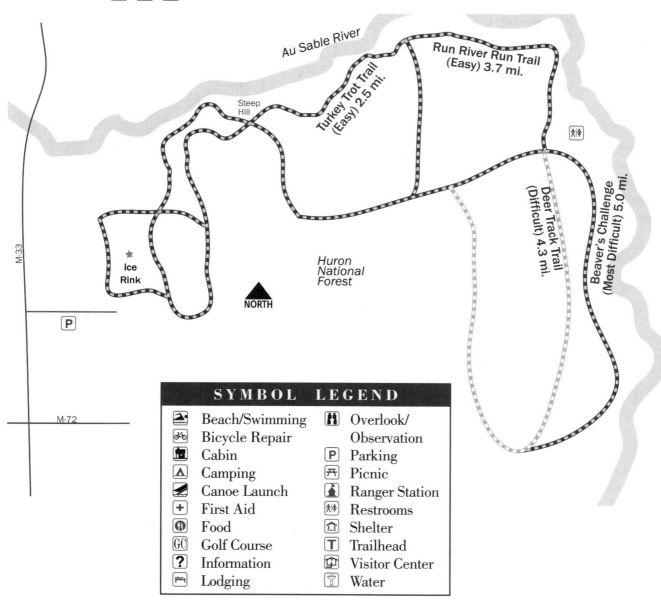

Au Sable River

Steep Hill

Turkey Trot Trail (Easy) 2.5 mi.

Run River Run Trail (Easy) 3.7 mi.

Deer Track Trail (Difficult) 4.3 mi.

Beaver's Challenge (Most Difficult) 5.0 mi.

Ice Rink

Huron National Forest

NORTH

M-33

P

M-72

SYMBOL LEGEND

(icon)	Beach/Swimming	(icon)	Overlook/
(icon)	Bicycle Repair		Observation
(icon)	Cabin	P	Parking
(icon)	Camping	(icon)	Picnic
(icon)	Canoe Launch	(icon)	Ranger Station
(icon)	First Aid	(icon)	Restrooms
(icon)	Food	(icon)	Shelter
GC	Golf Course	T	Trailhead
?	Information	(icon)	Visitor Center
(icon)	Lodging	(icon)	Water

Midland City Forest

Trail Uses			
Grid	F7 **Trail ID** 339	**Setting**	Woods, wetland, low ridges, open
Length	11 miles	**Location**	Midland
Surface	Natural	**Lat/Long**	43-41 / 84-15 Forest area
Difficulty	Easy to moderate	**County**	Midland
Acres	43,500	**Contact**	Midland City Forest 989-837-6930

Getting There From I-10 in Midland, take the Eastman Road exit. Go north two miles to Monroe Road. Turn left and go a half mile west to the city Forest main parking area on the south side of the road.

Trail Notes Midland City Forest is about a square mile of Saginaw Valley woodland. It is a mixture of wetland and low ridges, with pines and mixed hardwoods. The singletrack trail is marked. The north and south loops should be ridden in a counter-clockwise direction. The north and south creek-side sections are challenging and should be ridden clockwise. Watch for horses on the two track road intersections. Features include a 132' winding bridge.

Facilities P Drink vending machine

- ░░░░░░░░ **Gnu Loop**
- ▪▪▪▪▪▪▪▪ **Newell Creek**
- ▪▪▪▪▪▪▪▪ **North Loop**
- ▪▪▪▪▪▪▪▪ **South Loop**
- ▪▪▪▪▪▪▪▪ **Two Track Loop**

SYMBOL LEGEND

- Beach/Swimming
- Bicycle Repair
- Cabin
- Camping
- Canoe Launch
- First Aid
- Food
- Golf Course
- Information
- Lodging
- Overlook/Observation
- Parking
- Picnic
- Ranger Station
- Restrooms
- Shelter
- Trailhead
- Visitor Center
- Water

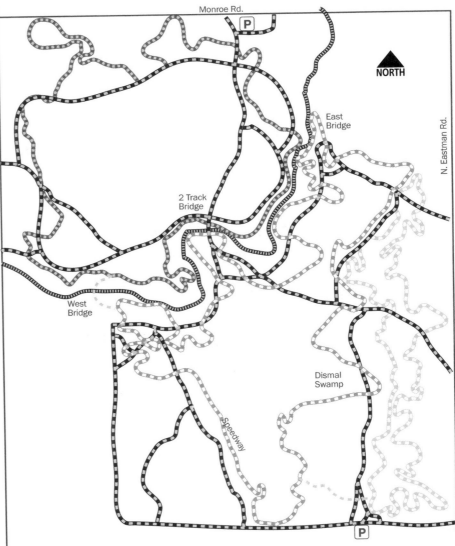

0   ¼
         Miles

Midland to Mackinac Trail

Trail Uses	🚵 🏃 ⛷️
Grid	AF7 **Trail ID** 209
Length	210 miles
Surface	Grass, dirt
Difficulty	Easy to difficult
Setting	Woods, open
Location	Midland, Cheboygan, Mackinaw City
Lat/Long	45-47 / 84-21 Midland trailhead area
Counties	Midland, Gladwin, Roscommon, Crawford, Otsego, Cheboygan
Contact	Mio Ranger District 517-826-3252
Getting There	South trailhead- From Midland 11 miles north to the Mills Community Center on Shearer Road and 2 miles west of Herner Road.
	North trailhead- Mackinaw City at the junction of Hwy 75 & 23.
Trail Notes	Effort level varies from easy to difficult. Setting is woods, open areas and farm land. There are many campgrounds along the route. It passes through the Huron-Manistee National Forest between Midland & Mackinaw City.
Facilities	🏕️ 🅿️ (Midland, Cheboygan & Mackinaw City – all facilities)

Norway Ridge Pathway

Trail Uses		**Setting**	Woods, open	
Grid	C8 **Trail ID** 226	**Location**	Alpena	
Length	7.5 miles	**Lat/Long**	45-01 / 83-31	Parking off Werth Rd
Surface	Natural	**County**	Alpena	
Difficulty	Easy	**Contact**	Atlanta DNR Field Office	989-785-4251

Getting There From Alpena, Southwest on US-23 for 4.5 miles.

Trail Notes Terrain is mostly level, with forested and open areas. Effort level is easy. Single and double track in a counter clockwise direction.

Facilities P

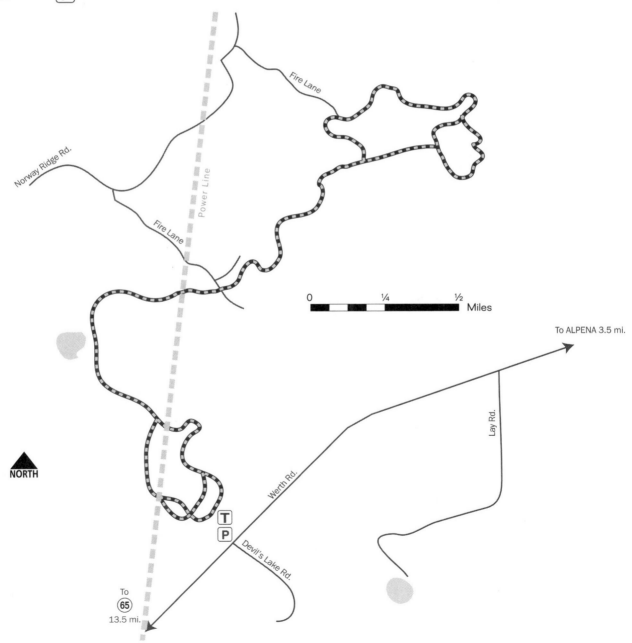

Ocqueoc Falls Bicentennial Pathway

Trail Uses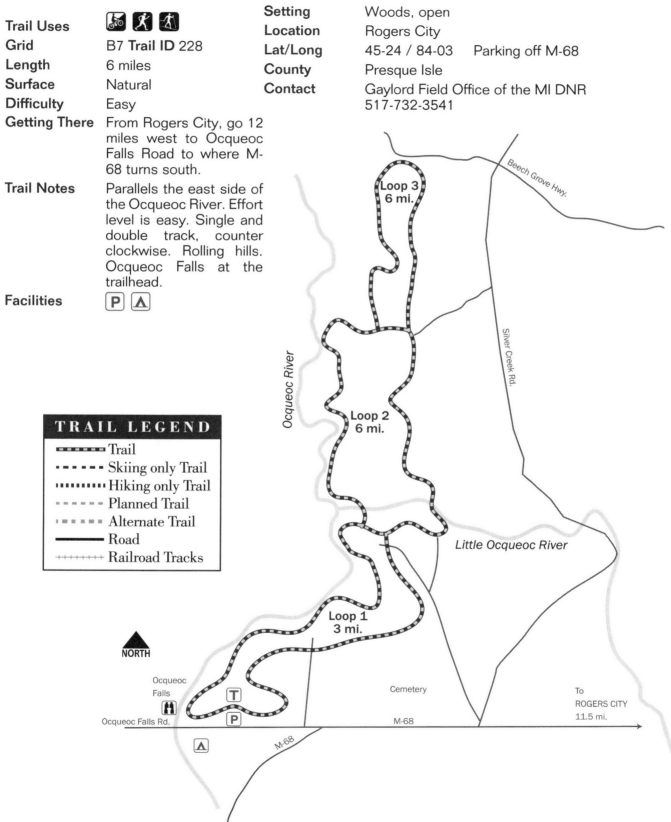

Grid B7 **Trail ID** 228

Length 6 miles

Surface Natural

Difficulty Easy

Getting There From Rogers City, go 12 miles west to Ocqueoc Falls Road to where M-68 turns south.

Trail Notes Parallels the east side of the Ocqueoc River. Effort level is easy. Single and double track, counter clockwise. Rolling hills. Ocqueoc Falls at the trailhead.

Facilities

Setting Woods, open

Location Rogers City

Lat/Long 45-24 / 84-03   Parking off M-68

County Presque Isle

Contact Gaylord Field Office of the MI DNR
517-732-3541

TRAIL LEGEND

- Trail
- Skiing only Trail
- Hiking only Trail
- Planned Trail
- Alternate Trail
- Road
- Railroad Tracks

NORTH

Beech Grove Hwy.

Loop 3
6 mi.

Silver Creek Rd.

Ocqueoc River

Loop 2
6 mi.

Little Ocqueoc River

Loop 1
3 mi.

Ocqueoc Falls

Ocqueoc Falls Rd.

M-68

Cemetery

M-68

To ROGERS CITY
11.5 mi.

Ogemaw Hills Pathway

Trail Uses		**Setting**	Wooded, hilly, rural
Grid	D7 **Trail ID** 229	**Location**	West Branch
Length	13.5	**Lat/Long**	41-21 / 84-14 Parking off CR-F7
Surface	Natural, groomed	**County**	Ogemaw
Difficulty	Easy to difficult	**Contact**	Roscommon Forest Area 571-275-5151

Getting There From West Branch, 5.5 miles north on Fairview Road (F7) to the entrance road on the right.

Trail Notes There are blue trail markers at the intersections. Effort level is easy to difficult. Setting is woody and hilly. Many loops.

Facilities P

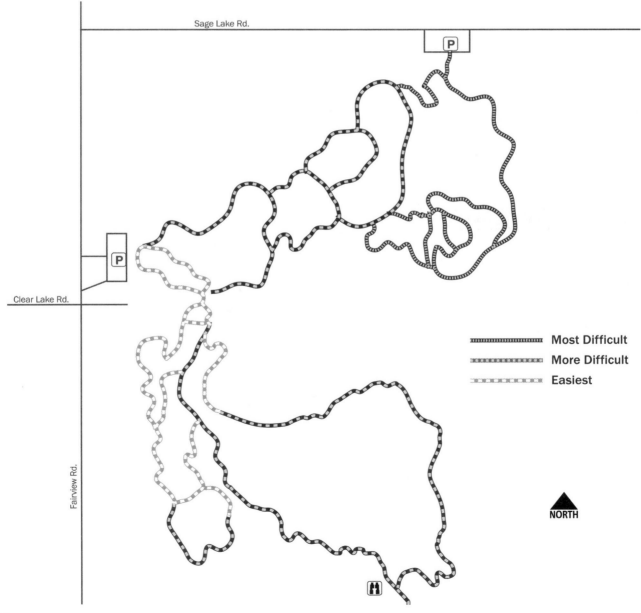

Pere-Marquette Rail-Trail

Trail Uses 🚲 ⛸ 🎿

Grid	F6	**Location**	Midland, Coleman, Clare
Length	30 miles	**Lat/Long**	43-37 / 84-15 Midland Trailhead at Hwy 20
Surface	Asphalt	**Counties**	Midland, Isabella
Difficulty	Easy	**Contact**	Midland County Parks & Recreation
Setting	Flat, open, farmland		989-832-6870

Getting There The Midland trailhead is located near the "tridge" (a bridge with three segments) at the confluence of the Tittabawassee and Chippewa River and the Farmers Market at the end of Ashman Road. The western trailhead is located on the outskirts of Clare off US 27 just south of Saginaw Road.

Trail Notes The trails spans from the Tridge in Midland to the outskirts of Clare. It parallels Saginaw Road and US 10 for almost its total distance. The surface is asphalt and 10 to 12 feet wide. The trail was built on old railroad bed.

Facilities P 🚰 🚻

	Miles
Tridge	0.0
Dublin Ave.	3.0
Averill Rollway	5.0
Sanford Staging Area	8.4
Verterans Park	9.3
Arbutus Bog	10.2
North Bradley	14.4
Coleman Staging Area	20.2
Loomis Staging Area	25.1
Clare	29.4

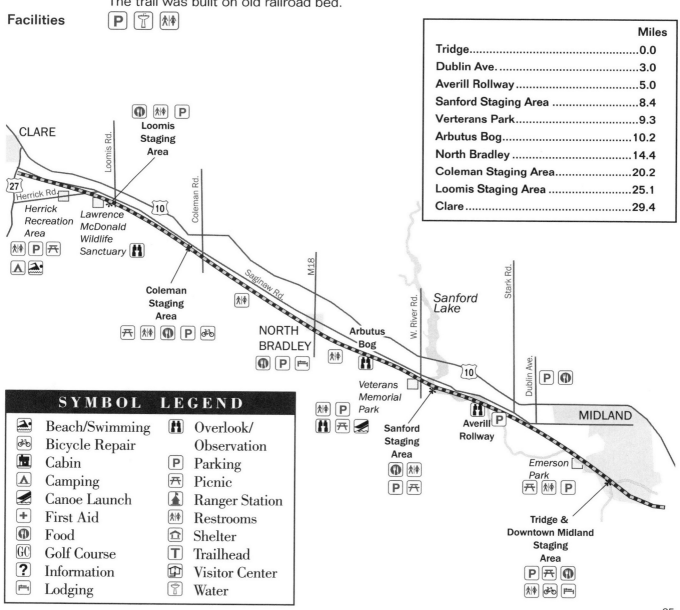

SYMBOL LEGEND

🏖	Beach/Swimming	🔭	Overlook/ Observation
🚲	Bicycle Repair		
🏠	Cabin	P	Parking
⛺	Camping	🪑	Picnic
🛶	Canoe Launch	🏛	Ranger Station
+	First Aid	🚻	Restrooms
🍴	Food	🏠	Shelter
GC	Golf Course	T	Trailhead
?	Information	🏛	Visitor Center
🛏	Lodging	🚰	Water

95

Pine Haven Recreation Area

Trail Uses		**Setting**	County Park, wooded, open
Grid	F6 **Trail ID** 241	**Location**	Midland
Length	10 miles	**Lat/Long**	43-41 / 84-24 Parking off Maynard Rd
Surface	Natural, groomed	**County**	Midland
Difficulty	Easy to moderate	**Contact**	Midland County Parks & Recreation 989-832-6874
Acres	325	**Fees**	Donations only

Getting There Take US-10 west to the West River Road exit. Turn south (left) and proceed back over the highway. Turn right on Maynard Road (just after the exit ramp). Pine Haven is at the end of Maynard Road.

Trail Notes Terrain is mostly moderate and flat, with a few steep descents. You'll find sections of sand where the trail skirts the Salt River at the south end. There are no water facilities. Effort level is easy. No entrance fee, but donations accepted at park entrance. The trail is straddled by US-10 to east and the Pere Marquette Rail Trail to the West.

Facilities

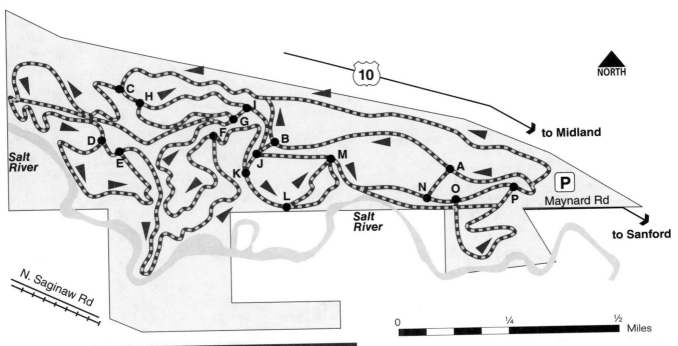

SYMBOL LEGEND

Beach/Swimming		Overlook/Observation	
Bicycle Repair		Parking	
Cabin		Picnic	
Camping		Ranger Station	
Canoe Launch		Restrooms	
First Aid		Shelter	
Food		Trailhead	
Golf Course		Visitor Center	
Information		Water	
Lodging			

TRAIL LEGEND

	Trail
	Skiing only Trail
	Hiking only Trail
	Planned Trail
	Alternate Trail
	Road
	Railroad Tracks

Rifle River Recreation Area

Trail Uses

Grid   D7 **Trail ID** 249

Length   13.5

Surface   Natural

Difficulty   Easy to difficult

Acres   4,329

Setting   Woods, open, hilly

Location   Rose City

Lat/Long   44-25 / 84-01   Entrance off CR-F28

County   Ogemaw

Contact   Rifle River Recreation Area   989-437-2258

Getting There   From Rose City go 5 miles east on Rose City Road (F28).

Trail Notes   Effort level is easy to difficult. Trail consists of single track and forest road. Trails on the south half of the park are flat. The trails east of Devoe and Grousenhaven Lakes are hilly.

Facilities

Map:

To LIPTON .75 Mi.

F-28

Ridge Rd.

Shady Shores Rd.

Ranch Rd.

Weir Rd.

Devoe Lake

Ridge Rd.

Grebe Lake

Rifle River Rd.

Lost Lake

Gravel Rd.

F-26

Shingle Mill Pathway

Trail Uses	🚲 🎿 🥾	**Setting**	Woods, open, marshland, ridges
Grid	C6 Trail ID 263	**Location**	Vanderbilt
Length	18 miles	**Lat/Long**	45-10 / 84-28 Parking off Sturgeon Valley Road
Surface	Natural	**Counties**	Otsego, Cheboygan
Difficulty	Moderate to difficult	**Contact**	Mackinaw State Forest 989-732-3541

Getting There   From Vanderbilt, proceed 9 miles on Sturgeon Valley Road to the entrance and trailhead.

Trail Notes   Single track, counter clockwise. A popular trail system, with a scenic overlook along the 10 mile loop. Part of the North Country Pathway enters the west side of the trail. Terrain is generally flat, with marshland areas, ridges.

Facilities   P 🚰 🏕

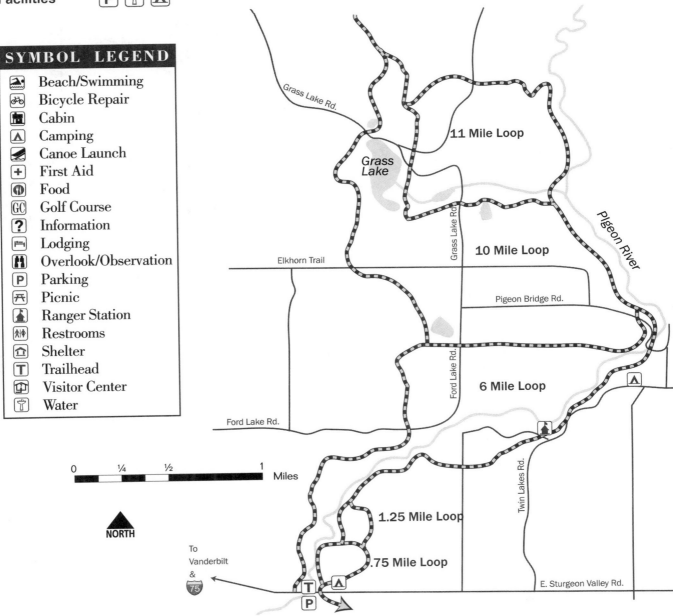

SYMBOL LEGEND

🏊	Beach/Swimming
🚲	Bicycle Repair
🏠	Cabin
🏕	Camping
🛶	Canoe Launch
➕	First Aid
🍴	Food
GC	Golf Course
❓	Information
🛏	Lodging
🔭	Overlook/Observation
P	Parking
🍱	Picnic
🧗	Ranger Station
🚻	Restrooms
🏠	Shelter
T	Trailhead
🏛	Visitor Center
🚰	Water

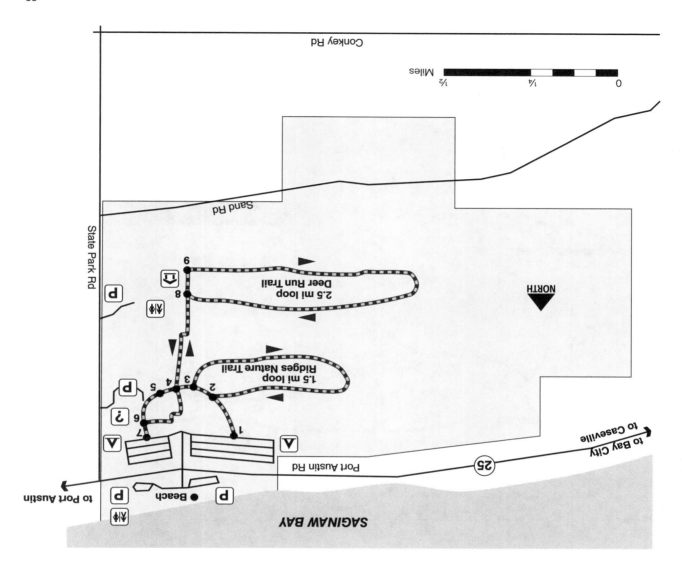

Sleeper State Park

Trail Uses		**Setting**	Woods, open, hilly, wetlands
Grid	E9 Trail ID 268	**Location**	Caseville, Bay City
Length	4.5 miles	**Lat/Long**	43-59 / 83-13 Parking area
Surface	Natural, groomed	**County**	Huron
Difficulty	Easy	**Contact**	Sleeper State Park 989-856-4411
Acres	1,003	**Fees**	Vehicle entrance fee

Getting There The Park is located in Huron County, 50 miles northeast of Bay City and 5 miles northeast of Caseville on M-25.

Trail Notes The setting consists of sandy ridges, uplands, and wetlands. Its 1,003-acres are heavily forested. The trails follow mainly old dune ridges with changing vegetation from upland to wetland type. Along the trails are a great variety of changing vegetation from upland to wetland type. There are two trails: Ridges Nature Trail - 1.5 miles; Deer Run - 2.5 miles. The trails are groomed in the winter for cross-country skiing.

Facilities

Tisdale Triangle Pathway

Trail Uses	🚴 🚶 🎿	**Setting**	Open, woods	
Grid	D6 **Trail ID** 284	**Location**	Roscommon	
Length	10 miles	**Lat/Long**	44-30 / 64-35	Parking area
Surface	Natural	**County**	Roscommon	
Difficulty	Easy	**Contact**	AuSable State Forest 989-275-4622	

Getting There From M-18 in Roscommon, go .5 miles east on Tisdale Road to the trailhead at the end of the road.

Trail Notes Terrain is flat, with forest and open areas. Effort level is easy. Trail is double track, counter clockwise.

Facilities P

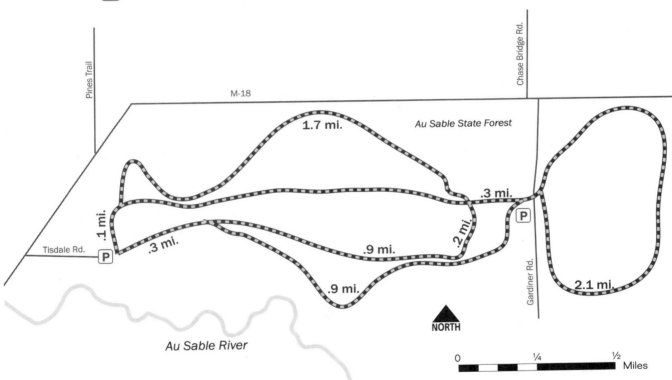

SYMBOL LEGEND

🏖	Beach/Swimming	🔭	Overlook/ Observation
🚲	Bicycle Repair	P	Parking
🏠	Cabin	🪑	Picnic
⛺	Camping	⛪	Ranger Station
🛶	Canoe Launch	🚻	Restrooms
✚	First Aid	🏠	Shelter
🅜	Food	T	Trailhead
GC	Golf Course	🏛	Visitor Center
❓	Information	🚰	Water
🛏	Lodging		

TRAIL LEGEND

▪▪▪▪▪	Trail
▪ ▪ ▪ ▪	Skiing only Trail
▪▪▪▪▪▪	Hiking only Trail
▪ ▪ ▪ ▪	Planned Trail
▪ ▪ ▪ ▪	Alternate Trail
▬▬▬	Road
++++++	Railroad Tracks

Wakeley Lake Quiet Area

Trail Uses	(icons)	**Setting**	Woods, open, hilly, marshland
		Location	Grayling
Grid	D6 **Trail ID** 291	**Lat/Long**	44-38 / 64-74 Parking off M-72
Length	16.5 miles	**County**	Crawford
Surface	Natural	**Contact**	USDA Forest Service 989-826-3252
Difficulty	Easy to moderate	**Fees**	Vehicle entrance fee

Getting There Entrance is off M-72, 1 mile east of Wakeley Bridge/Chase Bridge Road, and 10 miles east of Grayling or 22 miles west of Mio.

Trail Notes Effort level is easy to moderate. Single and double track, in a clockwise direction. Somewhat hilly. Woods and open areas.

Facilities P

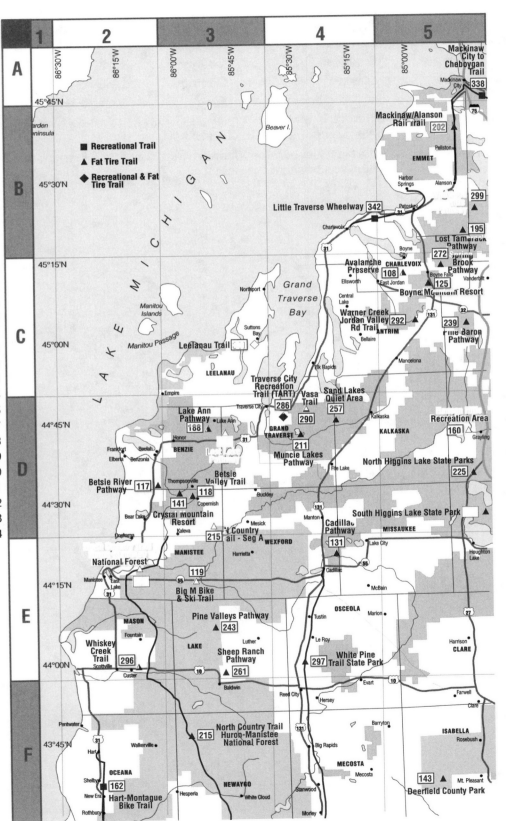

Avalanche Preserve Recreation Area

Trail Uses

Grid C5 **Trail ID** 108

Length 4.5 miles

Difficulty Moderate to difficult

Acres 300

Setting Wooded, hilly

Location Boyne City

Lat/Long 42-12 / 85-01   Parking area

County Charlevoix

Contact Boyne City Chamber of Commerce
231-582-6222

Getting There From Boyne City, go south on Lake Street to end of the road.

Trail Notes Gravel and natural surfaces. Effort level moderate to difficult. There is an overlook, with 462 steps to the top of Avalanche and a viewing platform.

Facilities [P]

TRAIL LEGEND

▪▪▪▪▪▪ Trail
- - - - - Skiing only Trail
▪▪▪▪▪▪ Hiking only Trail
- - - - - Planned Trail
◻▪◻▪◻▪ Alternate Trail
——— Road
+++++++ Railroad Tracks

BOYNE CITY

Division St.

Wilson

Hockey Rink & Warming House [P]

Pleasant Valley Rd.

NORTH

Davis Rd.

Betsie River Pathway

Trail Uses			
Grid	D2 **Trail ID** 117	**Location**	Thompsonville
Length	8 miles	**Lat/Long**	44-33 / 86-04 Parking-Longstreet Rd
Surface	Natural	**County**	Benzie
Difficulty	Easy to moderate	**Contact**	Pere Marquette State Forest 231-922-5280
Setting	Wooded, open	**Fees**	Trail use

Getting There   From Thompsonville, west on M115 for 5 miles, then south on King Road for half a mile to Longstreet Road, then left for .8 miles to the parking lot.

Trail Notes   Effort level is easy to moderate with the more difficult trails to the west of the parking lot. The trails connect to the Crystal Mountain Resort. There is a trail use fee.

Facilities

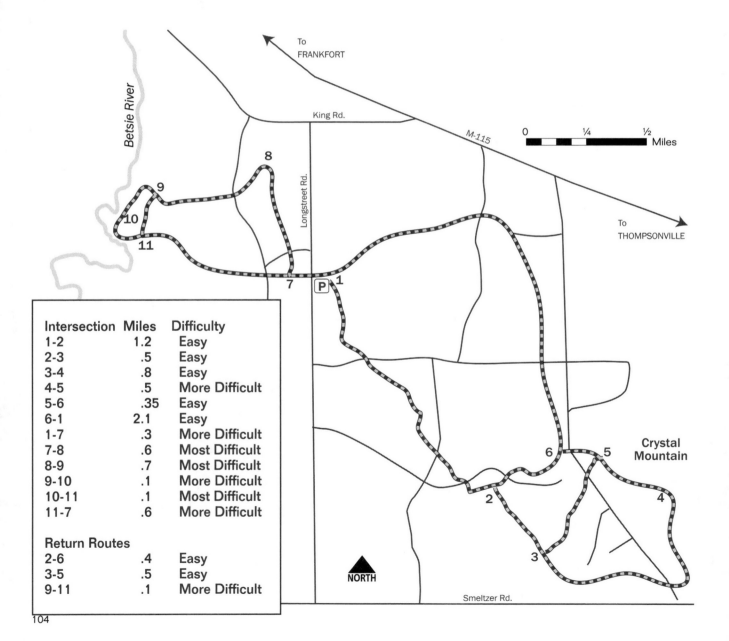

Intersection	Miles	Difficulty
1-2	1.2	Easy
2-3	.5	Easy
3-4	.8	Easy
4-5	.5	More Difficult
5-6	.35	Easy
6-1	2.1	Easy
1-7	.3	More Difficult
7-8	.6	Most Difficult
8-9	.7	Most Difficult
9-10	.1	More Difficult
10-11	.1	Most Difficult
11-7	.6	More Difficult
Return Routes		
2-6	.4	Easy
3-5	.5	Easy
9-11	.1	More Difficult

Betsie Valley Trails

Trail Uses

Grid   D3 **Trail ID** 118

Length   27 miles

Surface   Paved, Aggregate

Difficulty   Easy

Setting   Wooded, open, farmland

Location   Beulah, Frankfort, Thompsonville

Lat/Long   44-31 / 85-56   Thompsonville at CR-602

County   Benzie

Contact   Betsie Valley Trail Management Council
231-882-4844

Getting There   Trailheads are at Thompsonville, CR 602, and at Frankfort, M115.

Trail Notes   Effort level is easy. Terrain is flat. Developed on old railroad right-of-way. The surface is ballast and natural.

Facilities

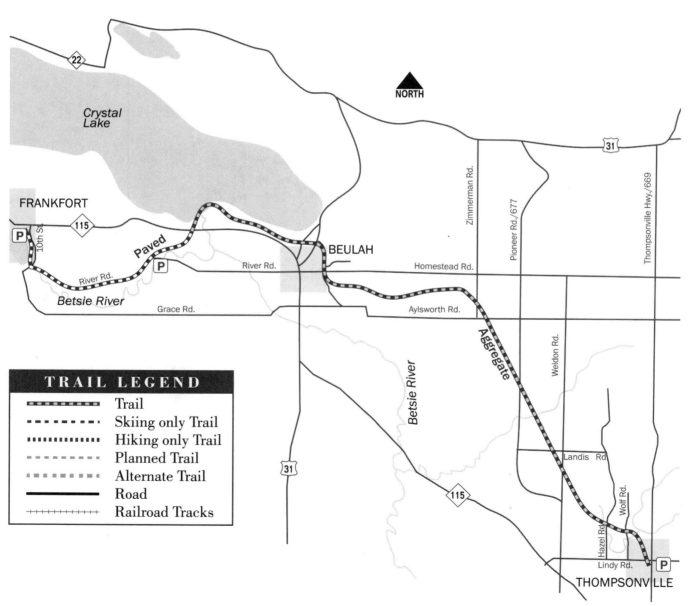

Big "M" Mountain Bike Trail

Trail Uses	🚵 🎿 🚶	**Setting**	Woods, open, hilly
Grid	E3 **Trail ID** 119	**Location**	Manistee, Wellston
Length	19 miles	**Lat/Long**	44-41 / 86-03 Entrance off Udell Hills Rd
Surface	Natural	**County**	Wellston
Difficulty	Moderate to difficulty	**Contact**	Manistee Ranger District 800-821-6263

Getting There From Wellston, head west on SR55 for 4 miles. Turn south on East Udell Hills Road for 3 miles to the entrance.

Trail Notes Located at the former Big M alpine ski area. The setting is wooded and hilly, with open areas. Effort level is moderate to difficult. There is a day use cabin at the site.

Facilities P

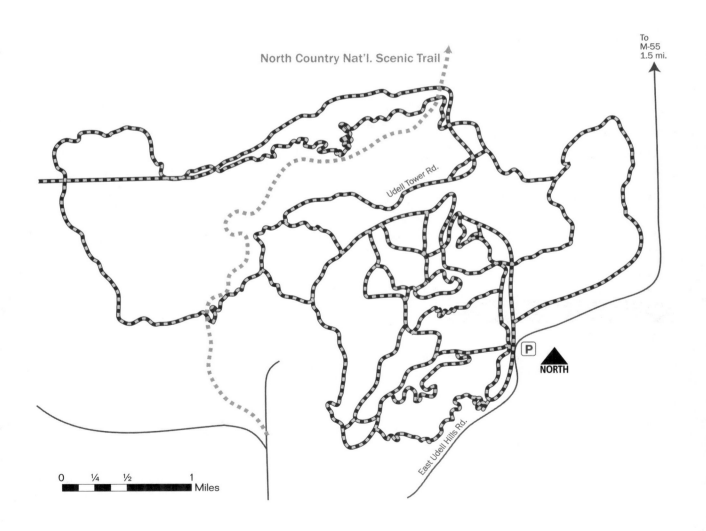

North Country Nat'l. Scenic Trail

To M-55 1.5 mi.

Udell Tower Rd.

East Udell Hills Rd.

NORTH

0   ¼   ½   1   Miles

Boyne Mountain Resort

Trail Uses

Grid	C5 **Trail ID** 125	**Location**	Boyne Falls	
Length	16 miles	**Lat/Long**	45-10 / 84-55	Boyne Mountain area
Surface	Natural	**County**	Charlevoix	
Difficulty	Easy to difficult	**Contact**	Boyne Mountain Resort	800-462-6963
Setting	Woods, open, hills	**Fees**	Trail use	

Getting There South edge of Boyne Falls, just southwest of US131 and M-75.

Trail Notes Boyne Nordican is a 4-season ski resort open to mountain biking. Effort level is moderate to difficult. Terrain is hilly and flat. The resort hosts mountain bike races, with restaurant and lodging facilities.

Facilities P ⚥ ◑ 🛏

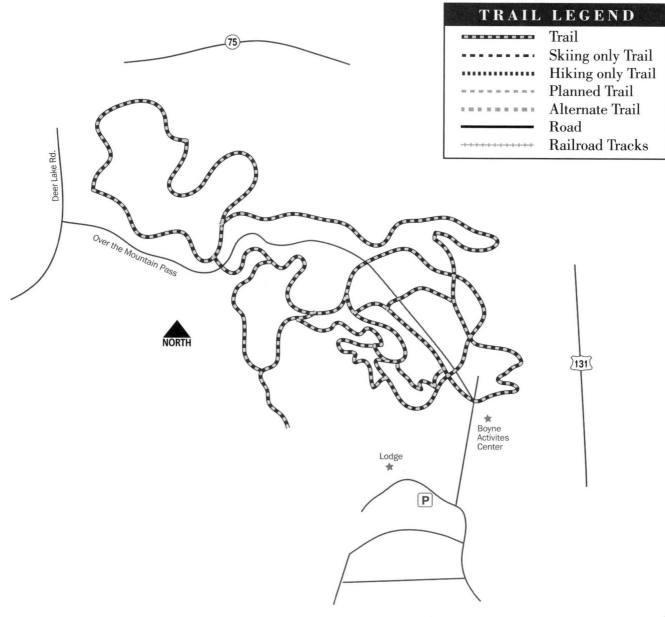

Cadillac Pathway

Trail Uses	(icons)	**Setting**	Wooded, open
Grid	E4 **Trail ID** 131	**Location**	Cadillac
Length	11 miles	**Lat/Long**	44-16 / 85-23 13th St. & Crosby Rd
Surface	Natural	**County**	Wexford
Difficulty	Easy to difficult	**Contact**	Pere Marquette State Forest 231-422-5280

Getting There From Cadillac, north on US131 to 34 Mile Road, then right on 13th Street for 1.5 miles to a playground where the road turns south. Trailhead is at the end of the playground.

Trail Notes Effort level varies from easy to difficult, with the west loops more interesting. The south loop is very hilly and challenging. Single track, counter clockwise, and mainly straightforward with just a few technical turns.

Facilities P 🚻

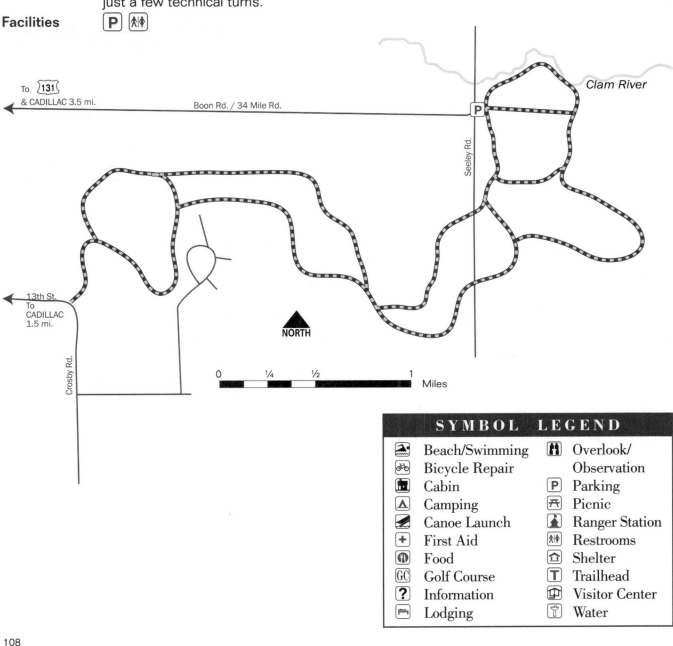

To 131
& CADILLAC 3.5 mi.

Boon Rd. / 34 Mile Rd.

Clam River

Seeley Rd.

P

13th St.
To
CADILLAC
1.5 mi.

Crosby Rd.

NORTH

0   ¼   ½   1   Miles

SYMBOL LEGEND

🏖	Beach/Swimming	🔭	Overlook/
🚲	Bicycle Repair		Observation
🏠	Cabin	P	Parking
⛺	Camping	🍴	Picnic
🛶	Canoe Launch	🏛	Ranger Station
✚	First Aid	🚻	Restrooms
🍲	Food	⌂	Shelter
GC	Golf Course	T	Trailhead
?	Information	🏢	Visitor Center
🛏	Lodging	🥤	Water

Cannonsburg State Game Area

Trail Uses	🚴 🏃 🎿	**Setting**	Woods, open, hilly
Grid	G4 **Trail ID** 132	**Location**	Grand Rapids
Length	10 miles	**Lat/Long**	43-02 / 85-30 State Game area
Surface	Natural	**County**	Kent
Difficulty	Moderate	**Contact**	Cannonsburg State Game Ares 616-794-2658
Acres	1,331	**Hours**	Daytime

Getting There Exit I-96 at M-44 (exit 38, East Belt Line) in Grand Rapids and head north past the Grand River. Go east on Cannonsburg Road for 5 miles, then south on Egypt Valley Road to Four Mile Road. East on Four Mile Road for a half mile to the parking lot and trailhead.

Trail Notes Effort level is easy to moderate. Setting is forests, hills. The trail is mostly single track, clockwise. Mountain biking is limited to daytime and non-winter months.

Facilities P

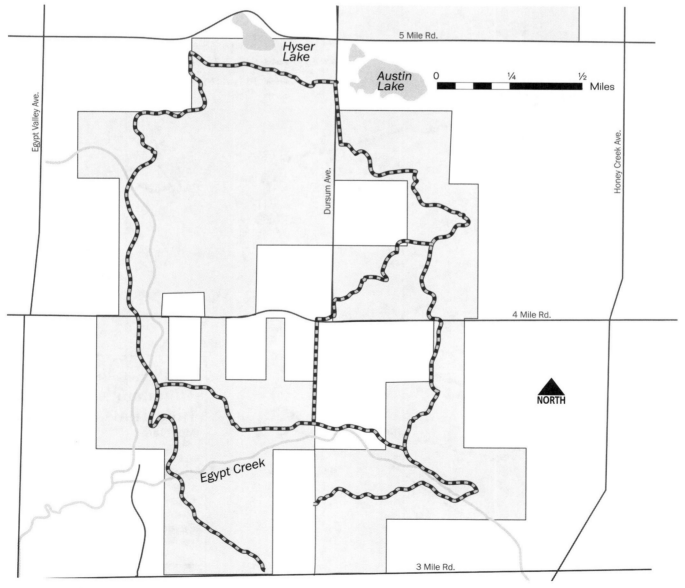

Crystal Mountain Resort

Trail Uses			
Grid	D3 Trail ID 141	**Location**	Thompsonville
Length	11 miles	**Lat/Long**	44-31 / 85-59 M-115 & Smeltzer Rd
Surface	Natural	**County**	Benzie
Difficulty	Easy to difficult	**Contact**	Crystal Mountain Resort 616-378-2911
Setting	Wooded, open, hilly	**Fees**	Trail use

Getting There Thompsonville area. From the intersection of M-115 and U.S. 71, take M-115 6 miles east to Crystal Mountain Drive. Turn southwest and continue back to the gravel parking lot near the Inn at the base of the ski lifts. From Cadillac, 36 miles northwest on M-115.

Trail Notes Privately operated resort. Terrain is hilly with many loops. Effort level is easy to difficult. There is a trail use fee with lift ticket privileges. Single and double track, clockwise

Facilities P

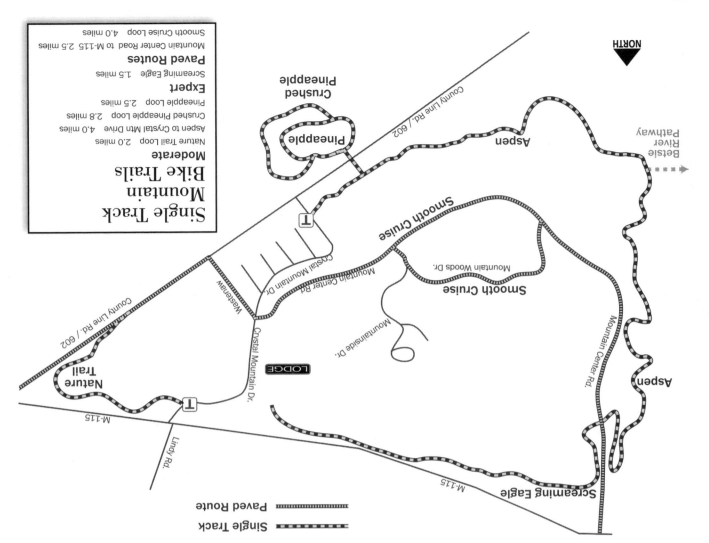

Single Track Mountain Bike Trails

Moderate
Nature Trail Loop 2.0 miles
Aspen to Crystal Mtn Drive 4.0 miles
Crushed Pineapple Loop 2.8 miles
Pineapple Loop 2.5 miles

Expert
Screaming Eagle 1.5 miles

Paved Routes
Mountain Center Road to M-115 2.5 miles
Smooth Cruise Loop 4.0 miles

Single Track ▬▬▬▬
Paved Route ▬▬▬▬

NORTH

Betsie River Pathway
Aspen
Smooth Cruise
Crushed Pineapple
Pineapple
County Line Rd. / 602
Mountain Woods Dr.
Mountain Center Rd
Crystal Mountain Dr.
Washtenaw
Mountainside Dr.
LODGE
Nature Trail
County Line Rd. / 602
M-115
Lindy Rd.
Aspen
Mountain Center Rd.
Screaming Eagle
M-115

Deerfield Nature Park

Trail Uses	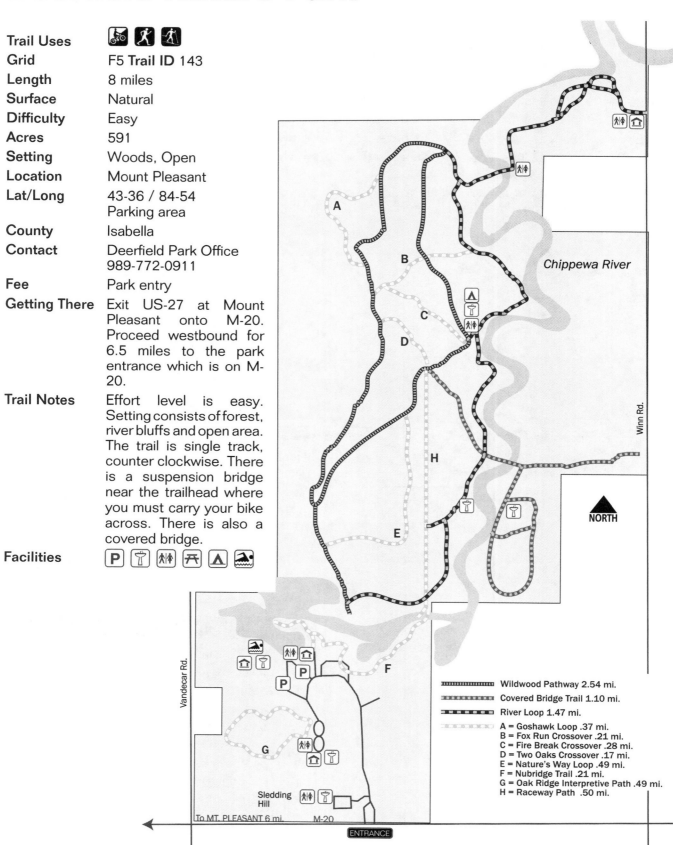
Grid	F5 **Trail ID** 143
Length	8 miles
Surface	Natural
Difficulty	Easy
Acres	591
Setting	Woods, Open
Location	Mount Pleasant
Lat/Long	43-36 / 84-54 Parking area
County	Isabella
Contact	Deerfield Park Office 989-772-0911
Fee	Park entry
Getting There	Exit US-27 at Mount Pleasant onto M-20. Proceed westbound for 6.5 miles to the park entrance which is on M-20.
Trail Notes	Effort level is easy. Setting consists of forest, river bluffs and open area. The trail is single track, counter clockwise. There is a suspension bridge near the trailhead where you must carry your bike across. There is also a covered bridge.
Facilities	

Chippewa River

NORTH

Wildwood Pathway 2.54 mi.
Covered Bridge Trail 1.10 mi.
River Loop 1.47 mi.

A = Goshawk Loop .37 mi.
B = Fox Run Crossover .21 mi.
C = Fire Break Crossover .28 mi.
D = Two Oaks Crossover .17 mi.
E = Nature's Way Loop .49 mi.
F = Nubridge Trail .21 mi.
G = Oak Ridge Interpretive Path .49 mi.
H = Raceway Path .50 mi.

Vandecar Rd.

Winn Rd.

Sledding Hill

To MT. PLEASANT 6 mi.   M-20

ENTRANCE

Green Pine Lake Pathway

Trail Uses	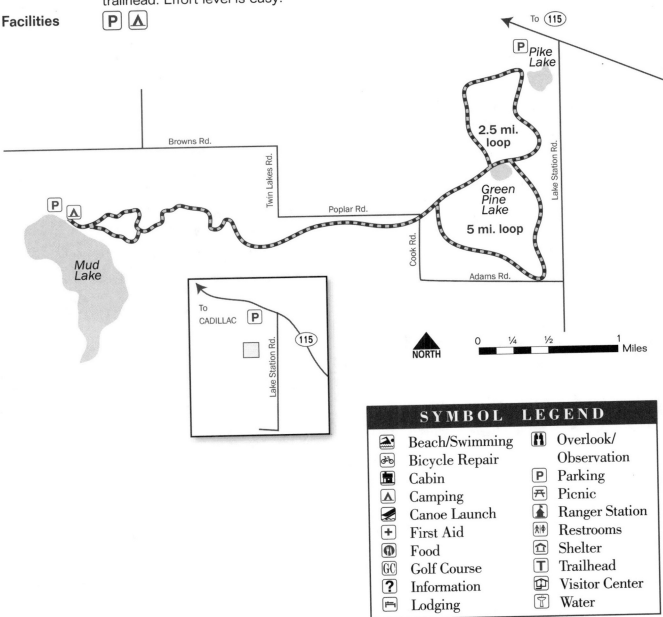	**Setting**	Woods, open	
Grid	E5 **Trail ID** 157	**Location**	Clare	
Length	10 miles	**Lat/Long**	43-54 / 85-05	Mud Lake parking area
Surface	Natural	**County**	Clare	
Difficulty	Easy	**Contact**	Gladwin Forest Area	517-426-9205

Getting There From Clare, go 14 miles northwest on Hwy 115 to the Pike Lake State Forest Campground.

Trail Notes Setting is flat to slightly rolling, woods and open areas. There is a campground at the trailhead. Effort level is easy.

Facilities P A

To (115)

P *Pike Lake*

Browns Rd.

Twin Lakes Rd.

2.5 mi. loop

Green Pine Lake

Poplar Rd.

5 mi. loop

P A

Mud Lake

Cook Rd.

Lake Station Rd.

Adams Rd.

To CADILLAC P

Lake Station Rd.

115

NORTH

0   ¼   ½   1
Miles

SYMBOL LEGEND

Beach/Swimming		Overlook/ Observation	
Bicycle Repair		Parking	
Cabin		Picnic	
Camping		Ranger Station	
Canoe Launch		Restrooms	
First Aid		Shelter	
Food		Trailhead	
Golf Course		Visitor Center	
Information		Water	
Lodging			

Hanson Hills Recreation Area

Trail Uses	🚴 🏃 ⛷	**Setting**	Woods, open, hilly
Grid	D5 **Trail ID** 160	**Location**	Grayling
Length	11 miles	**Lat/Long**	44-39 / 44-39 Parking area
Surface	Natural, groomed	**County**	Crawford
Difficulty	Easy to moderate	**Contact**	Hanson Hills Recreation Park 989-348-9260
Acres	1,500 acres	**Fees**	Trail use pass

Getting There Take I-75 to the Downtown Grayling exit. Follow the I-75 business loop to M-72 West. Take M-72 West toward Traverse City. Turn left on M-93 (towards Camp Grayling) proceed ½ mile, then turn left at the Hanson Hills Ski Area sign. Park at the main lodge. The trailhead starts next to the pond.

Trail Notes Most of the trail is singletrack. Look for long climbs, switch backs, fast downhills . There are a couple of more difficult routes for the adventurous who look for the challenge of long climbs, short hairy hill climbs and tight twisty trails.

Facilities P T ⚦ 🅸 🛏

TRAIL LEGEND

- ▪▪▪▪▪ Trail
- ▪ ▪ ▪ ▪ Skiing only Trail
- ▪▪▪▪▪▪ Hiking only Trail
- ▪ ▪ ▪ ▪ Planned Trail
- ▪ ▪ ▪ ▪ Alternate Trail
- —— Road
- ++++++ Railroad Tracks

93

P
LODGE

Military Rd.

*Hanson State
Game Refuge*

Hart-Montague Bicycle Trail State Park

Trail Uses

Grid F2 **Trail ID** 162

Length 22 miles

Surface Asphalt

Difficulty Easy

Setting Fields, orchards, woods

Location Montague, Hart, New Era, Shelby, Whitehall, Mears

Lat/Long 43-42 / 86-21
Hart at Katheryn & Park

County Oceana, Muskegon

Contact Silver Lake State Park
616-873-3083

Fees Trail use

Getting There South trailhead - Just off Stanton Road in Montague. The cities of Montague and Whitehall at White Lake are joined by a bridge less than a mile from the trailhead.

North trailhead - John Gurney Park off Business Hwy 31, as you enter Hart. The city portion of the route continues on, winding past Hark Lake and following city streets to the parking area on Polk Road, which is a common northern beginning area.

Trail Notes The Hart-Montague Trail runs between the towns of Montague and Hart near Lake Michigan. The trail was built on railroad right-of-way and is the first state park rail-trail with an improved surface. There are mile markers. The terrain is flat, with open spaces, small communities and some wooded areas.

Facilities John Gurney Park (north trailhead)

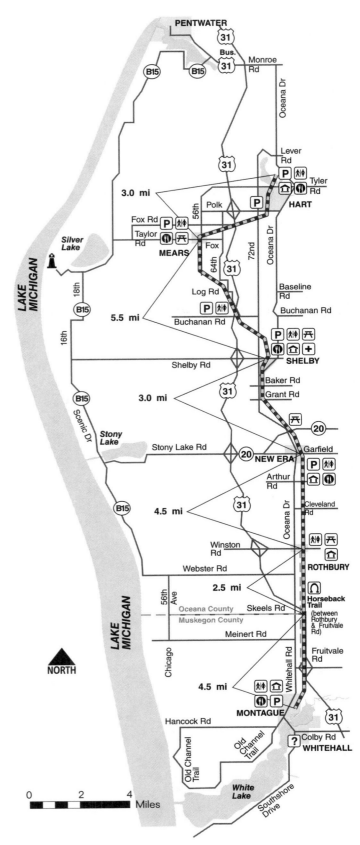

Lake Ann Pathway

Trail Uses	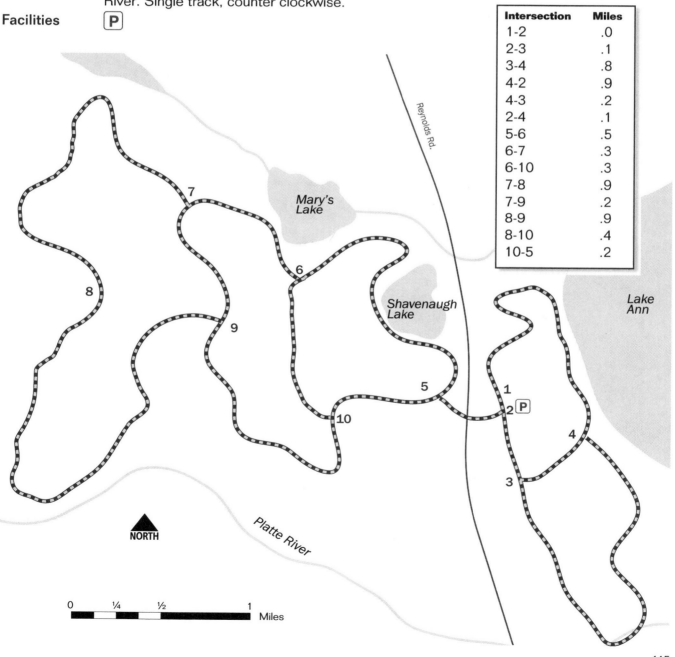
Grid	D3 **Trail ID** 188
Length	5.5
Surface	Natural
Difficulty	Easy to difficult

Setting	Woods, open, mostly flat
Location	Lake Ann, Traverse City
Lat/Long	44-43 / 85-52 Parking area off Reynolds Rd
County	Benzie
Contact	Traverse City Forest Area 231-922-5280

Getting There From Traverse City west between M72 and US31. From Lake Ann west on Almira Road to Reynolds Road, then south 2.5 miles to Lake Ann State Forest.

Trail Notes Effort level is easy to difficult. Terrain is mostly flat, with a few hills, lakes and the Platte River. Single track, counter clockwise.

Facilities P

Intersection	Miles
1-2	.0
2-3	.1
3-4	.8
4-2	.9
4-3	.2
2-4	.1
5-6	.5
6-7	.3
6-10	.3
7-8	.9
7-9	.2
8-9	.9
8-10	.4
10-5	.2

Leelanau Trail

Trail Uses	
Grid	D3 Trail ID 341
Length	15 miles
Surface	Asphalt, gravel, dirt
Difficulty	Easy
Setting	Forest, meadows orchards, lakes, ponds
Location	Traverse City, Suttons Bay
Lat/Long	44-57 / 85-39 Suttons Bay
County	Grand Traverse, Leelanau
Contact	TART Trails 231-941-4300
Getting There	A good point to pick up the trail going south is the old railroad depot in Suttons Bay. Parking is available off Carter Road in Traverse City and Fourth Street in Suttons Bay.
Trail Notes	The trail connects Traverse City and Suttons Bay, stretching over 15 miles through railway corridors. The trail route features rolling hills, forests, meadows, and several lakes, streams and ponds. The surface varies from asphalt and gravel to dirt.
Facilities	

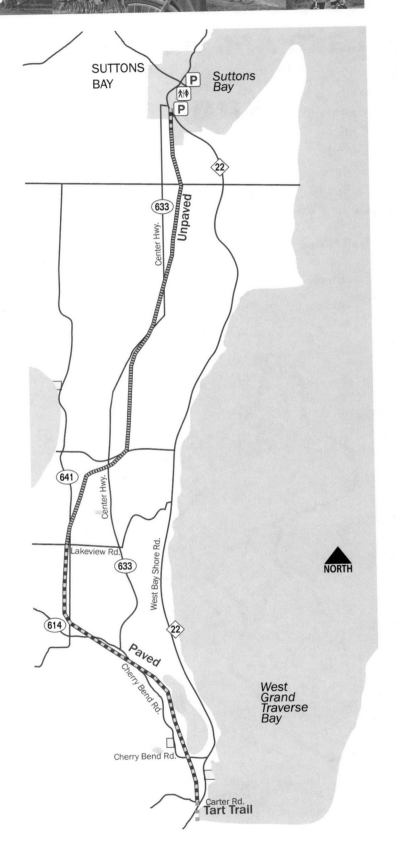

TRAIL LEGEND

▪▪▪▪▪▪▪	Trail
– – – – –	Skiing only Trail
▪▪▪▪▪▪▪	Hiking only Trail
– – – – –	Planned Trail
▪▪▪▪▪▪	Alternate Trail
——————	Road
+++++++	Railroad Tracks

ROAD SYMBOLS

🛡39	Interstate Highway
12	U.S. Highway
26	State Highway
K	County Highway

AREA LEGEND

▨	City, Town
▢	Parks, Preserves
▨	Waterway
▬▬	Mileage Scale
★	Points of Interest
– –	County/State
🌲	Forest/Woods

TRAIL LEGEND

▪▪▪▪▪▪	Trail
- - - - -	Skiing only Trail
▪▪▪▪▪▪▪▪	Hiking only Trail
▪ ▪ ▪ ▪	Planned Trail
▪ ▪ ▪ ▪	Alternate Trail
———	Road
++++++	Railroad Tracks

TRAIL USES

🚵	Mountain Biking
🚲	Leisure Biking
⛸	In Line Skating
🎿	Cross-Country Skiing
🚶	Hiking
⛑	Horseback Riding
🛷	Snowmobiling

SYMBOL LEGEND

🏖	Beach/Swimming
🚲	Bicycle Repair
🏠	Cabin
⛺	Camping
🛶	Canoe Launch
✚	First Aid
🍴	Food
GC	Golf Course
?	Information
🛏	Lodging
🔭	Overlook/Observation
P	Parking
🞃	Picnic
🗼	Ranger Station
🚻	Restrooms
⌂	Shelter
T	Trailhead
🏛	Visitor Center
🚰	Water

Little Traverse Wheelway

Trail Uses		**Setting**	Woods, open
Grid	B4-5 Trail ID 342	**Location**	Charlevoix, Harbor Springs, Petoskey
Length	29 miles	**Lat/Long**	45-20 / 85-15 Charlevoix area
Surface	Asphalt	**Counties**	Charlevoix, Emmet
Difficulty	Easy	**Contact**	Petoskey City Planner 816-347-2500

Getting There   The western trailhead is located at Mt. McSauba Road & Division Street in Charlevoix.

Trail Notes   The trail runs for about 29 miles between Charlevoix and Harbor Springs, and is mostly asphalt and dedicated. The park between Bayfront Park in Petoskey and Petoskey State Park closely follows the path of the original Little Traverse Wheelway rail line. The trail is multi-use except for horses and snowmobiles.

Facilities   P 🍵 🚻 🍴

TRAIL LEGEND

▪▪▪▪▪▪▪	Trail
– – – – – –	Skiing only Trail
▪▪▪▪▪▪▪▪▪▪	Hiking only Trail
▬ ▬ ▬ ▬	Planned Trail
▪ ▬ ▪ ▬ ▪	Alternate Trail
▬▬▬▬	Road
++++++++++	Railroad Tracks

SYMBOL LEGEND

🏊	Beach/Swimming
🚲	Bicycle Repair
🏚	Cabin
⛺	Camping
🛶	Canoe Launch
✚	First Aid
🍴	Food
GC	Golf Course
?	Information
🛏	Lodging
🔭	Overlook/Observation
P	Parking
⛟	Picnic
🧍	Ranger Station
🚻	Restrooms
⌂	Shelter
T	Trailhead
🏛	Visitor Center
🍵	Water

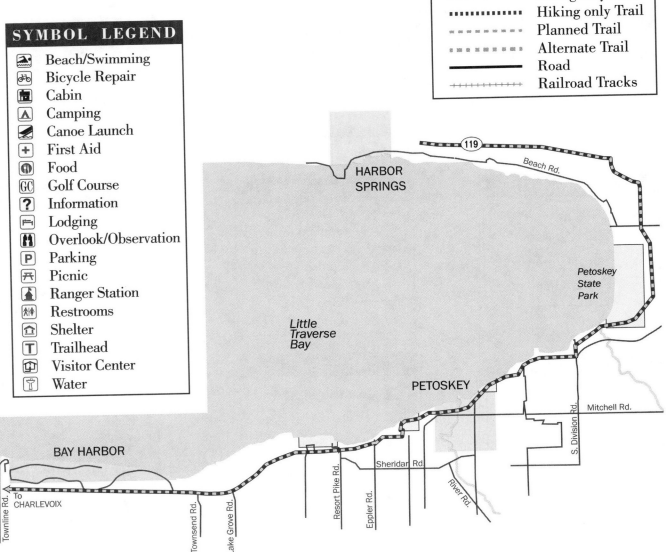

Charlevoix County Segment of the Little Traverse Wheelway

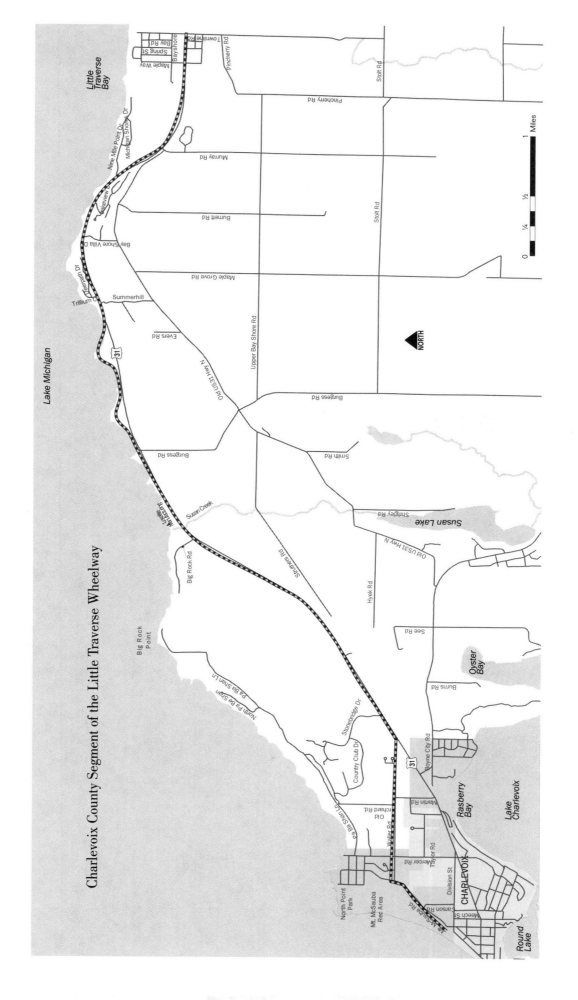

Lost Lake Pathway

Trail Uses		**Setting**	Woods, open
Grid	D3 **Trail ID** 194	**Location**	Interlochen
Length	6.5 miles	**Lat/Long**	44-41 / 85-46 Campground
Surface	Natural	**County**	Traverse
Difficulty	Easy	**Contact**	Traverse City DNR 231-946-4920

Getting There   From Interlocken, go 1.5 miles west on US31 to Wildwood Road, then north 1 mile to state forest campground.

Trail Notes   Effort level is easy. Single track, clockwise and counter clockwise. Terrain is largely flat. Setting is open and wooded.

Facilities   [P] [A]

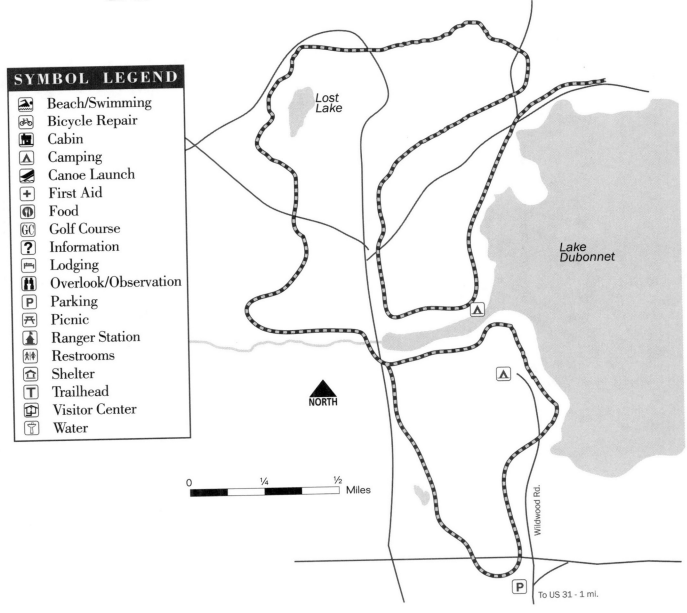

SYMBOL LEGEND

- Beach/Swimming
- Bicycle Repair
- Cabin
- Camping
- Canoe Launch
- First Aid
- Food
- GC Golf Course
- Information
- Lodging
- Overlook/Observation
- Parking
- Picnic
- Ranger Station
- Restrooms
- Shelter
- Trailhead
- Visitor Center
- Water

Lost Lake

Lake Dubonnet

NORTH

0   ¼   ½   Miles

Wildwood Rd.

To US 31 - 1 mi.

Lost Tamarack Pathway

Trail Uses	🚵 🎿 🥾
Grid	B5 **Trail ID** 195
Length	5 miles
Surface	Natural
Difficulty	Easy
Setting	Woods, open, rolling
Location	Wolverine
Lat/Long	45-21 / 84-45 Campground
County	Cheboygan
Contact	Indian River Forest Area 231-238-9313
Getting There	From Wolverine, go 6.5 miles west on C58 at Weber Lake State Forest Campground.
Trail Notes	Effort level is easy. The terrain is rolling and there are 2 loops. There is also a 1.5 mile connector trail to the Wildwood Hills Pathway.
Facilities	P ⛺

TRAIL LEGEND

▪▪▪▪▪▪▪▪	Trail
– – – – –	Skiing only Trail
••••••••••	Hiking only Trail
– – – – –	Planned Trail
▪ ▪ ▪ ▪ ▪	Alternate Trail
———	Road
+++++++++	Railroad Tracks

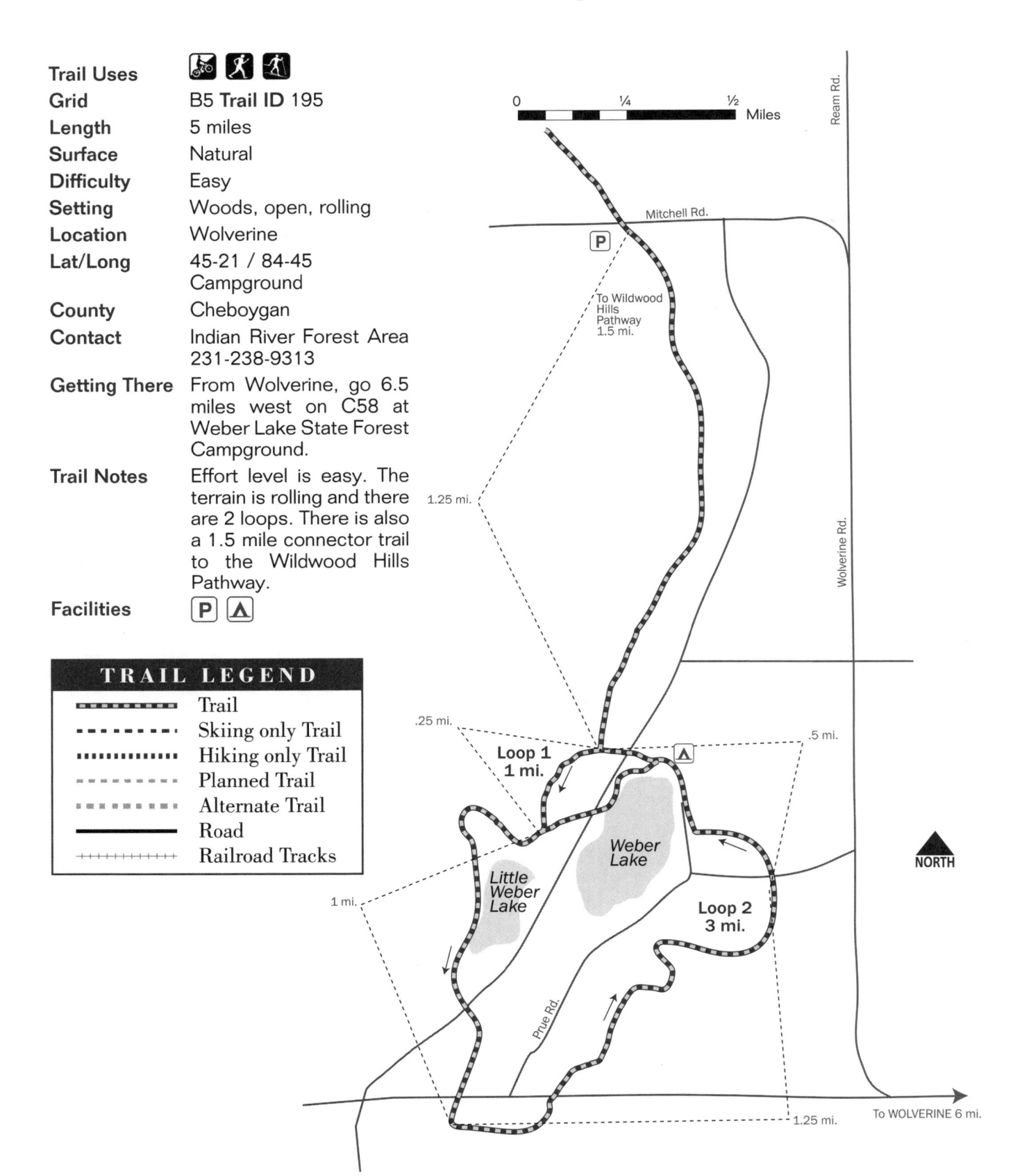

121

Mackinaw City to Cheboygan Trail

Trail Uses		**Setting**	Woods, open
Grid	AB5-6 **Trail ID** 338	**Location**	Alanson, Mackinaw
Length	15.5	**Lat/Long**	45-47 / 84-45 Mackinaw City
Surface	Crushed stone, natural	**County**	Emmet
Difficulty	Easy to moderate	**Contact**	Top of Michigan Trails Council 231-348-8280

Getting There Mackinaw trailhead - I-75 at Central Avenue.

Cheboygan trailhead - Lincoln Avenue

Trail Notes The trail is 12 miles of crushed stone from just south of the DNR Trailhead to 3.5 north of Cheboygan, from where it reverts to dirt and cinders. It follows US 23, providing views of Lake Huron. Mill Creek State Park is adjacent to the trail to the south.

Facilities

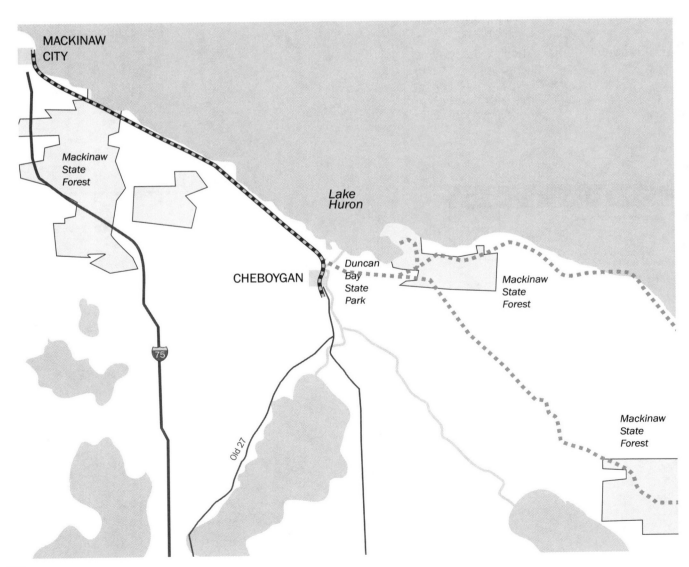

Mackinaw/Alanson Rail-Trail

Trail Uses	
Grid	B5 **Trail ID** 202
Length	27 miles
Surface	Ballast, natural
Difficulty	Easy to moderate
Setting	Woods, open, rural
Location	Alanson, Levering, Mackinaw City
Lat/Long	44-27 / 84-47 Alanson
County	Emmet
Contact	Indian River Forest Area 616-238-9313
Getting There	South trailhead - Hillside Gardens in Alanson.
	Levering - Trailhead west of US31.
	North trailhead - Mackinaw City, west of I-75 behind the Chalet House Motel.
Trail Notes	Effort level is easy. Surface is gravel, ballast and dirt on old railroad bed. The entire surface is 'bikeable', although the trail between Alanson and Levering not in good condition. The North Country Trail joins this trail about a mile south of the trailhead in Mackinaw City. Use US-31 to get around the gap in the trail from Robinson Road north to Ely Road in the village of Pellston.
Facilities	P T (I)

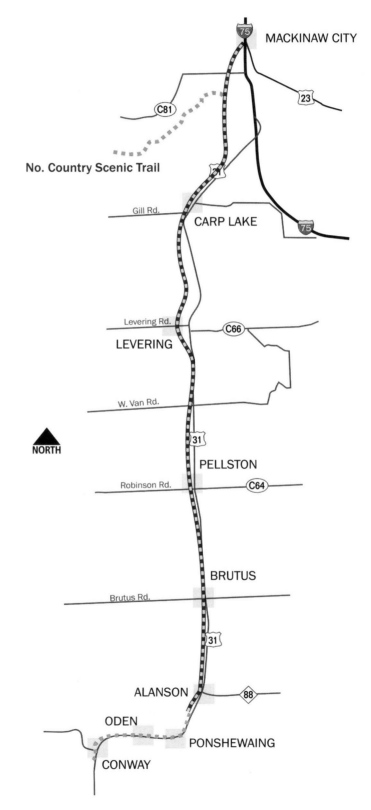

No. Country Scenic Trail

MACKINAW CITY
CARP LAKE
Gill Rd.
Levering Rd.
LEVERING
W. Van Rd.
NORTH
PELLSTON
Robinson Rd.
BRUTUS
Brutus Rd.
ALANSON
ODEN
PONSHEWAING
CONWAY

Muncie Lakes Pathway

Trail Uses	🚲 🎿 🚶	**Setting**	Woods, open, flat
Grid	D4 **Trail ID** 211	**Location**	Traverse City
Length	11.5	**Lat/Long**	44-41 / 85-27 Parking area
Surface	Natural	**County**	Grand Traverse
Difficulty	Easy to moderate	**Contact**	Muncie Lakes Pathway 231-946-4920

Getting There From Traverse City take Garfield Avenue south to Hammond Road, then east to High Lake Road, then south .5 miles to Supply Road. Go east on Supply Road 3 miles to Rennie Lake Road, then south until it ends. Turn left for 2 miles to the parking lot.

Trail Notes Effort level is easy to moderate. Terrain is largely flat. Single track, clockwise. There is a trail connection to Ranch Rudolf for food and lodging.

Facilities P 🅟 ⛺ 🛏

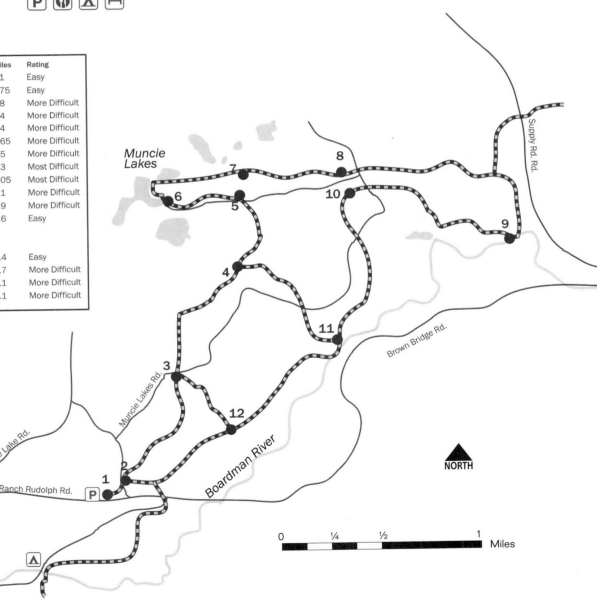

Intersection	Miles	Rating
1-2	.1	Easy
2-3	.75	Easy
3-4	.8	More Difficult
4-5	.4	More Difficult
5-6	.4	More Difficult
6-7	.65	More Difficult
7-8	.5	More Difficult
8-9	1.3	Most Difficult
9-10	1.05	Most Difficult
10-11	1.1	More Difficult
11-12	.9	More Difficult
12-2	.6	Easy

Return Routes		
3-12	.4	Easy
4-11	.7	More Difficult
5-7	.1	More Difficult
8-10	.1	More Difficult

North Country Trail Huron-Manistee National Forest

Trail Uses

Grid	E-G3	**Location**	Marilla, Baldwin, Brohlan, White Cloud, Newaygo
Length	110 miles	**Lat/Long**	Marilla 44-20 / 85-51
Surface	Natural		Croton Dam 43-26 / 85-40
Difficulty	Easy to moderate	**Counties**	Manistee, Mason, Newaygo, Oceana
Setting	Forest, open, rural	**Contact**	Manistee Ranger District 616-723-2211

Getting There Trailheads:

Marilla From Marilla, go .5 miles north and take Beers Road about 2 miles east. The trailhead is located on the south side of the road.

Udell From Wellston, go about 6 miles west on M-55. The trailhead is located on the south side of the highway.

FreeSoil From FreeSoil, go 9.5 miles east on FreeSoil Road. The Trailhead is located on the south side of the road.

Timber Creek From Baldwin, go north on M-37 to US-10, then west 7.5 miles to the Timber Creek Campground.

Bowman Lake From Baldwin, go west on 56th Street for 5 miles to Bowman Bridge Campground Spur. Continue west 1.5 miles to Bowman Lake Trailhead.

76th Street From Baldwin go south 3 miles on M-37 to Big Start Lake Road (76th), then 2.5 miles to where the trail crosses the road.

Nichols Lake From Brohman go north 2 miles on M-37, then west on 11 Mile Road for 1.5 miles to the entrance of Nichols Lake Recreation Area. Turn north for .4 miles to the boat launch turnoff, then west for .1 mile to the trail.

M-20 From White Cloud go north 1 mile on M-37 to M-20, then west on M-20 for 2.75 miles.

40th Street From White Cloud go south for 5 miles on M-37 to 40th Street, then .75 miles west on 40th Street to the trailhead.

Corton Dam From Newaygo go east on Croton Drive to the dam site.

Trail Notes The North Country Trail is a National Scenic Hiking Trail being constructed across public and private lands. When completed, it will extend 3,200 miles from near Crown Point, New York to Lake Sakakawea in North Dakota. This segment illustrates the trail located on the Huron-Manistee National Forest. Topography varies from flat to rolling hills. The trail passes by a variety of breathtaking views, rivers and streams, and through a wide variety of vegetation types. Camping is permitted along the trail, but stay at least 200 feet off the trail and away from water sources. Water sources are limited. Gray diamonds designate the North Country Trail, as well as posts with NCT stickers at road crossings.

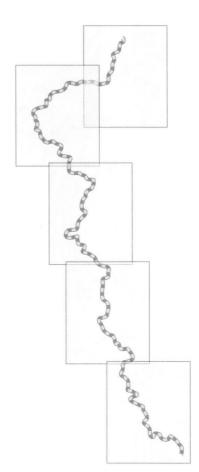

Facilities

North Country Trail Huron-Manistee National Forest (continued)

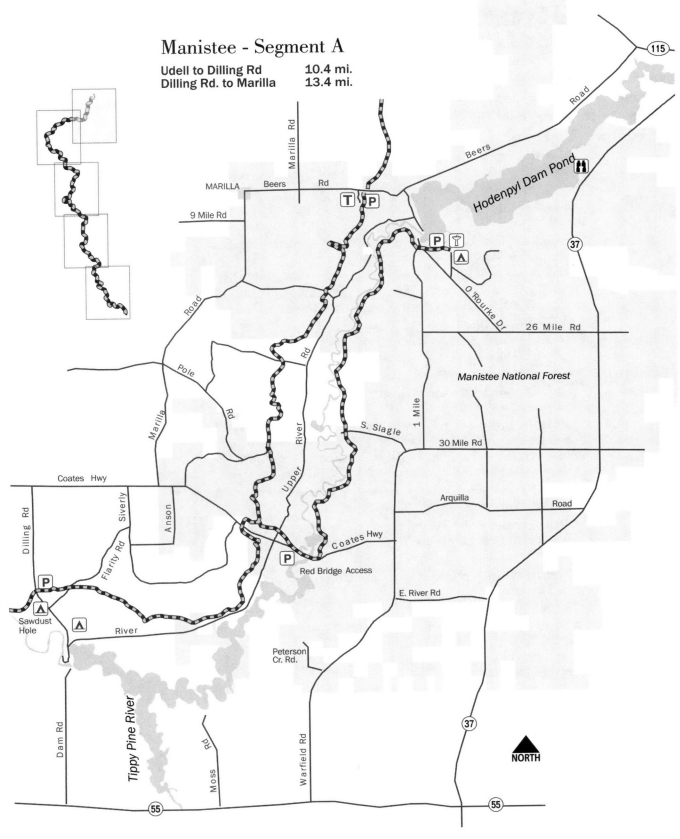

Manistee - Segment A

Udell to Dilling Rd   10.4 mi.
Dilling Rd. to Marilla   13.4 mi.

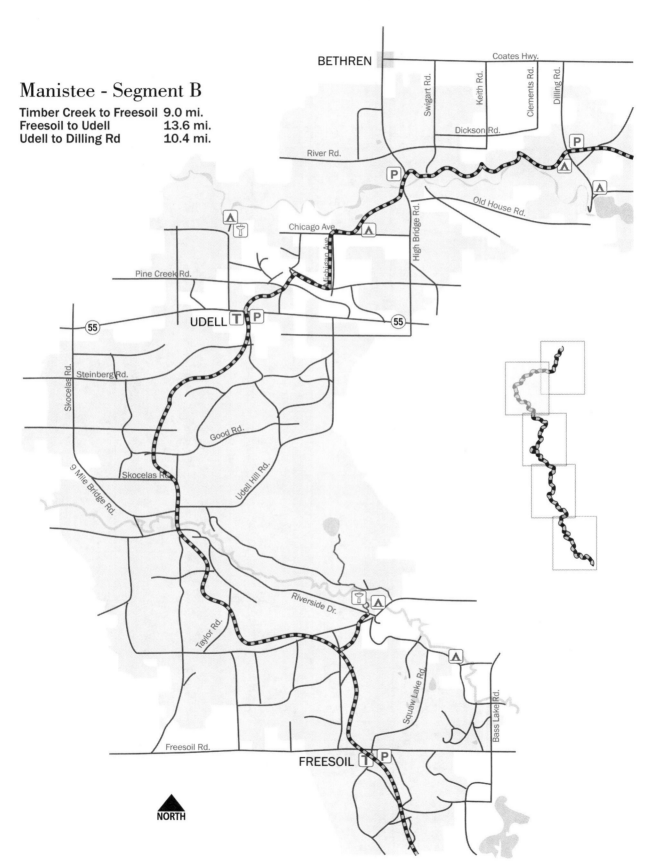

Manistee - Segment B

Timber Creek to Freesoil 9.0 mi.
Freesoil to Udell 13.6 mi.
Udell to Dilling Rd 10.4 mi.

BETHREN

Coates Hwy.

Swigart Rd.

Keith Rd.

Clements Rd.

Dilling Rd.

Dickson Rd.

River Rd.

P

P

Old House Rd.

Chicago Ave.

Michigan Ave.

High Bridge Rd.

Pine Creek Rd.

55

UDELL T P

55

Skocelas Rd.

Steinberg Rd.

Good Rd.

9 Mile Bridge Rd.

Skocelas Rd.

Udell Hill Rd.

Riverside Dr.

Taylor Rd.

Squaw Lake Rd.

Bass Lake Rd.

Freesoil Rd.

FREESOIL T P

NORTH

North Country Trail Huron-Manistee National Forest (continued)

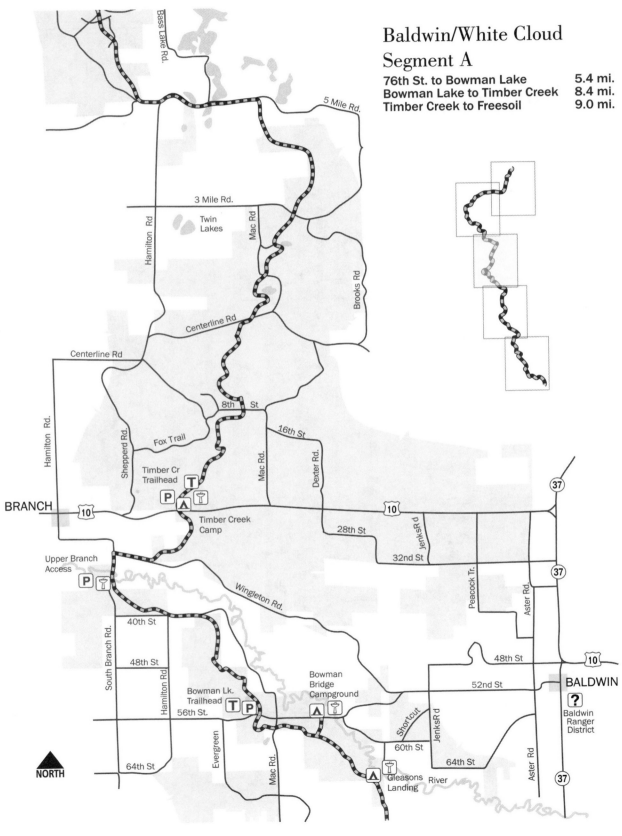

Baldwin/White Cloud

Segment A

76th St. to Bowman Lake	5.4 mi.
Bowman Lake to Timber Creek	8.4 mi.
Timber Creek to Freesoil	9.0 mi.

Bass Lake Rd.

5 Mile Rd.

3 Mile Rd.

Twin Lakes

Hamilton Rd

Mac Rd

Brooks Rd

Centerline Rd

Centerline Rd

Hamilton Rd.

8th St

Shepperd Rd.

Fox Trail

16th St

Mac Rd.

Dexter Rd.

Timber Cr Trailhead

P T

BRANCH 10

Timber Creek Camp

28th St

Jenks Rd

10

32nd St

37

37

Upper Branch Access

P

Wingleton Rd.

Peacock Tr.

Aster Rd.

South Branch Rd.

40th St

48th St

Hamilton Rd

48th St

10

52nd St

BALDWIN

Bowman Bridge Campground

Shortcut

Jenks Rd

?

Baldwin Ranger District

Bowman Lk. Trailhead

T P

56th St.

Evergreen

Mac Rd.

64th St

60th St

64th St

Aster Rd

37

Gleasons Landing

River

NORTH

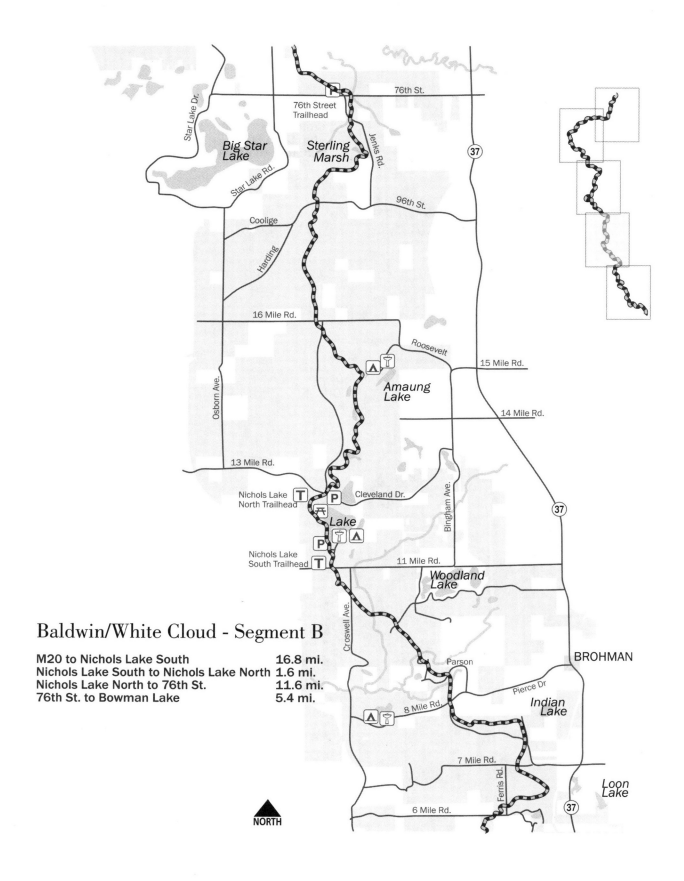

Baldwin/White Cloud - Segment B

M20 to Nichols Lake South	16.8 mi.
Nichols Lake South to Nichols Lake North	1.6 mi.
Nichols Lake North to 76th St.	11.6 mi.
76th St. to Bowman Lake	5.4 mi.

NORTH

North Country Trail Huron-Manistee National Forest (continued)

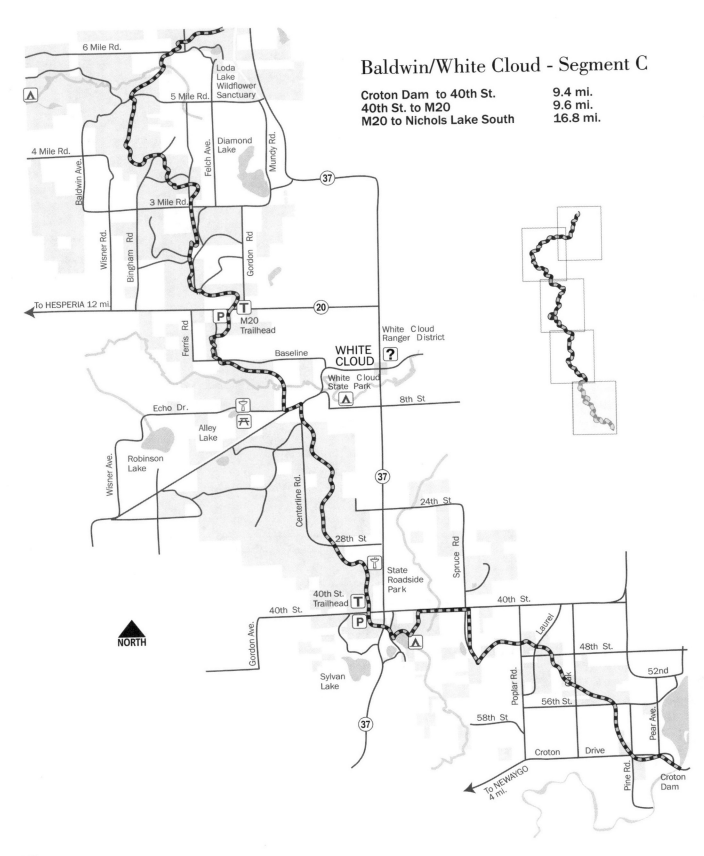

Baldwin/White Cloud - Segment C

Croton Dam to 40th St.	9.4 mi.
40th St. to M20	9.6 mi.
M20 to Nichols Lake South	16.8 mi.

North Higgins Lake State Park

Trail Uses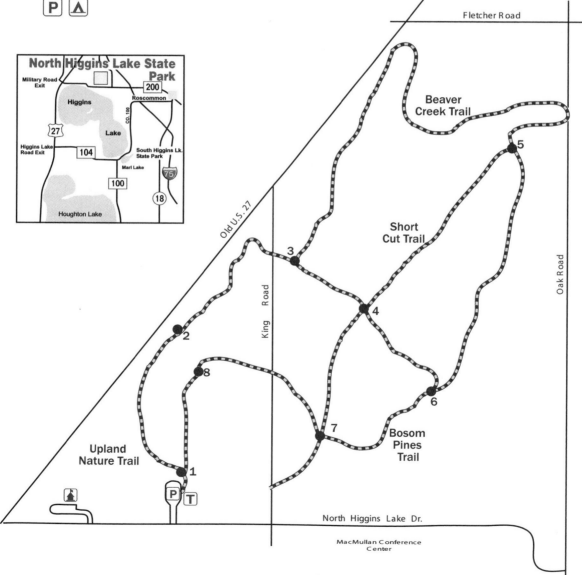

Grid	D5 **Trail ID** 225	**Location**	Higgins Lake
Length	6.5 miles	**Lat/Long**	44-31 / 84-46 Parking area
Surface	Natural	**County**	Crawford
Difficulty	Easy	**Contact**	North Higgins Lake State Park 517-821-6125
Setting	Woods, open	**Fees**	Vehicle entry

Getting There   Located on the north end of Higgins Lake, 1.5 miles east of US-27 or 4.5 miles west of I-75 on CR 200 (Roscommon Road).

Trail Notes   Effort level is easy. Terrain is flat and sometimes hilly, and the setting wooded and open. Most trails are two-track. There are several loops. The CCC Museum and historical exhibit is located of the north side of the entrance road.

Facilities   P A

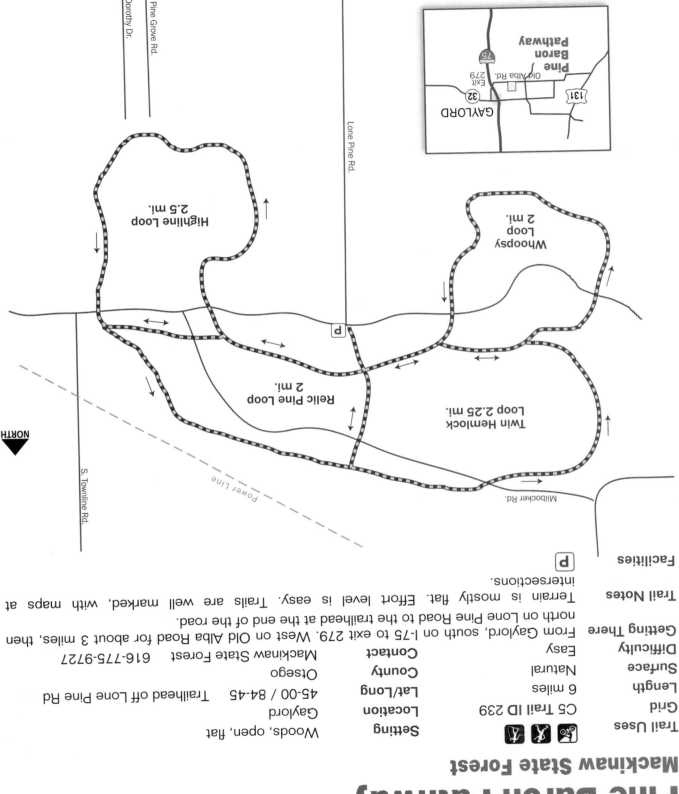

Pine Baron Pathway

Mackinaw State Forest

Trail Uses		**Setting**	Woods, open, flat
Grid	C5 Trail ID 239	**Location**	Gaylord
Length	6 miles	**Lat/Long**	45-00 / 84-45 Trailhead off Lone Pine Rd
Surface	Natural	**County**	Otsego
Difficulty	Easy	**Contact**	Mackinaw State Forest 616-775-9727
Getting There	From Gaylord, south on I-75 to exit 279. West on Old Alba Road for about 3 miles, then north on Lone Pine Road to the trailhead at the end of the road.		
Trail Notes	Terrain is mostly flat. Effort level is easy. Trails are well marked, with maps at intersections.		
Facilities	P		

Pine Valleys Pathway

Trail Uses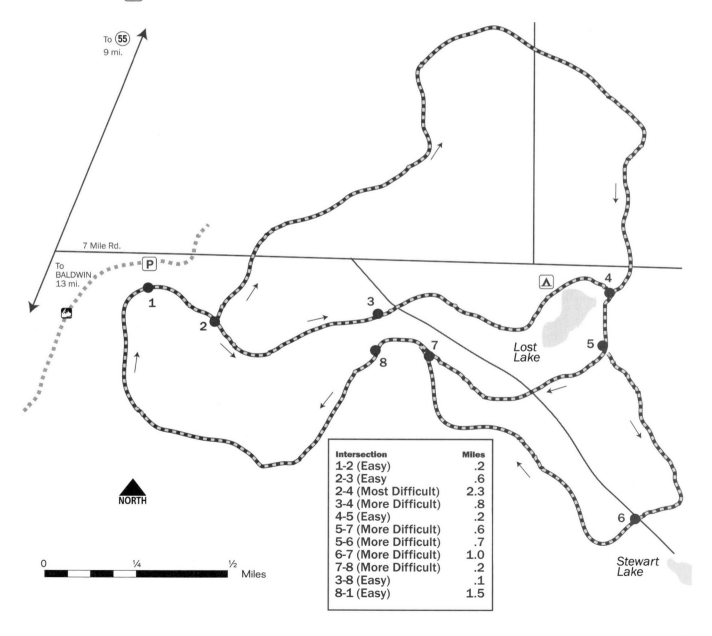

Grid E3 **Trail ID** 243

Length 8 miles

Surface Natural

Difficulty Easy to moderate

Setting Woods, open, rolling

Location Baldwin

Lat/Long 44-05 / 85-49   Parking off 4 Mile Rd

County Clare

Contact Pere Marquette State Forest, Baldwin
231-775-9727

Getting There From Baldwin, 16 miles north on M-37 to 7 mile Road, then east .2 miles to parking lot.

Trail Notes Effort level is easy to moderate. Single track, clockwise. Setting is rolling to flat with woods and open areas.

Facilities P

To (55)
9 mi.

7 Mile Rd.

To
BALDWIN
13 mi.

P

Lost
Lake

NORTH

0   ¼   ½   Miles

Stewart
Lake

Intersection	Miles
1-2 (Easy)	.2
2-3 (Easy)	.6
2-4 (Most Difficult)	2.3
3-4 (More Difficult)	.8
4-5 (Easy)	.2
5-7 (More Difficult)	.6
5-6 (More Difficult)	.7
6-7 (More Difficult)	1.0
7-8 (More Difficult)	.2
3-8 (Easy)	.1
8-1 (Easy)	1.5

Sand Lakes Quiet Area

Trail Uses		**Acres**	2,800	
Grid	D4 **Trail ID** 257	**Setting**	Woods, open, hilly	
Length	11 miles	**Location**	Kalkaska, Williamsburg	
Surface	Natural	**Lat/Long**	44-42 / 85-22 Parking off Broomhead Rd	
Difficulty	Easy to moderate	**Counties**	Grand Traverse, Kalkaska	
		Contact	Traverse City Forest Area 616-922-5280	

Getting There From Kalkaska, west on Island Lake Road for about 9 miles to the Guernsey Lake State Forest Campground.

Trail Notes The terrain varies from flat to very hilly. Effort level is easy to moderate. Single track, clockwise. The Quiet Area is closed to motorized vehicles. Loops.

Facilities P ⛲ 🚻 ⛺

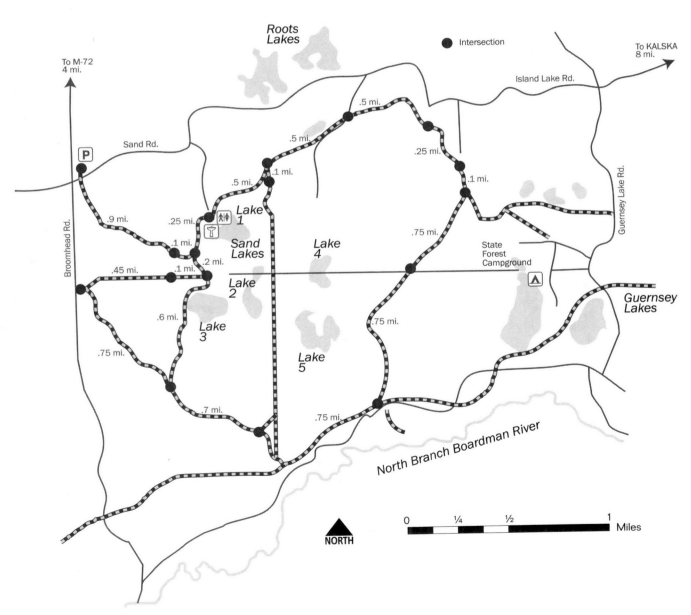

Sheep Ranch Pathway

Trail Uses	(icons)	**Setting**	Open, marsh
Grid	E3 **Trail ID** 261	**Location**	Baldwin
Length	4.5 miles	**Lat/Long**	43-54 / 85-49 Parking off Mud Trail Rd
Surface	Natural	**County**	Lake
Difficulty	Easy	**Contact**	Pere Marquette State Forest 616-775-9727

Getting There From Baldwin, go 2 miles east on US10, then north on Mud Trail Road to parking a short distance on the left.

Trail Notes The setting is mostly flat, with low hills, swamps and small creeks. Effort level is easy. There are two loops.

Facilities P

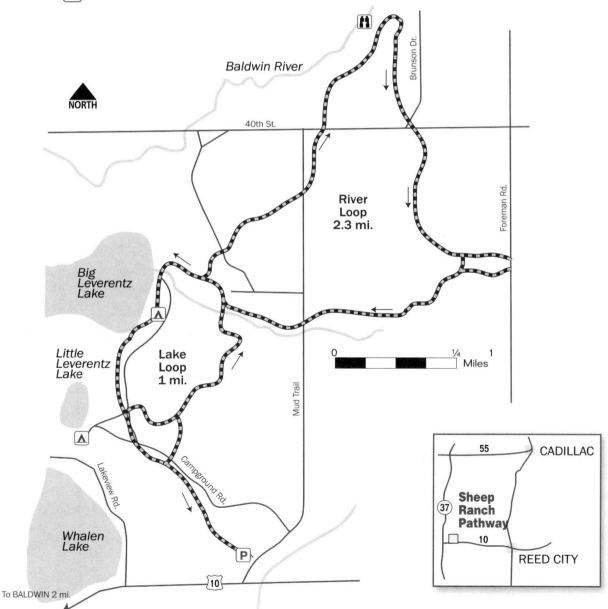

Sinkholes Pathways

Trail Uses	🚵 🚶		
Grid	B7 **Trail ID** 344	**Setting**	Woods, open
Length	2.5 miles	**Location**	Atlanta, Onaway
Surface	Natural	**Lat/Long**	45-14 / 84-10 Sinkhole area
Difficulty	Easy to moderate	**County**	Prasque Isle
Acres	2,600	**Contact**	Mackinaw State Forest 989-785-4251

Getting There Access the Sinkhole Pathway from Mohawk Lake Hwy. Tomahawk Lake Campground is located just south of the Sinkhole Area.

Trail Notes The 2,600 acre Sink Holes Area consists of a network of fire lanes that can provide access. There are two loops. Loop 1 is .75 miles and loop 2 is 1.25 miles. These loops form a circle around five of the sinkholes. Sinkholes are formed as large circular caves in the limestone collapse as the water dissolves the rock.

Facilities P △

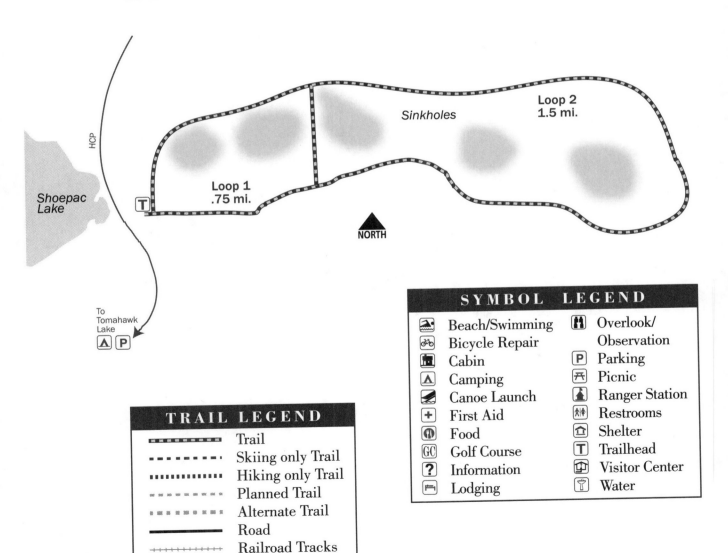

TRAIL LEGEND

▪▪▪▪▪▪	Trail
▬ ▬ ▬ ▬	Skiing only Trail
▪▪▪▪▪▪▪▪	Hiking only Trail
▬ ▬ ▬ ▬	Planned Trail
▪ ▪ ▪ ▪	Alternate Trail
▬▬▬▬	Road
++++++++	Railroad Tracks

SYMBOL LEGEND

🏊	Beach/Swimming	🏔	Overlook/
🚲	Bicycle Repair		Observation
🏠	Cabin	P	Parking
△	Camping	🪑	Picnic
🛶	Canoe Launch	🧍	Ranger Station
+	First Aid	🚻	Restrooms
🍴	Food	🏠	Shelter
GC	Golf Course	T	Trailhead
?	Information	🏛	Visitor Center
🛏	Lodging	🚰	Water

South Higgins Lakes State Pathway

Trail Uses

Grid	D5 **Trail ID** 271	**Location**	Sharps Corner
Length	6 miles	**Lat/Long**	44-25 / 84-41 Parking area
Surface	Natural	**County**	Roscommon
Difficulty	Easy	**Contact**	Traverse City Tourism 800-872-3541
Setting	Woods, open	**Fees**	Vehicle entry

Getting There From Higgins Lake, tale CR 104 to the parking area.

Trail Notes Effort level is easy. The trail forms a loop around the southern half of Marl Lake.

Facilities P · picnic · camp · swim · boat

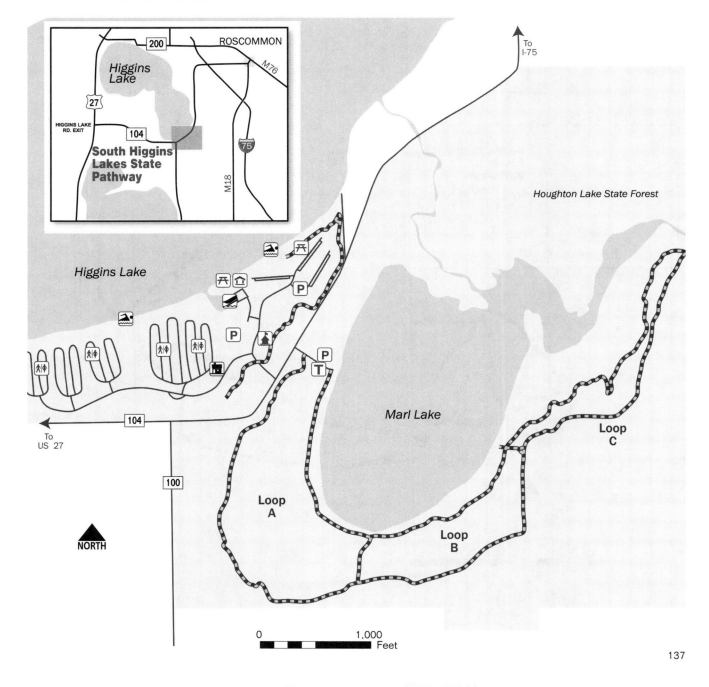

Spring Brook Pathway

Trail Uses		**Setting**	Woods, open, hilly
Grid	C5 **Trail ID** 272	**Location**	Boyne Falls
Length	6 miles	**Lat/Long**	45-13 / 84-49 Parking off Chandler Rd
Surface	Ballast, dirt	**County**	Charlevoix
Difficulty	Moderate	**Contact**	Gaylord Forest Area 517-732-3541

Getting There   From Boyne Falls, 5 miles on Thumb Lake Road to Slashing Road, then north 2.5 miles to the end of the road (Chandler Road) junction. West .5 miles to parking lot on the south side.

Trail Notes   Effort level is moderate. Terrain varies from flat to hilly. Setting is wooded and open.

Facilities   P

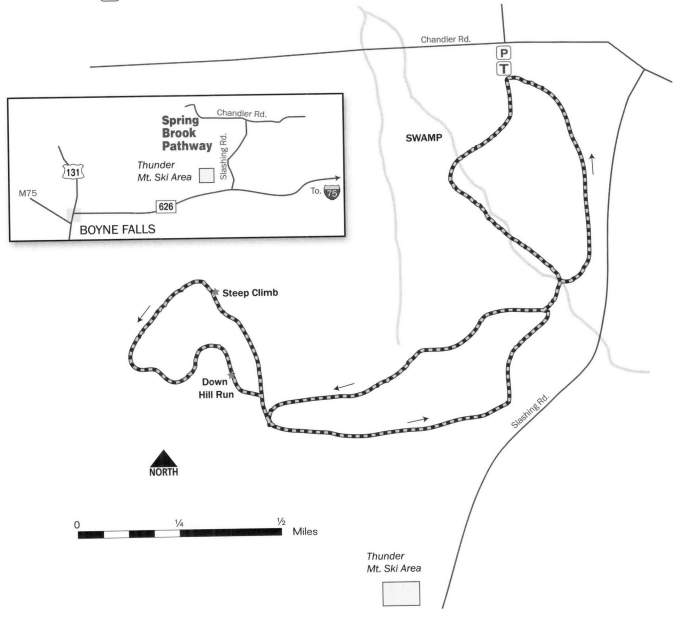

TART & Boardman Lake Trails

Trail Uses		**Difficulty**	Easy
Grid	D4	**Setting**	Urban, Parks
Length	TART 10 miles,	**Location**	Traverse City
	Boardman Lake	**Lat/Long**	44-36 / 85-36
	5 miles	**County**	Grand Transverse
Surface	Paved	**Contact**	Traverse Trails 231-941-4300

Getting There The are many access points. The TART Trail runs between Bunker Hill Road in Acme Township and M-22/M72 intersection in Traverse City. It is being extended from eastward from Lautner to Bates. The Boardman Lake Trail runs from Hull Park south to Medalie Park.

Trail Notes The TART and Boardman Lake Trails are paved urban transportation corridors running along Grand Traverse Bay and through downtown Traverse City neighborhoods.

Facilities

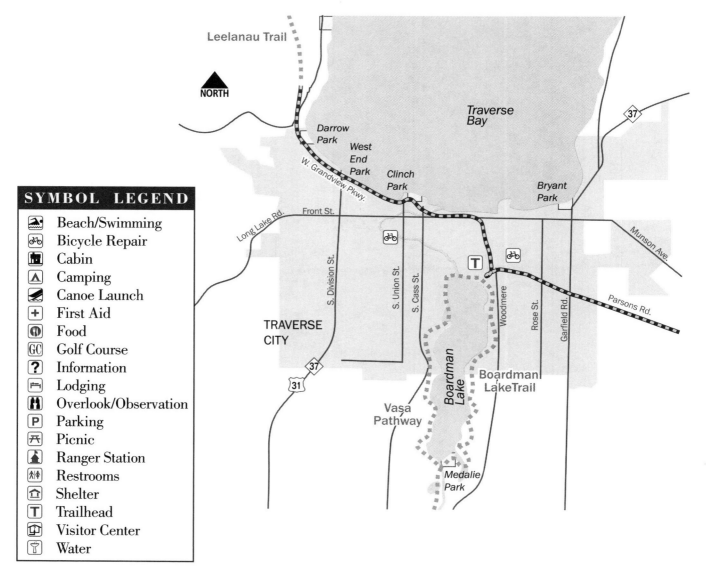

SYMBOL LEGEND

- Beach/Swimming
- Bicycle Repair
- Cabin
- Camping
- Canoe Launch
- First Aid
- Food
- Golf Course
- Information
- Lodging
- Overlook/Observation
- Parking
- Picnic
- Ranger Station
- Restrooms
- Shelter
- Trailhead
- Visitor Center
- Water

Vasa Trail

Trail Uses			
Grid	D4 **Trail ID** 290	**Location**	Acme, Traverse City
Length	18 miles	**Lat/Long**	44-45 / 85-30 Trailhead off Bartlett Rd
Surface	Natural	**County**	Grand Traverse
Difficulty	Easy to moderate	**Contact**	Traverse City Forest Area 616-946-4920
Setting	Woods, open, hilly	**Fees**	Donations accepted

Getting There From US-31, just south of its intersection with M-72, head east on Bunker Hill Road for a mile to Bartlett Road. Turn right and follow Bartlett Road to the trailhead and parking lot.

Trail Notes Located in the hills above East Bay. Effort level is easy to moderate. The surrounding forest roads are also popular for mountain biking. Terrain varies from hilly and flat. Trail is single track, clockwise.

Facilities P

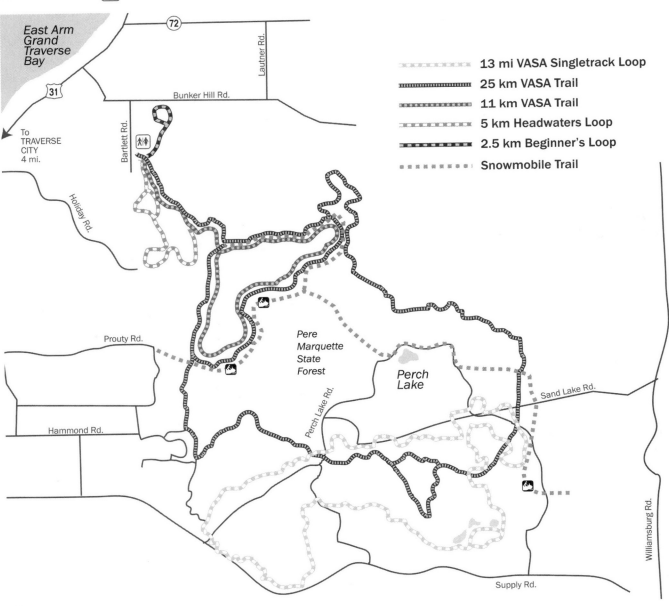

Warner Creek Pathway

Trail Uses	🚴 🥾 ⛷️	**Setting**	Woods, open
Grid	C5 **Trail ID** 292	**Location**	East Jordan
Length	3.8 miles	**Lat/Long**	45-04 / 84-56 Parking off M-32
Surface	Natural	**County**	Antrim
Difficulty	Easy	**Contact**	Gaylord Tourism Bureau 989-732-4000

Getting There The Warner Creek Pathway is located on M-32 about 2 miles west of US-131.

Trail Notes Effort level is easy. There are many exposed roots and soft areas along the riverbank. From the north trailhead of Warner Creek Pathway, south along the Jordan River to Cascade Road, where camping is available.

Facilities P ⛺

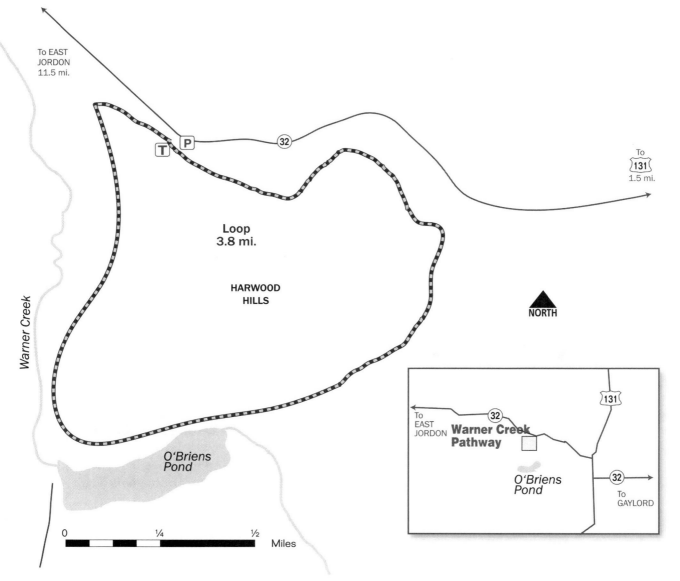

Whiskey Creek

Trail Uses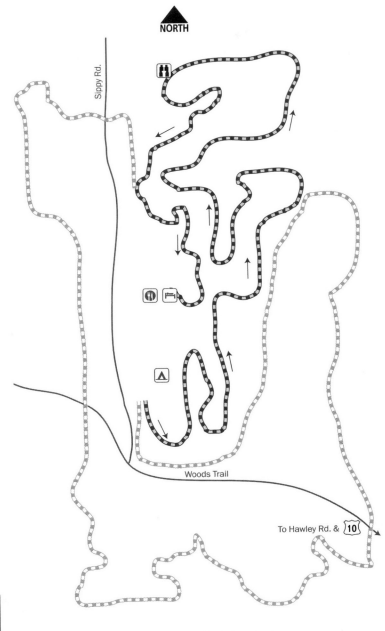

Grid E2 **Trail ID** 296

Length 6 miles

Surface Natural, groomed

Difficulty Easy to difficult

Setting Woods, hilly

Location Custer

Lat/Long 43-52 / 86-08
Hawley & Woods Rd.

County Mason

Contact Whiskey Creek
800-792-7335

Fees Trail use

Getting There Exit M-37 onto US-10 and proceed west for about 10 miles to Walhalla Road. Go south on Walhalla Road to Hawley Road, then west to Woods Trail. South on Woods Trail where signs will direct you to the lodge.

Trail Notes Trail is single track, counter clockwise. The setting is wooded and hilly. The effort level ranges from easy to difficult. The trail is centered around a lodge with full facilities.

Facilities

NORTH

Sippy Rd.

Woods Trail

To Hawley Rd. & 10

White Pine Trail State Park

Trail Uses	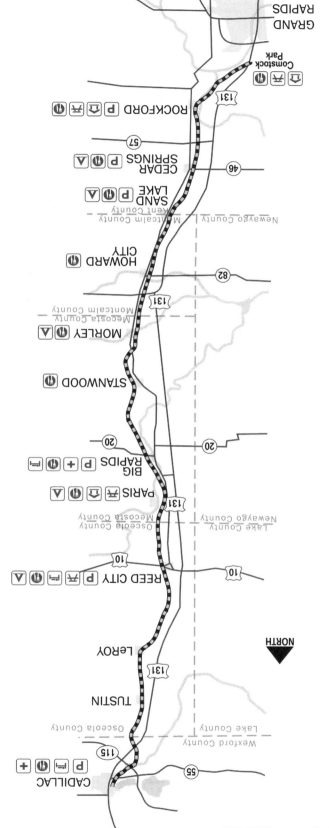 (trail use icons)
Grid	EFG4 Trail ID 297
Length	88 miles
Surface	Asphalt, packed gravel, ballast
Difficulty	Easy to moderate
Setting	Woods, open
Location	Cadillac, Grand Rapids, Cedar Springs, Reed City
Lat/Long	43-02 / 85-40 Comstock Park
Counties	Kent, Montcalm, Mecosta, Osceola, Wexford
Contact	DNR Parks & Recreation 517-373-1270
Getting There	Cadillac Trailhead: Take US-131 north to the M-115 exit and go northwest a half mile. Take North 41 Road one mile north to North 44 Road. Go west on North 44 Road for about a half mile. Rogue River Park, Belmont Trailhead: Take US-131 to exit 95 (Post Drive). Go on Post Drive east to Belmont Road. Take Belmont road a quarter mile south to the Rogue River Park entrance and turn left.
Trail Notes	This north-south rail-trail runs between Grand Rapids and Cadillac. There are 13 miles of asphalt surface from Reed City to Big Rapids and 7 miles of asphalt from Cadillac to Belmont. The remaining surface is hard packed gravel and natural ballast. The surface is ballast and natural, and flat.
Facilities	Most facilities available in the communities along the route

Wildwood Hills Pathway

Trail Uses		**Setting**	Woods, open, hilly
Grid	B5 **Trail ID** 299	**Location**	Indian River, Petoskey
Length	9.5 miles	**Lat/Long**	45-22 / 84-43 Wildwood & Ream Rd
Surface	Natural	**Counties**	Emmet, Cheboygan
Difficulty	Easy to moderate	**Contact**	Indian River Forest Area 616-238-9313

Getting There   From Indian River take M-68 to old US-27, south to Wildwood Road, then west for 3 miles to the parking lot.

From Petoskey on C58 (Mitchell Rd), go 9.5 miles east to Wildwood Road (left fork), then 3 miles to the parking lot.

Trail Notes   Effort level is easy to moderate. Terrain is steep and hilly in some areas. Woods and open fields. Snowmobilers use the area.

Facilities

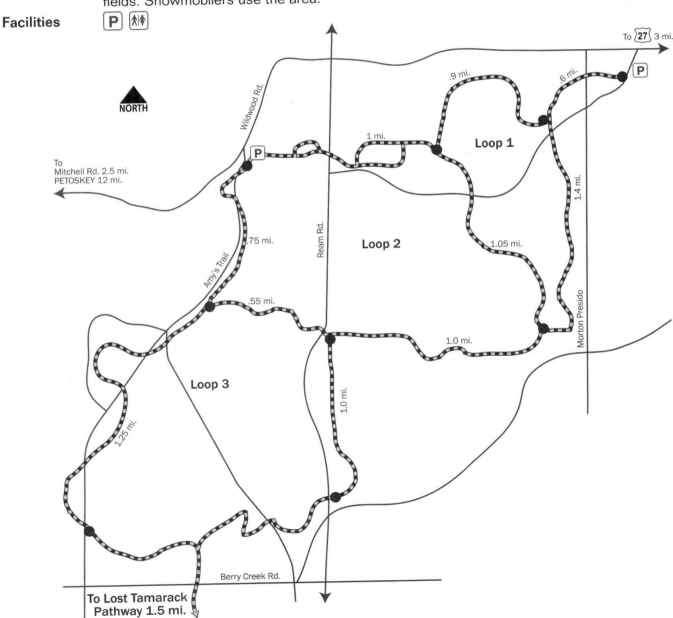

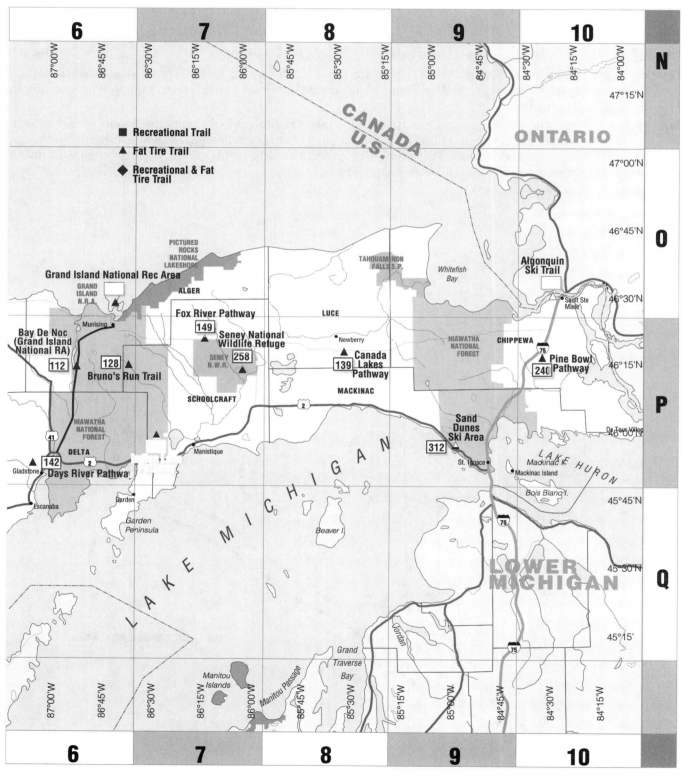

Algonquin Ski Trail

Trail Uses	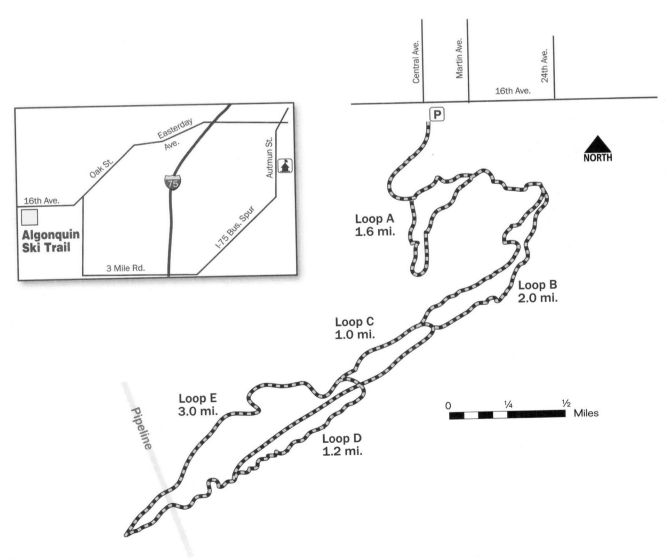		
Grid	O10 **Trail ID** 314	**Location**	Sault Sainte Marie
Length	10 miles	**Lat/Long**	46-29 / 84-25 Trailhead off 16th Ave.
Surface	Natural	**County**	Chippewa
Difficulty	Moderate	**Contact**	Algonquin Cross Country Ski Trail 906-635-1367
Setting	Woods, open, marsh	**Fees**	Donations only

Getting There   From Sault Sainte. Marie, go south for 2 miles on I-75 to the Three Mile Road exit, then west for a mile to Baker Road. North on Baker Road to 16th Ave, then west for a mile to the trailhead.

Trail Notes   Located in Chippewa County, about 4 miles southwest of Sault Ste. Marie. Effort level is moderate, single and two-track. Direction is counter clockwise. Setting is forests, wetlands, hills and sandy areas. Bisecting this trail is the Soo-Strongs Rail Trail, extending 20 miles from the west side of Sault Sainte Marie.

Facilities   P

Bay De Noc – Grand Island Trail

Trail Uses

Grid P6 **Trail ID** 112

Length 40 miles

Surface Natural, sandy

Difficulty Easy

Getting There South trailhead - From Rapid River take US-2 east to CR 509, then north for 1.5 miles to the trailhead and parking.

North trailhead - From Munising and the M28/M94 intersection, take M-94 8 miles west to trailhead at Ackerman Lake.

Trail Notes Effort level is easy, but the surface is natural and sandy. The terrain varies between hilly and flat.

Facilities P | 🚰 | 🚻 | 🛏

Setting Woods, open, hills

Location Munising, Rapid City

Lat/Long 45-55 / 86-56   Trailhead at Hwy D5, Rapid River

Counties Alger, Delta

Contact Hiawatha National Forest   906-786-4062

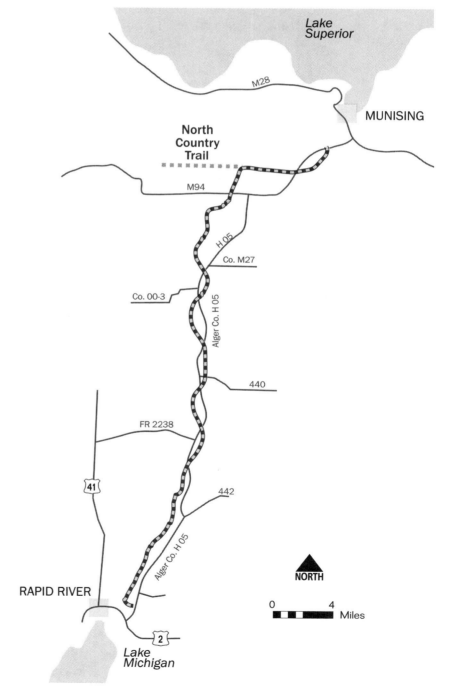

Bruno's Run Trail

Trail Uses		**Setting**	Woods, open, hilly	
Grid	P6 **Trail ID** 128	**Location**	Munising, Wetmore	
Length	7.5 miles	**Lat/Long**	46-14 / 86-87	Trailhead off CR-13
Surface	Natural	**Counties**	Alger, Schoolcraft	
Difficulty	Moderate to difficult	**Contact**	Hiawatha National Forest	906-387-2512

Getting There From Wetmore, 11 miles south on H-13 to the Moccasin Lake Picnic Area and trailhead.

Trail Notes Effort level is moderate to difficult. Terrain is mostly flat. Many lakes and bridges. Rolling terrain and scenic views.

Facilities P 🏕

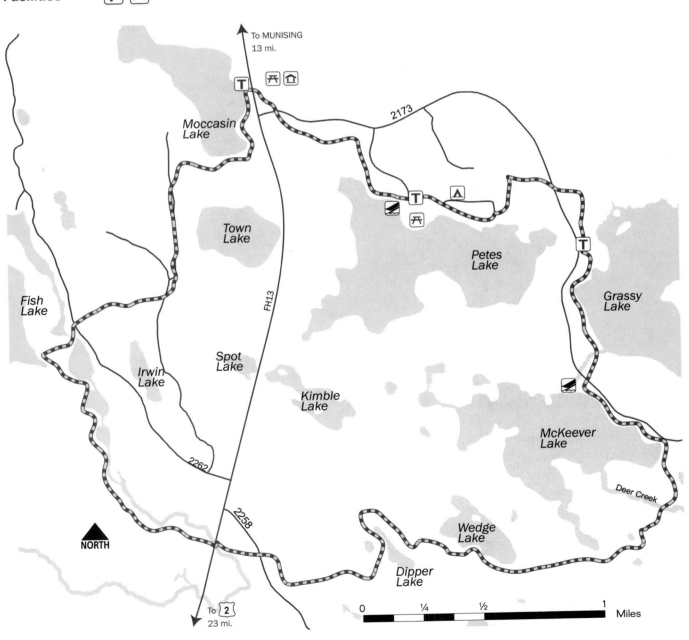

Canada Lakes Pathway

Trail Uses	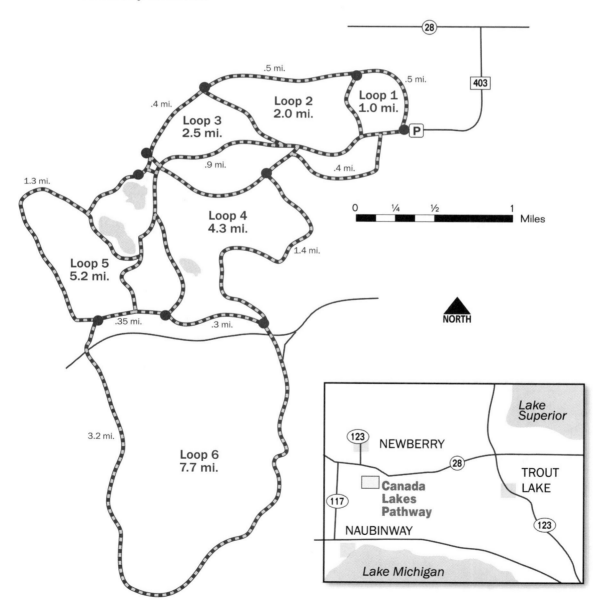	**Setting**	Woods, open
Grid	P8 Trail ID 139	**Location**	Newberry
Length	14 miles	**Lat/Long**	46-17 / 85-29 Entrance off CR-403
Surface	Natural	**County**	Luce
Difficulty	Easy	**Contact**	Lake Superior State Forest 906-293-3293

Getting There   Located four miles southeast of Newberry. From the junction of M-123 and M-28, go east 1 mile to CR 403, then south 1.5- miles to parking and the trailhead.

Trail Notes   Effort level is easy. Wooded and open.

Facilities   P A (Campgrounds – 2 miles west of Newberry off CR 405, and 4 miles north of Newberry on M123)

Days River Pathway

Trail Uses	
Grid	P6 **Trail ID** 142
Length	10.5 miles
Surface	Natural, groomed
Difficulty	Easy
Setting	Woods, open
Location	Gladstone
Lat/Long	45-53 / 87-03 Parking area
County	Delta
Contact	Escanaba River State Forest 906-786-2354
Getting There	From Gladstone, go 3 miles north on US-2/41, then west 2 miles on Days River Road to the entrance.
Trail Notes	Several loops. Effort level is easy. Terrain is rolling hills to flat. Single track, in a clockwise direction. Parallels the west side of the Days River with views of the river at several points.
Facilities	P

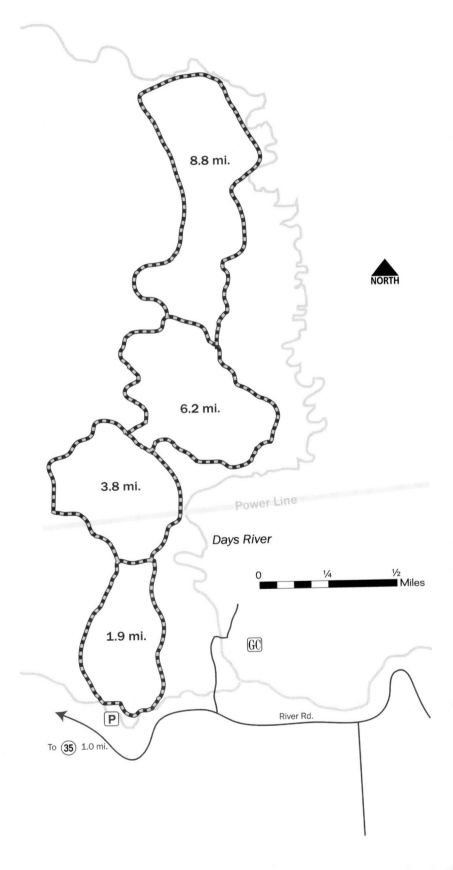

8.8 mi.

NORTH

6.2 mi.

3.8 mi.

Power Line

Days River

0   ¼   ½
Miles

1.9 mi.

GC

P

River Rd.

To 35 1.0 mi.

228
41
35
2
GLADSTONE
Days River Pathway
412
ESCANABA
41
2
35
Lake Michigan

Fox River Pathway

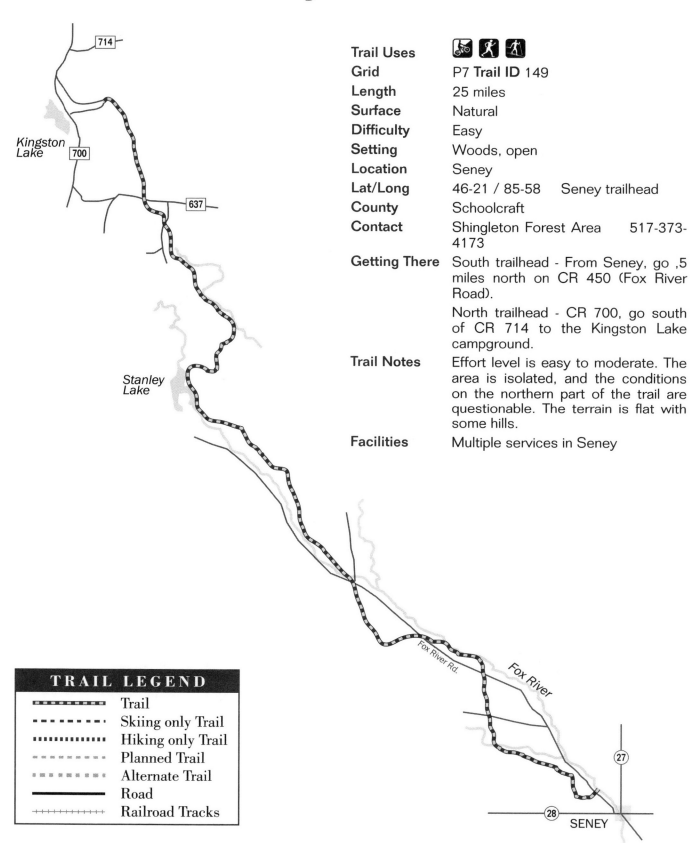

Trail Uses	
Grid	P7 **Trail ID** 149
Length	25 miles
Surface	Natural
Difficulty	Easy
Setting	Woods, open
Location	Seney
Lat/Long	46-21 / 85-58 Seney trailhead
County	Schoolcraft
Contact	Shingleton Forest Area 517-373-4173
Getting There	South trailhead - From Seney, go ,5 miles north on CR 450 (Fox River Road).
	North trailhead - CR 700, go south of CR 714 to the Kingston Lake campground.
Trail Notes	Effort level is easy to moderate. The area is isolated, and the conditions on the northern part of the trail are questionable. The terrain is flat with some hills.
Facilities	Multiple services in Seney

TRAIL LEGEND

- ▪▪▪▪▪ Trail
- – – – – Skiing only Trail
- ▪▪▪▪▪▪ Hiking only Trail
- – – – – Planned Trail
- ▪ ▪ ▪ ▪ Alternate Trail
- —————— Road
- ++++++++++ Railroad Tracks

Grand Island Trails

Trail Uses		**Setting**	Woods, open
Grid	O6 **Trail ID** 152	**Location**	Munising
Length	30 miles	**Lat/Long**	47-27 / 86-34 Williams Landing
Surface	Natural	**County**	Alger
Difficulty	Easy	**Contact**	Munising Ranger District 906-387-3700
Acres	13,000	**Fees**	Ferry fee to access the Island

Getting There   From Munising, there is ferry service to Williams Landing at the south end of the island.

Trail Notes   Grand Island is located off shore from Munising. Terrain is moderate to flat. Effort level is easy. There is a campground on the island. Be aware that bears also reside here.

Facilities   P ⊤ ⋔ ⛺

SYMBOL LEGEND

🏊	Beach/Swimming
🚲	Bicycle Repair
▥	Cabin
⛺	Camping
🛶	Canoe Launch
+	First Aid
⏣	Food
GC	Golf Course
?	Information
⊨	Lodging
⋔	Overlook/Observation
P	Parking
⊼	Picnic
⌂	Ranger Station
⋔	Restrooms
⌂	Shelter
⊤	Trailhead
⌂	Visitor Center
⊤	Water

TRAIL LEGEND

▪▪▪▪	Trail
- - - -	Skiing only Trail
▪▪▪▪▪▪	Hiking only Trail
- - - -	Planned Trail
▪ ▪ ▪ ▪	Alternate Trail
———	Road
++++++	Railroad Tracks

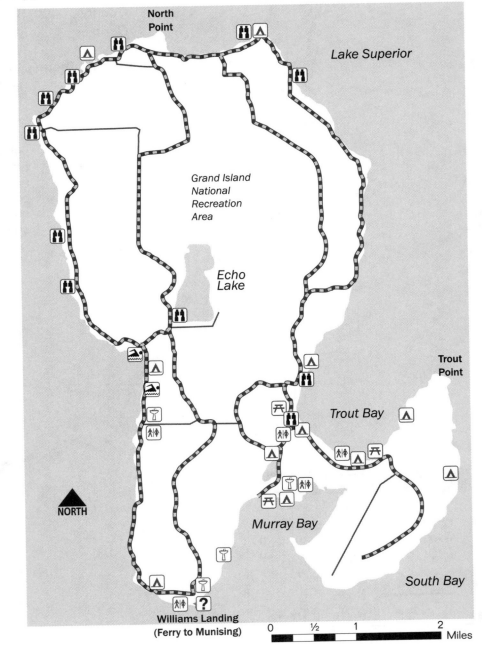

South Bay

Williams Landing
(Ferry to Munising)

0   ½   1   2
Miles

Granite Pointe Nordic Ski Area

Trail Uses	🚴 🏃 ⛷️	**Location**	Marquette	
Grid	O5 **Trail ID** 308	**Lat/Long**	46-35 / 87-57	Ski Lodge area
Length	13 miles	**County**	Marquette	
Surface	Natural	**Contact**	Granite Pointe Nordic Ski Center	
Difficulty	Moderate to difficult		906-475-8200	
Setting	Woods, open	**Fees**	Trail use	

Getting There From Marquette, take US-41 west for 2 miles from a Wal-Mart stop light to CR-502, then right a half mile to CR-510, then 4 miles to North Basin Road. Left 1.5 miles to Snowy Ridge Road, then right a half mile to Granite Ridge.

Trail Notes Effort level is moderate to difficult. The terrain is hilly with some steep areas. There is a trail use fee.

Facilities Nordic Ski Center P ⊤ 🚻 🛏️

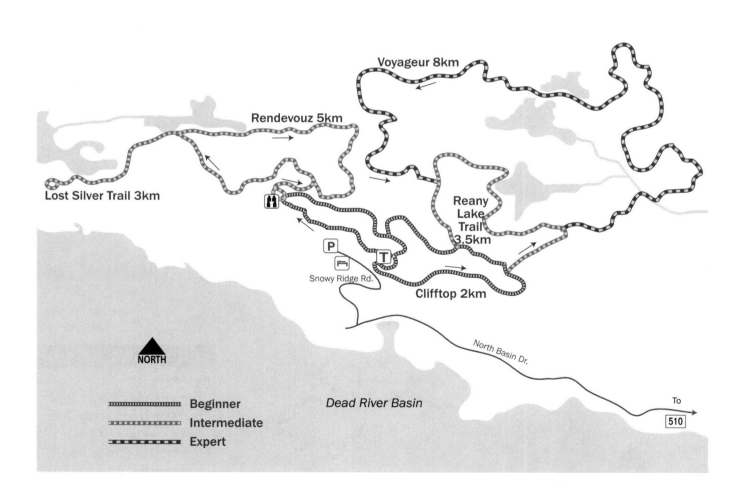

153

Pine Bowl Pathway

Trail Uses
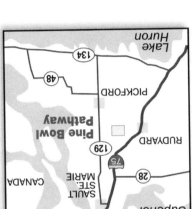

Grid	P10 Trail ID 240	**Location**	Sault Ste. Marie	
Length	12.5 miles	**Lat/Long**	46-15 / 84-26	Parking area off Wilson Rd.
Surface	Natural, groomed	**County**	Chippewa	
Difficulty	Easy	**Contact**	Munuscong State Forest	906-635-5281
Setting	Woods, open	**Fees**	Donations only	

Getting There From Sault Ste. Marie, go south for 16 miles on I-75 on Tone Road, then east for 4 miles to Wilson Road. Proceed south less than a mile to the parking lot.

Trail Notes Effort level is easy. Topography is rolling and wooded. Single and two-track, counter clockwise. Chippewa County airport is within 2 miles.

Facilities P 🚻 (In Kinross)

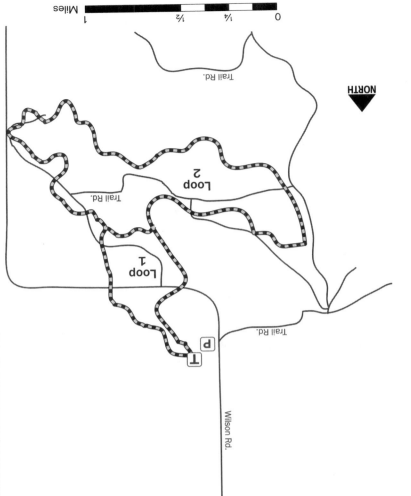

To 75 4 mi.

To KINCHELOE 2 mi.

To 129 3 mi.

Wilson Rd.

Trail Rd.

Loop 1

Loop 2

Trail Rd.

Trail Rd.

NORTH

Miles

0 ¼ ½ 1

TRAIL LEGEND

Trail	▪▪▪▪
Skiing only Trail	– – – –
Hiking only Trail	▪▪▪▪▪▪
Planned Trail	░░░░
Alternate Trail	░░░░
Road	———
Railroad Tracks	+++++

Lake Superior

CANADA

SAULT STE. MARIE

75

28

129

RUDYARD

Pine Bowl Pathway

PICKFORD

48

134

Lake Huron

Sand Dunes Cross Country Ski Trail

Trail Uses	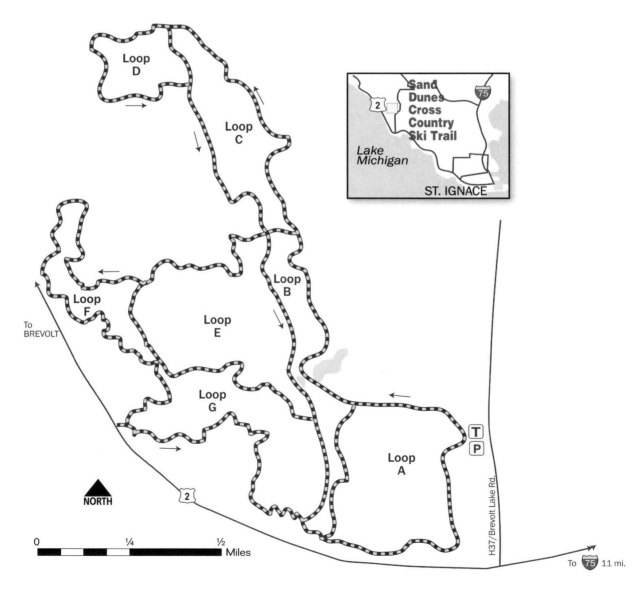		**Setting**	Woods, open, sand dunes
Grid	P9 **Trail ID** 312		**Location**	St. Ignace
Length	9.5 miles		**Lat/Long**	45-56 / 84-56 Trailhead off Brevort Lake Rd
Surface	Natural		**County**	Mackinac
Difficulty	Easy to difficult		**Contact**	Hiawatha National Forest 906-786-4062

Getting There From the Mackinac Island bridge at St. Ignace, go 11 miles northwest on Hwy 2, then north on Bevoort Lake Road for a half mile to the entrance and trailhead.

Trail Notes The topography of the Sand Dunes Ski Trail is forested dunes and sandy. The effort level varies from easy to difficult. Direction is counter clockwise and both singe and two-track.

Facilities P

Seney National Wildlife Refuge

Trail Uses			
Grid	P7 **Trail ID** 258	**Setting**	Woods, open
Length	52 miles	**Location**	Germfask
Surface	Natural	**Lat/Long**	44-17 / 85-56 Entrance off M-77
Difficulty	Easy	**County**	Schoolcraft
Acres	95,500	**Contact**	Seney National Wildlife Refuge 906-586-9851

Getting There Just north of the town of Germfask on M-77

Fees Vehicle entry

Trail Notes Effort level is easy. There are many loops and small lakes. Terrain is mostly flat.

Facilities Germfask P [T] [A] (O) Bike & ski rentals

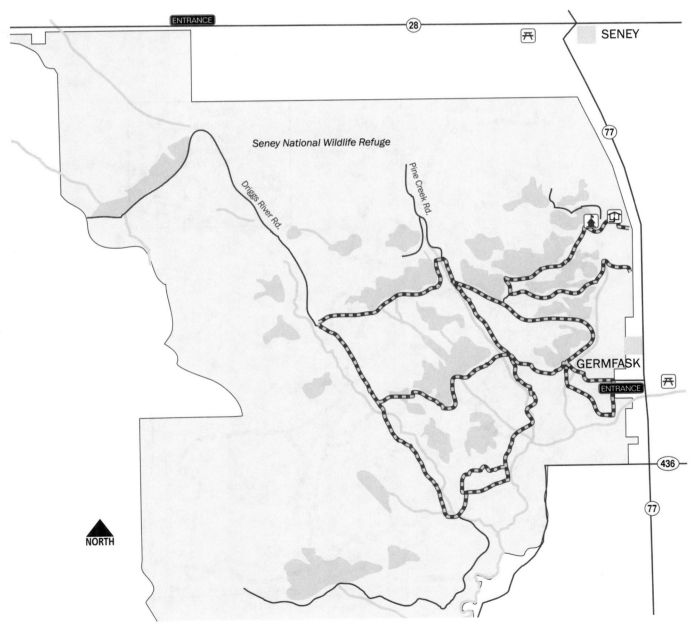

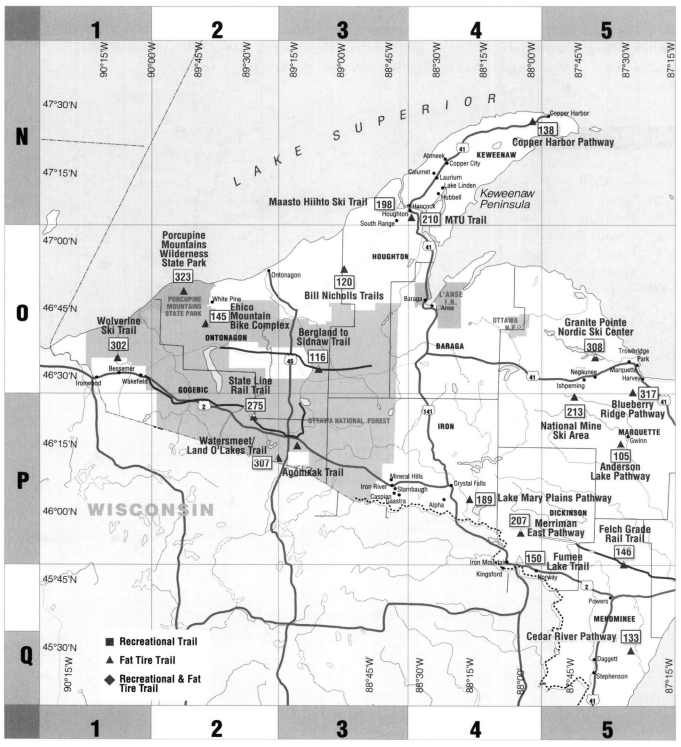

Agonikak Trail

Trail Uses		**Setting**	Woods, Open
Grid	P3 **Trail ID** 102	**Location**	Watersmeet, Land O' Lakes (WI)
Length	10.5 miles	**Lat/Long**	46-10 / 89-12 Trailhead at a roadside park
Surface	Natural	**County**	Gogebic
Difficulty	Easy to moderate	**Contact**	Ottawa National Forest 906-932-1330
Getting There	Forest Service Visitor Center at the intersection of Hwy 2 & 45 in Watersmeet.		
Trail Notes	Ungroomed. Effort level is easy to moderate. Surface is natural.		
Facilities			

SYMBOL LEGEND

- Beach/Swimming
- Bicycle Repair
- Cabin
- Camping
- Canoe Launch
- First Aid
- Food
- GC Golf Course
- ? Information
- Lodging
- Overlook/Observation
- P Parking
- Picnic
- Ranger Station
- Restrooms
- Shelter
- T Trailhead
- Visitor Center
- Water

TRAIL LEGEND

- ▪▪▪▪▪ Trail
- ▪ ▪ ▪ ▪ Skiing only Trail
- ▪▪▪▪▪▪▪ Hiking only Trail
- ▪ ▪ ▪ ▪ Planned Trail
- ▪ ▪ ▪ ▪ Alternate Trail
- ——— Road
- +++++++ Railroad Tracks

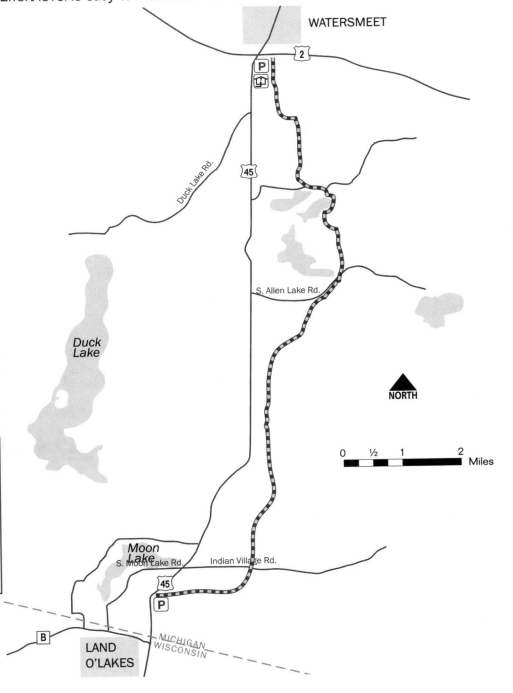

WATERSMEET

Duck Lake Rd.

Duck Lake

S. Allen Lake Rd.

NORTH

0   ½   1   2 Miles

Moon Lake

S. Moon Lake Rd.   Indian Village Rd.

LAND O'LAKES

MICHIGAN
WISCONSIN

Anderson Lake Pathway

Trail Uses	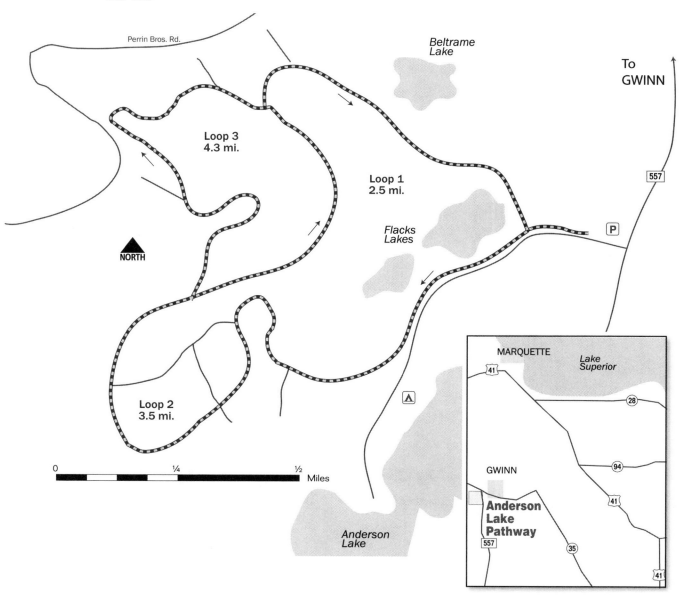	**Setting**	Woods, open, hilly
Grid	P5 **Trail ID** 105	**Location**	Gwinn
Length	6 miles	**Lat/Long**	46-16 / 87-29 Parking off CR-557
Surface	Natural, groomed	**County**	Marquette
Difficulty	Easy to difficult	**Contact**	Escanaba River State Forest 906-786-2351

Getting There   From Gwinn take M-35 west for 2.5 miles to CR-557, then south for 2.5 miles to the entrance.

Trail Notes   The terrain is mostly flat with some hilly and steep areas in the forest. Loops are in a clockwise direction. Loop 1 is easy, loop 2 is moderate, and loop 3 is more difficult. Parking and the campground is located at the trailhead

Facilities

Perrin Bros. Rd.

Beltrame Lake

To GWINN

557

Loop 3
4.3 mi.

Loop 1
2.5 mi.

NORTH

Flacks Lakes

P

Loop 2
3.5 mi.

0   ¼   ½   Miles

MARQUETTE

Lake Superior

41

28

94

GWINN

41

Anderson Lake Pathway

557

35

41

Anderson Lake

Bergland to Sidnaw Trail

Trail Uses			
Grid	O2-3 **Trail ID** 116	**Location**	Bergland, Bruce Crossing, Ewen, Kenton,
Length	43 miles		Matchwood, Paynesville, Sidnaw, Trout Creek
Surface	Ballast, cinder, dirt	**Lat/Long**	46-35 / 89-32 Bergland at East Shore Rd
Difficulty	Moderate	**Counties**	Ontonagon, Houghton
Setting	Woods, open, farmland	**Contact**	Copper Country State Forest 906-353-6651

Getting There   Multiple accesses from SR-28 and the numerous communities along its route.

Trail Notes   The Bergland to Sidnaw Rail-Trail follows a former railroad grade. The surface consists of gravel, sand, dirt, original ballast. The setting is forest, wet area, pasture and farmland, land bridges. You will be crossing extensive bridges towering over streams and rivers, the most spectacular of which is Agate Falls, at the Middle Branch of the Ontonagon River. The trail generally follows State Route 28.

Facilities   Most services are available in the communities along the route

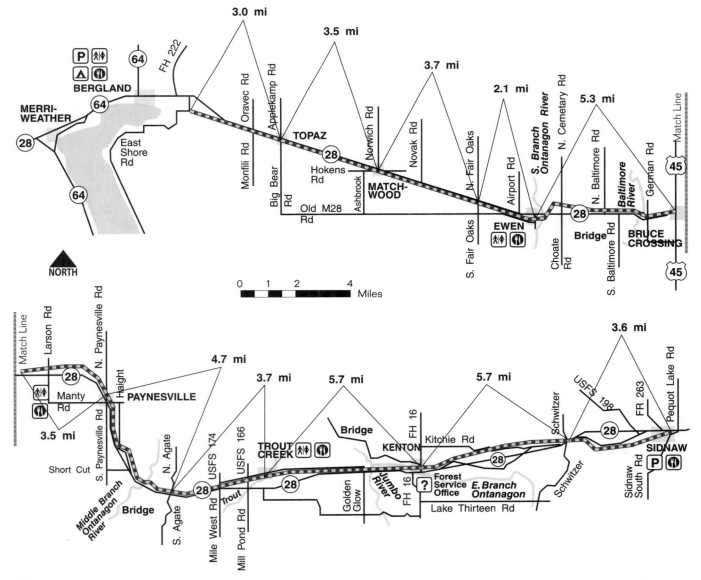

Bill Nichols Trails

Trail Uses

Grid O3 **Trail ID** 120

Length 41.5

Surface Cinder, ballast, dirt

Difficulty Easy

Setting Woods, open, rural

Location Greenland, Hancock, Atlantic Mine, Painesdale

Lat/Long 46-44 / 89-07 Trailhead off H-26 by Greenland

County Houghton, Ontonagon

Contact Copper County State Forest 906-353-6651

Getting There South Trail - Greenland, at Adventure Mountain Ski Area.

North Trailhead - From Houghton, west of town on Canal Drive and Houghton's Waterfront Trail.

Trail Notes Built on old railroad bed. Effort level is easy and the terrain is flat. Surface consists of ballast, sand, and clay. The trail runs northeast from Greenland to Hancock.

Facilities Most services can be found in the communities along the route.

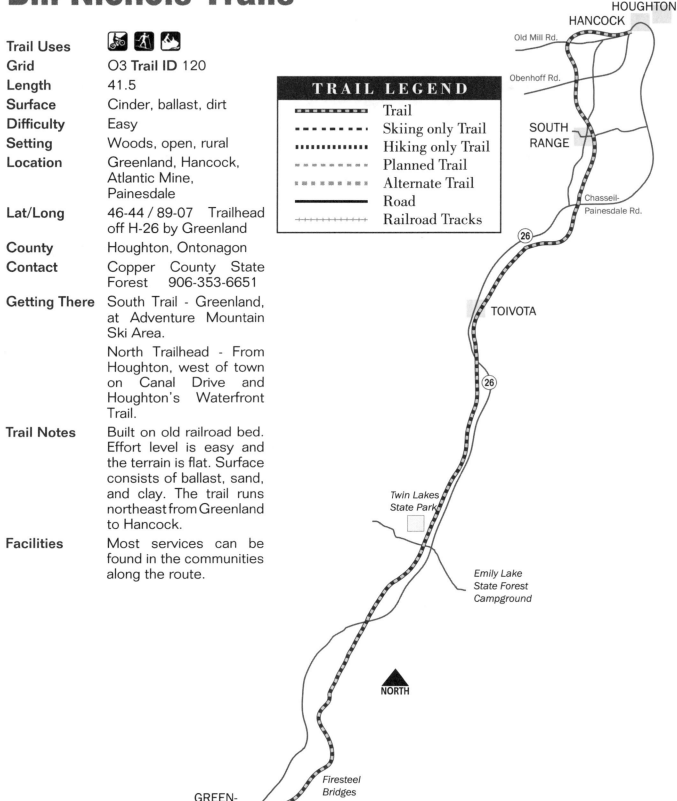

TRAIL LEGEND

- ▬▬▬ Trail
- - - - - Skiing only Trail
- ▪▪▪▪▪ Hiking only Trail
- - - - - Planned Trail
- ▪ ▪ ▪ ▪ Alternate Trail
- ▬▬▬ Road
- +++++++ Railroad Tracks

HOUGHTON
HANCOCK
Old Mill Rd.
Obenhoff Rd.
SOUTH RANGE
Chasseil-Painesdale Rd.
26
TOIVOTA
26
Twin Lakes State Park
Emily Lake State Forest Campground
NORTH
Firesteel Bridges
GREEN-LAND
MASS CITY

Blueberry Ridge Pathway

Trail Uses	🚴 🏃 ⛷	**Setting**	Forest, open, sandy areas
Grid	O5 **Trail ID** 317	**Location**	Marquette
Length	15 miles	**Lat/Long**	46-28 / 87-25 Entrance off CR-553
Surface	Natural	**County**	Marquette
Difficulty	Moderate	**Contact**	Escanaba River State Forest 908-485-1031
		Fees	Donations only

Getting There   The trail is located 6 miles south of Marquette via CR-553 at CR-480. Parking at the trailhead on the east side of CR-553.

Trail Notes   Setting is sandy and forested. The trail is single and two-track, and clockwise. There are seven loops.

Facilities   P

TRAIL LEGEND

- ▪▪▪▪▪ Trail
- ▪ ▪ ▪ ▪ Skiing only Trail
- ∙∙∙∙∙∙ Hiking only Trail
- ▫ ▫ ▫ ▫ Planned Trail
- ▪ ▪ ▪ ▪ Alternate Trail
- ──── Road
- ++++++ Railroad Tracks

To MARQUETTE 6 mi.

P

480

Crossroads Loop
1.5 mi.
(Easy)

Husky Loop
1.5 mi.
(Medium)

Spartan Loop
1.6 mi.
(Expert)

Wildcat Loop
1.7 mi.
(Expert)

553

Superior Loop
2.8 mi.
(Expert)

Wolverine Loop
2.7 mi.
(Medium)

Lighted Loop
1.7 mi.
(Easy)

P

To SANDS 1.3 mi.

MARQUETTE

41

Lake Superior

480

28

35

Blueberry Ridge Pathway

553

41

Cedar River Pathway

Trail Uses	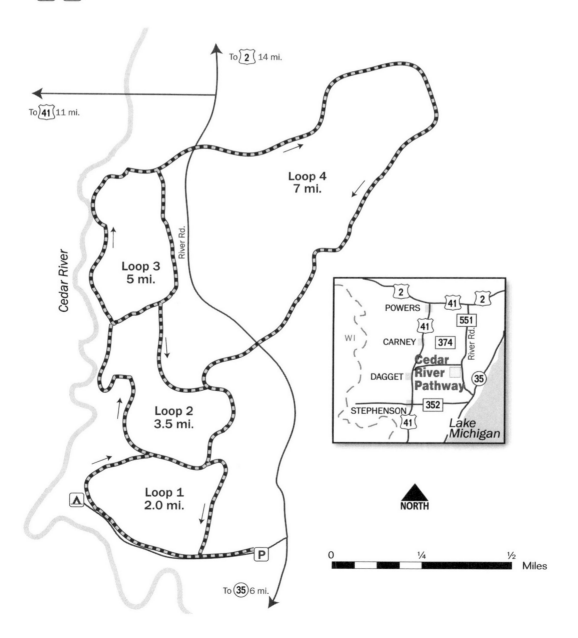	**Setting**	Woods	
Grid	Q5 **Trail ID** 133	**Location**	Cedar River	
Length	8 miles	**Lat/Long**	45-26 / 87-23	Entrance off CR-551
Surface	Natural	**County**	Memoninee	
Difficulty	Easy	**Contact**	Escanaba River State Forest	908-786-2351

Getting There From Cedar River, go 1.5 miles north on M-35, then continue north on CR-551 (River Road) for 6 miles to the entrance and trailhead.

Trail Notes Effort level is easy. Terrain is flat. Setting is wooded and open. There is a campground along the trail. Single track, running clockwise.

Facilities P A

163

Copper Harbor Pathway

Trail Uses			
Grid	N4 Trail ID 138	**Location**	Copper Harbor
Length	12 miles	**Lat/Long**	47-28 / 87-53 Entrance off Hwy 41
Surface	Natural	**County**	Keweenaw
Difficulty	Moderate to difficult	**Contact**	Copper Country State Forest 906-353-6651
Getting There	From Copper Harbor, go to the west end of Lake Fanny Hooe by the Lake Fanny Hooe Resort.		
Trail Notes	Effort level is moderate to difficult. Terrain it hilly. Lodging with facilities available at Lake Fanny Hooe at the west end. Single track and dirt road, running clockwise.		
Facilities	P Lodging, food at the Lake Fanny Hooe Resort (906-289-4451)		

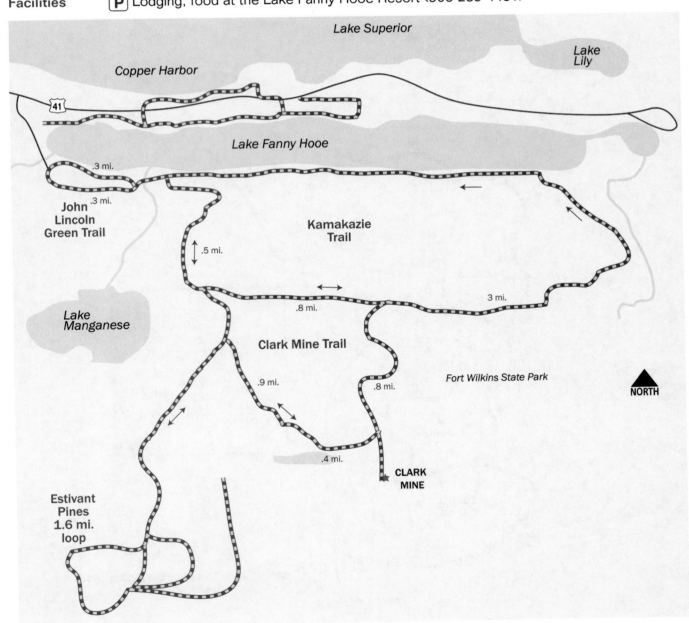

Ehico Mountain

Trail Uses	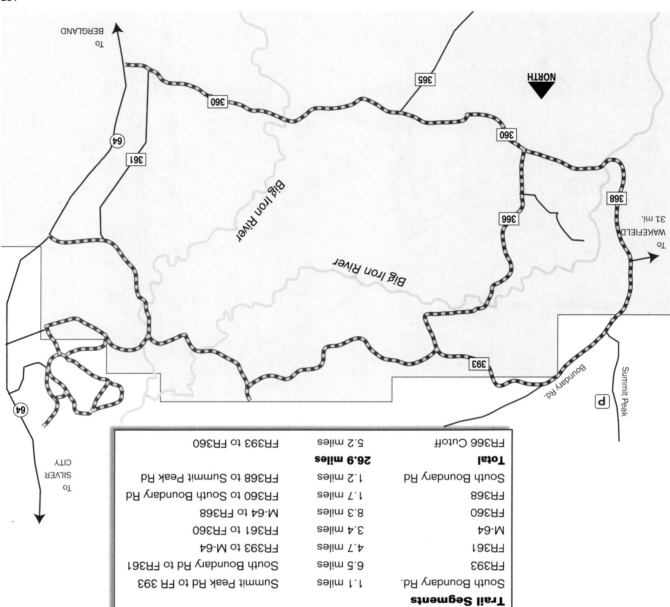	**Setting**	Woods, open	
Grid	O2 Trail ID 145	**Location**	Bergland	
Length	27 miles	**Lat/Long**	46-40 / 89-36	Hwy 64 & FR-360
Surface	Crushed stone, natural	**County**	Ontonagon	
Difficulty	Easy to difficult	**Contact**	Ottawa National Forest	906-932-1330

Getting There Located north of Bergland and south of Silver City. From Bergland go 5 miles north on FR-360 and west of M64.

Trail Notes Trail consists of gravel and old logging roads through speed hardwood forests. Beaver dams and deep ruts are frequent obstructions. Effort level is easy to difficult. Direction is clockwise.

Facilities [P]

Trail Segments

South Boundary Rd.	1.1 miles	Summit Peak Rd to FR 393	
FR393	6.5 miles	South Boundary Rd to FR361	
FR361	4.7 miles	FR393 to M-64	
M-64	3.4 miles	FR361 to FR360	
FR360	8.3 miles	M-64 to FR368	
FR368	1.7 miles	FR360 to South Boundary Rd	
South Boundary Rd	1.2 miles	FR368 to Summit Peak Rd	
Total	**26.9 miles**		
FR366 Cutoff	5.2 miles	FR393 to FR360	

Felch Grade Rail Trail

Trail Uses	🚵 🏂 🏃 🔥	**Setting**	Woods, open, rural
Grid	PQ5 **Trail ID** 146	**Location**	Escanaba, Felch, LaBranche, Schaffer
Length	45 miles	**Lat/Long**	45-60 / 87-50 Trailhead
Surface	Gravel, dirt	**Counties**	Delta, Menominee, Dickinson
Difficulty	Moderate	**Contact**	Copper Country State Forest 906-563-9247

Getting There   East trailhead - From Pine Ridge go about 1.5 miles on US-2 to the trail.

West trailhead - From the Felch Township Community Center on M-69, take Andy's Lane to Van Lear Drive, then right to Old Dump Road, then left 2 blocks. Turn right to the trail grade.

Trail Notes   The trail is an old railroad bed running between Escanaba and Felch, with a surface of ballast and gravel that can be rough. It mostly parallels M-69, but your awareness of this lightly-traveled road is masked by the vegetation separating the road from the trail. The terrain is flat, with surroundings including woods, sand, creek and rivers.

Facilities   Communities in route; No parking at the eastern trailheads; Small stores in LaBranche and Schafter

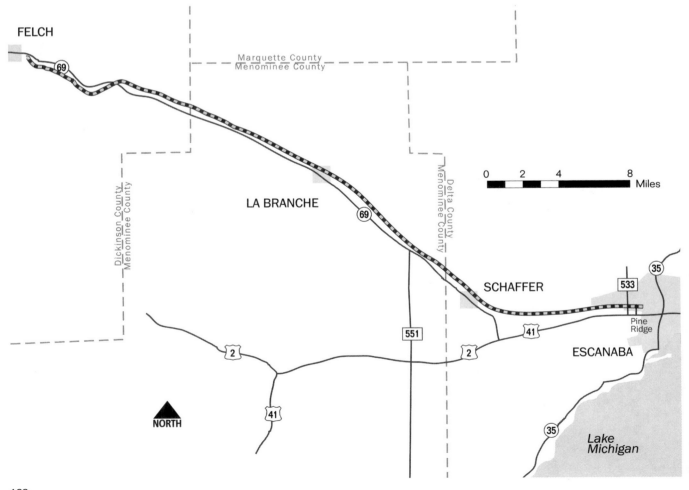

Fumee Lake Trails

Trail Uses	🚵 🚶 ⛷️
Grid	P4 **Trail ID** 150
Length	18 miles
Surface	Natural
Difficulty	Easy to moderate
Setting	Woods, open

Location	Norway, Quinnesec
Lat/Long	45-49 / 87-57 Trailhead
County	Dickinson
Contact	Dickinson Conservations District
	906-774-1550

Getting There Between Norway and Quinnesec. From US-2, take Upper Pine Creek Rd for 1 mile to the entrance.

Trail Notes Terrain is rolling. The trails surround two lakes. The path is two-track, running clockwise. The South Ridge Trail is more difficult, and involves a gradual climb of about 330 feet above Fumee Lake. The Fumee Mountain Trail has recently been completed and offers a view of Fumee Lake and the Pine Creek Bluff Chain after a rather difficult climb.

Facilities P

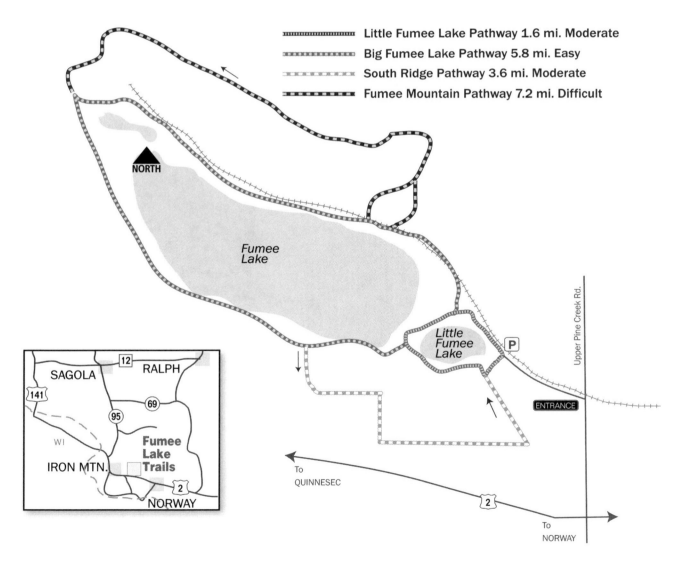

▬▬▬▬▬▬	Little Fumee Lake Pathway 1.6 mi. Moderate
▬▬▬▬▬▬	Big Fumee Lake Pathway 5.8 mi. Easy
▬▬▬▬▬▬	South Ridge Pathway 3.6 mi. Moderate
▬▬▬▬▬▬	Fumee Mountain Pathway 7.2 mi. Difficult

Indian Lake Pathway

Trail Uses	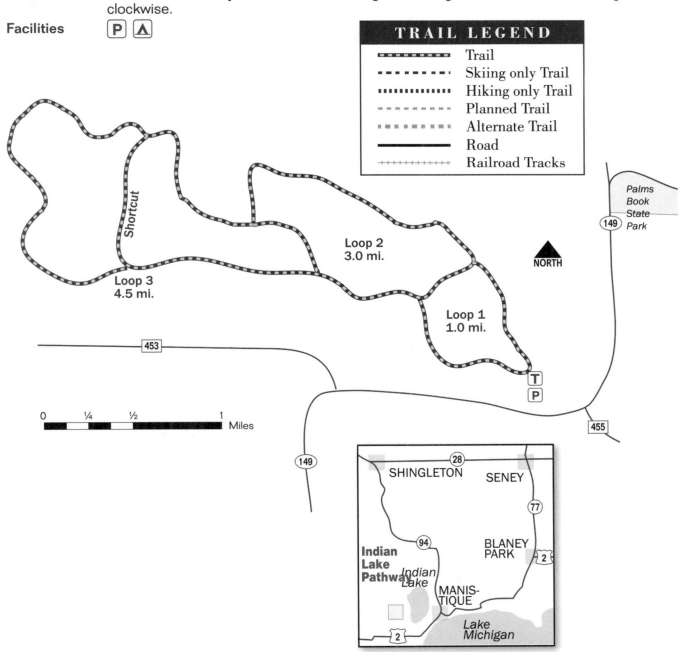	**Setting**	Woods, open	
Grid	P7 Trail ID 178	**Location**	Thompson	
Length	8.5 miles	**Lat/Long**	46-00 / 86-23	Parking area
Surface	Natural	**County**	Schoolcraft	
Difficulty	Easy to moderate	**Contact**	Lake Superior State Forest	906-452-6236

Getting There From Thompson, go 9 miles northwest on M-149 to the entrance. Palms Brook State Park is located 1 mile to the east.

Trail Notes Effort level is easy to moderate. Rolling hills. Single and two-track, running counter clockwise.

Facilities P A

TRAIL LEGEND

- Trail
- Skiing only Trail
- Hiking only Trail
- Planned Trail
- Alternate Trail
- Road
- Railroad Tracks

Shortcut

Loop 2
3.0 mi.

Loop 3
4.5 mi.

Loop 1
1.0 mi.

NORTH

Palms Book State Park

149

453

455

T
P

0   ¼   ½   1   Miles

149

28
SHINGLETON   SENEY

77

94

BLANEY PARK

2

Indian Lake Pathway   Indian Lake

MANIS-TIQUE

Lake Michigan

2

Lake Mary Plains Pathway

Trail Uses	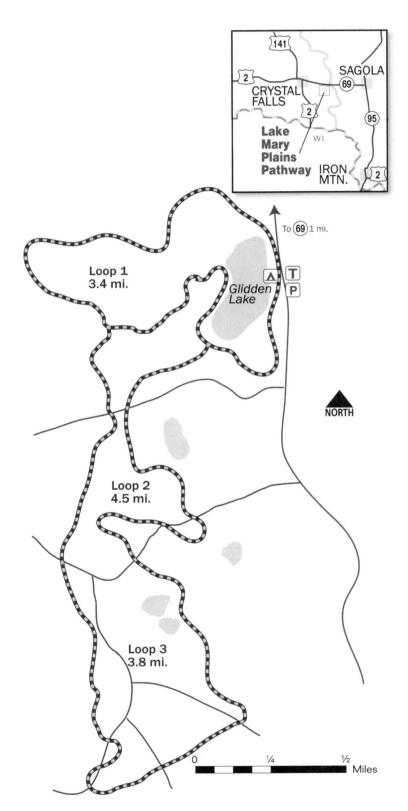
Grid	P4 **Trail ID** 189
Length	9.5 miles
Surface	Natural
Difficulty	Moderate
Setting	Woods, open, rolling hills
Location	Crystal Falls
Lat/Long	46-04 / 88-14 Parking off Lake Mary Rd
County	Dickinson
Contact	Copper County State Forest 906-353-6651
Getting There	From Crystal Falls, go east on M-69 for 4 miles to Lake Mary Plains Road, then south to Glidden Lake Campground where there is day-use parking and the trailhead.
Trail Notes	Setting is rolling hills and wooded. Effort level is moderate. Single track, running clockwise.
Facilities	P A

Maasto Hiihto Ski Trail

Trail Uses		**Setting**	Woods, open, hilly
Grid	N3 **Trail ID** 198	**Location**	Hancock
Length	12 miles	**Lat/Long**	48-08 / 88-36 Parking off Poplar St.
Surface	Natural	**County**	Houghton
Difficulty	Easy to difficult	**Contact**	Keweenaw Tourism Council 906-482-5240
		Fees	Trail use

Getting There The trail is located in the city of Hancock, and can be accessed from many points. The main trailhead is located at the Houghton County Areas at Birch and Ingot Street.

Trail Notes Effort level is easy to difficult. Terrain is hilly with meadows and stream crossings. Single, two-track and gravel road. The 1.5 mile Quincy Loop is easy and gently rolling; the 1.5 mile St. Urho's Loop is easy, the 4.3 mile Gorge Loop is moderate to difficult; the 2.3 mile Austrailia Loop is moderate and rolling; the 1 mile Yooper Looper Loop is moderate and rolling; and the short Mieto Loop is difficult with steep descents and climbs with hairpin turns.

Facilities

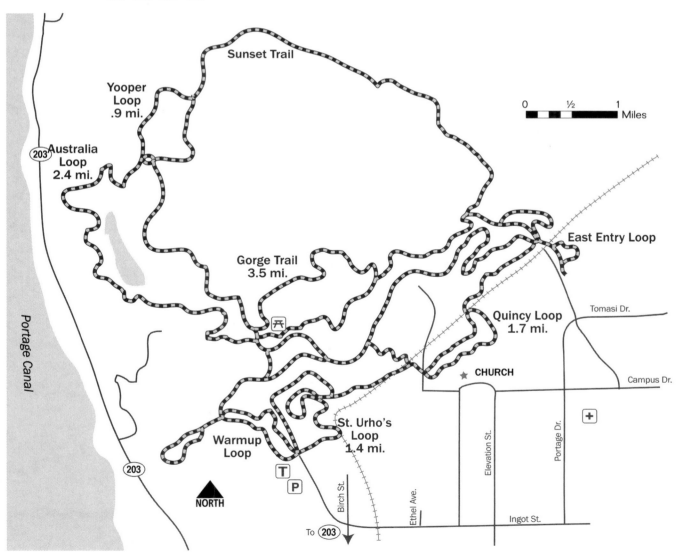

170

Merriman East Pathway

Trail Uses

Grid P4 **Trail ID** 207

Length 9.5 miles

Surface Natural

Difficulty Easy

Setting Woods, open, hilly

Location Iron Mountain, Merriman

Lat/Long 45-56 / 87-56   Parking area

County Dickinson

Contact Copper Country State Forest   906-353-6651

Fees Trail use

Getting There From Iron Mountain, go north for 6 miles to the Merriman Truck Trail, then east 7 miles to the trailhead just before the Mitchell Creek bridge.

Trail Notes Effort level is easy. Terrain is hilly. The "A' Loop is 3.3 miles long, and the "B" Loop is 5.6 miles long. There is a .7 mile connector from the trailhead and parking.

Facilities P

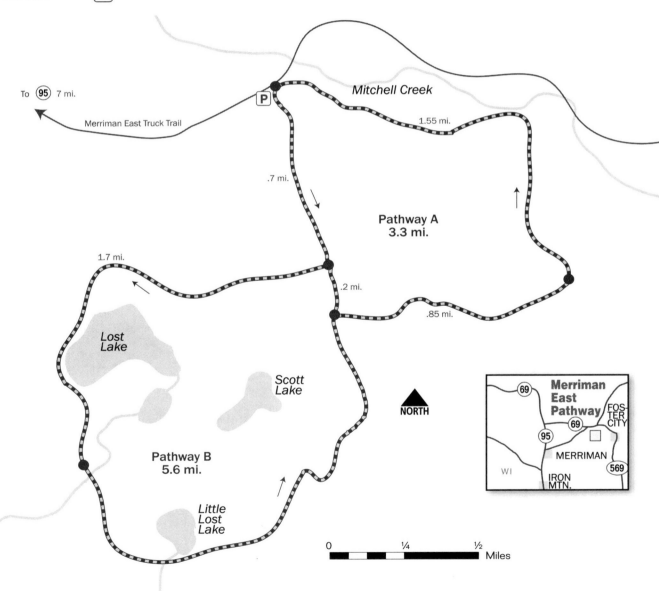

MTU Trail

Trail Uses		**Setting**	Woods, open, hilly
Grid	N4 **Trail ID** 210	**Location**	Houghton
Length	12 miles	**Lat/Long**	47-06 / 88-33 Parking off W. Haron Ave.
Surface	Natural	**County**	Houghton
Difficulty	Easy to difficult	**Contact**	Keweenaw Tourism Council 800-338-7982

Getting There   Located on the MTU campus, between Sharon Avenue and Manninen Road with the entrance on Sharon Avenue.

Trail Notes   Effort level is easy to difficult, with hilly and flat areas. There are many loops. There are cut offs allowing you to bypass the more difficult areas.

Facilities   P

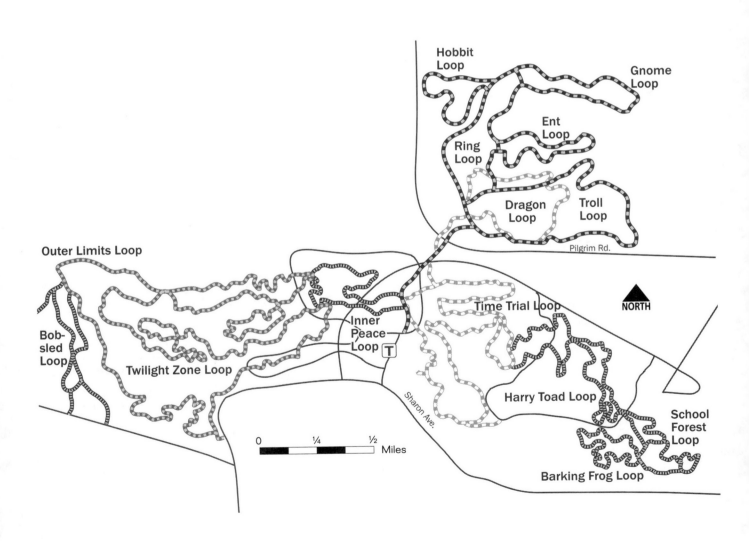

National Mine Ski Area

Trail Uses	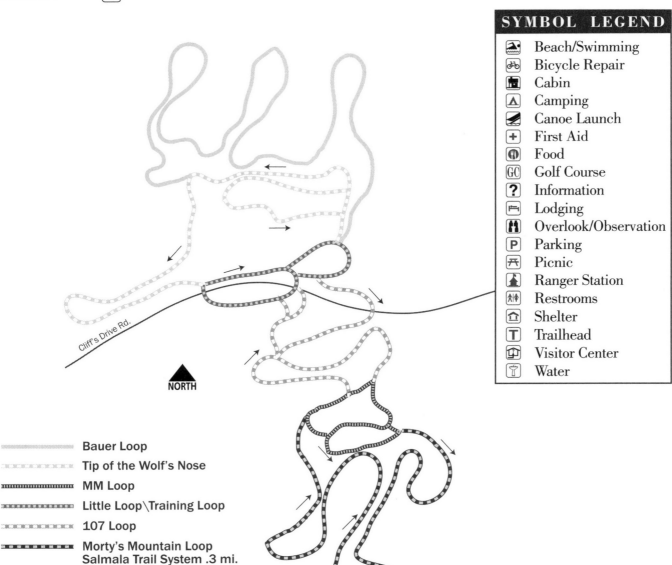		
Grid	P5 **Trail ID** 213	**Location**	Ishpeming, National Mine
Length	7 miles	**Lat/Long**	46-28 / 87-46 National Mine area
Surface	Natural	**County**	Marquette
Difficulty	Moderate to difficult	**Contact**	Trail information 906-486-8080
Setting	Woods, open, hilly	**Fees**	Donations

Getting There From Ishpeming on US-41, go 1 mile west to a yellow blinker, then turn south on Lakeshore Drive. Go .4 miles to Washington Street and turn right (west). Continue for 2.7 miles to the National Mine. The trailhead is 65 yards west on the road to Tilden Mine, and past the A-frame.

Trail Notes Trail area is steep and hilly. Effort level varies from moderate to difficult. Setting is wooded and open. Surface is natural. There is an A-frame with toilets. Trails are not well signed.

Facilities P

SYMBOL LEGEND

🏊	Beach/Swimming
🚲	Bicycle Repair
🏠	Cabin
⛺	Camping
🛶	Canoe Launch
✚	First Aid
🍴	Food
GC	Golf Course
?	Information
🛏	Lodging
🔭	Overlook/Observation
P	Parking
🪑	Picnic
🏛	Ranger Station
🚻	Restrooms
🏠	Shelter
T	Trailhead
🏚	Visitor Center
⛲	Water

Cliff's Drive Rd.

NORTH

Bauer Loop
Tip of the Wolf's Nose
MM Loop
Little Loop\Training Loop
107 Loop
Morty's Mountain Loop
Salmala Trail System .3 mi.

Porcupine Mountains Wilderness State Park

Trail Uses		**Setting**	Forest, open area
Grid	O2 **Trail ID** 323	**Location**	Silver City
Length	35 miles	**Lat/Long**	46-47 / 89-41 Parking area
Surface	Natural	**County**	Ontonagon
Difficulty	Easy to difficult	**Contact**	Western UP Visitors Bureau 906-932-4850
Park Size	92 square miles	**Fees**	Vehicle entry

Getting There From Silver City, go west on M-107 for 10 miles to its end. The Visitors Center is located on South Boundary Road, just south of M-107.

Trail Notes The setting is forest, waterfalls and rocky cliffs. Effort level is easy to difficult. Trail direction is counter clockwise.

Facilities [P] [?] [T] [♦♦] [bed] Ski Lodge

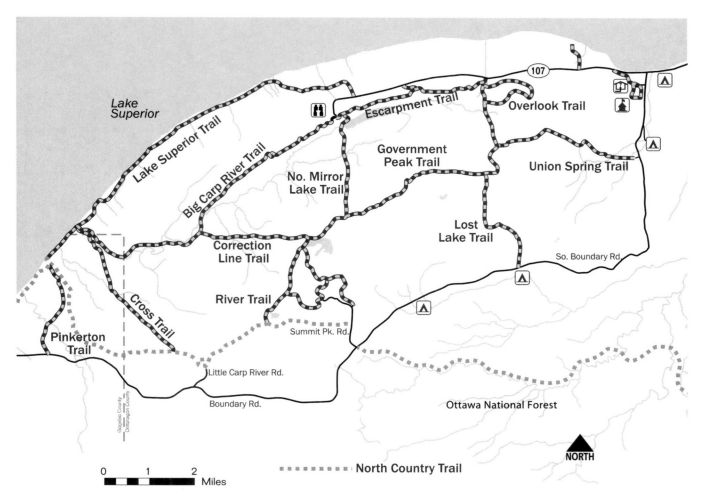

State Line Trail

Trail Uses	🚲 🚶 ⛰️		
Grid	P2-3 **Trail ID** 275	**Location**	Crystal Falls, Beechwood, Iron River, Marenisco, Pentoga, Stambaugh, Wakefield, Watersmeat
Length	102.5		
Surface	Ballast, wood chips, dirt	**Lat/Long**	46-03 / 88-38 Caspian trailhead
Difficulty	Easy to moderate	**County**	Gogebic, Iron
Setting	Woods, open, farmland	**Contact**	Copper Country State Forest 908-353-6651

Getting There   East trailhead - west of US-2 at the Brule River Bridge.

West trailhead - from Wakefield, go 5 miles east on US-2, then south on Korpela Road, then .4 miles south.

Trail Notes   This is an old railroad bed connecting Crystal Falls and Wakefield, with many communities between. It's Michigan's longest rail-trail. There are over 50 bridges on the trail, often with scenic vistas over rivers. Surface is gravel base, original ballast, sand, wood chips and natural. Effort level is easy to moderate. Setting is forests, farmland, lakes, and old iron mines.

Facilities   Most facilities can be found in the many communities along the route.

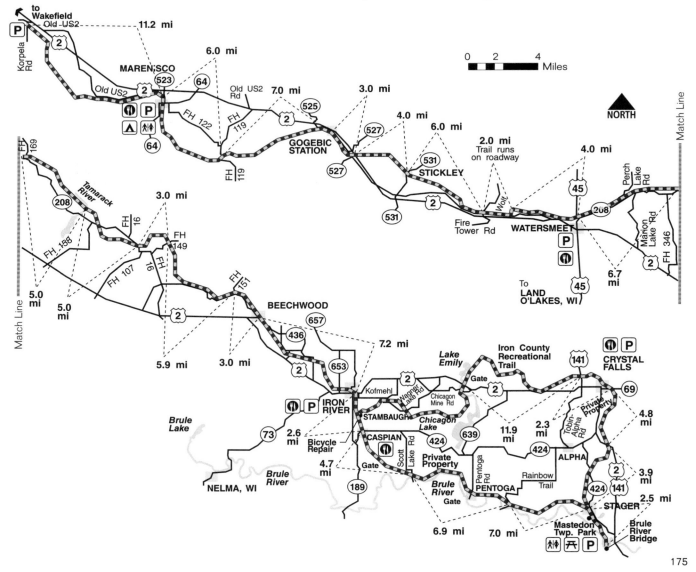

Western Upper Peninsula Trails

Watersmeet – Land O'Lakes Trail

Trail Uses	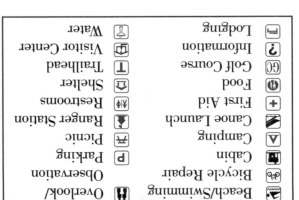		
Grid	P3 Trail ID 307	**Location**	Watersmeet, Land O'Lakes Wisconsin
Length	18 miles	**Lat/Long**	46-16 / 89-12 Land O'Lakes trailhead at SSR B
Surface	Gravel, sand, dirt, ballast	**County**	Gogebic
Difficulty	Easy	**Contact**	Ottawa National Forest 906-932-1330
Setting	Forest, open, ponds	**Fees**	Donations
Getting There	The north trailhead is 1 mile west of Watersmeet at Sylvania Outfitters.		
Trail Notes	This trail is on an abandoned railroad bed. There are no facilities between the trailhead towns of Watersmeet and Land O'Lakes. You can camp in the Ottawa National Forest without a permit, other than in designated campgrounds.		
Facilities	Most services are available in Watersmeet and Land O'Lakes.		

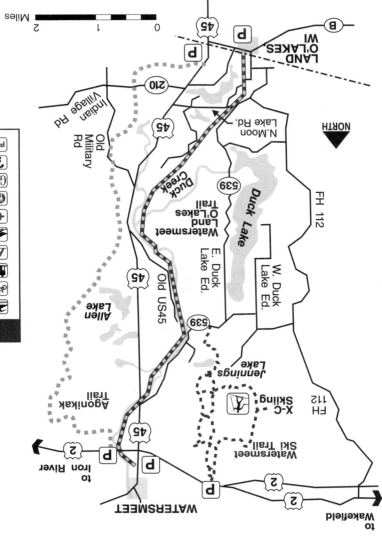

TRAIL LEGEND

▪▪▪▪▪	Trail
▪ ▪ ▪ ▪	Skiing only Trail
▪▪▪▪▪▪▪▪	Hiking only Trail
▪ ▪ ▪ ▪ ▪	Planned Trail
▪ ▪ ▪ ▪ ▪	Alternate Trail
——	Road
+++++++	Railroad Tracks

SYMBOL LEGEND

🏖	Beach/Swimming	🔭	Overlook/Observation
🔧	Bicycle Repair	P	Parking
🏠	Cabin	🏕	Camping
🛶	Canoe Launch	⛺	Picnic
✚	First Aid	🔽	Ranger Station
🍴	Food	🚻	Restrooms
⛳	Golf Course	🛖	Shelter
ℹ	Information	T	Trailhead
🛏	Lodging	🏛	Visitor Center
		⛲	Water

Wolverine Ski Trail

Trail Uses			
Grid	O1 **Trail ID** 302	**Location**	Ironwood
Length	8 miles	**Lat/Long**	46-30 / 90-07 Parking off Sunset Rd
Surface	Natural, groomed	**County**	Gogebic
Difficulty	Easy to moderate	**Contact**	Trail information 906-932-4465
Setting	Woods, open	**Fees**	Donations

Getting There   From Ironwood, east on US-2, then north 1.3 miles on Section 12 Road. Turn east a half mile on Sunset Road to the ski jump and Big Powderhorn trailhead.

Trail Notes   Loops, with easy to moderate effort level. Terrain is hilly with flat areas. Facilities at Powderhorn Lodge. Loops.

Facilities   Powderhorn Lodge:

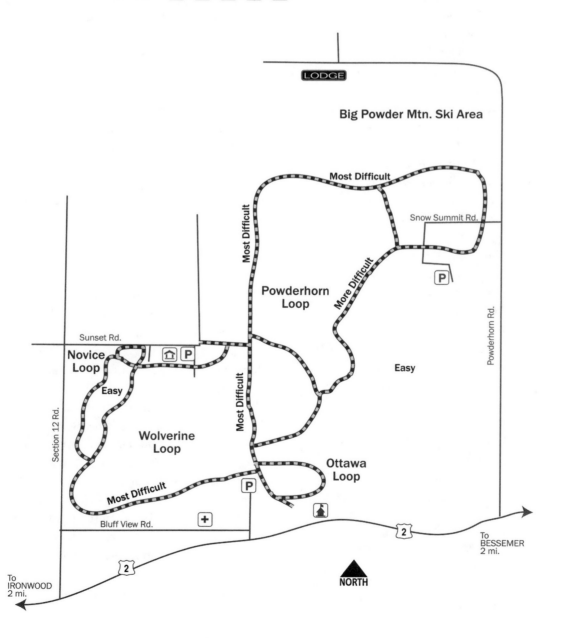

County Name	Trail Name	County Name	Trail Name
Alger	Bruno's Run Trail	Emmet	Mackinaw City to Cheboygan Trail
Alger	Bay De Noc (Grand Island National RA)	Emmet	Wildwood Hills Pathway
		Emmet	Little Traverse Wheelway
Alger	Grand Island National Rec Area	Genesee	Clio Area Bike Path
Allegan	Allegan State Game Area	genesee	Flint River Trail
Alpena	Chippewa Hills Pathway	Gladwin	Midland-Mackinac Trail
Alpena	Norway Ridge Pathway	Gogebic	Wolverine Ski Trail
Antrim	Warner Creek/Jordan Valley Rd Trail	Gogebic	State Line Rail Trail
Barry	Yankee Springs Recreational Area	Gogebic	Agonikak Trail
Barry	Thornapple Rail Trail	Gogebic	Watersmeet/Land O'Lakes Trail
Bay	Bay Hampton Rail Trail	Grand Traverse	TART & Boardmand Lake Trails
Bay	Bay City State Park (Tobico Marsh)	Grand Traverse	Sand Lakes Quiet Area
Benzie	Betsie Valley Trail	Grand Traverse	Muncie Lakes Pathway
Benzie	Lake Ann Pathway	Grand Traverse	Leelandau
Benzie	Betsie River Pathway	Grand Traverse	Lost Lake Pathway
Benzie	Crystal Mountain Resort	Grand Traverse	Vasa Trail
Cass	T K Lawless County Park	Gratiot	Fred Meijer Heartland Trail
Charlevoix	Spring Brook Pathway	Gratiot	Ithaca Jailhouse Trail
Charlevoix	Avalanche Preserve	Hillsdale	Baw Beese Trail
Charlevoix	Boyne Mountain Resort	Houghton	Maasto Hiihto Ski Trail
Charlevoix	Little Traverse Wheelway	Houghton	MTU Trail
Cheboygan	Shingle Mill Pathway	Houghton	Bill Nicholls Trails
Cheboygan	High Country Pathway	Houghton	Bergland to Sidnaw Trail
Cheboygan	Wildwood Hills Pathway	Huron	Sleeper State Park
Cheboygan	Lost Tamarack Pathway	Ingham	Lakelands Trail State Park
Cheboygan	Black Mountain Forest Rec Area	Ingham	Lansing River Trail
Cheboygen	Midland-Mackinac Trail	Ingham	Burchfield (Grand River Park)
Chippewa	Algonquin Ski Trail	Ionia	Portland Riverwalk Trail
Chippewa	Pine Bowl Pathway	Ionia	Ionia State Recreational Trail
Clare	Pine Valleys Pathway	Iron	State Line Rail Trail
Clare	Green Pine Lake Pathway	Isabella	Deerfield County Park
Clinton	Sleepy Hollow State Park	Isabella	Pere Marquette Rail-Trail - mid MI
Clinton	Rose Lake Wild Life Research Area	Jackson	Ella Sharp Single Track
Crawford	Hartwick Pines State Park	Jackson	Lakelands Trail State Park
Crawford	North Higgins Lake State Parks	Kalamazoo	Fort Custer Recreational Trail
Crawford	Midland-Mackinac Trail	Kalamazoo	Kal-Haven State Trail
Crawford	Wakeley Lake Quiet Area	Kalkaska	Sand Lakes Quiet Area
Crawford	Hanson Hills Recreation Area	Kent	Thornapple Rail Trail
Delta	Days River Pathway	Kent	White Pine Trail State Park
Delta	Felch Grade Rail Trail	Kent	Cannonsburg State Game Area
Delta	Bay De Noc (Grand Island National RA)	Kent	Kent Trail - Grand Rapids
		Keweenaw	Copper Harbor Pathway
Dickinson	Merriman East Pathway	Lake	Sheep Ranch Pathway
Dickinson	Lake Mary Plains Pathway	Lapeer	Ortonville Recreation Area
Dickinson	Felch Grade Rail Trail	Leelanau	Leelandau
Diskinson	Fumee Lake Trail	Lenawee	Heritage Park
Emmet	Mackinaw/Alanson Rail Trail	Lenawee	Kiwanis Trail

County Name	Trail Name	County Name	Trail Name
Livingston	Kensington-Metro Park Trail	Oakland	Huron Valley Trail
Livingston	Lakelands Trail State Park	Oakland	Paint Creek Trail
Livingston	Brighton State Recreation Area	Oceana	North Country Trail (Huron-Manistee NF)
Livingston	Pinckney State Recreational Trail	Oceana	Hart-Montague Bike Trail
Livingston	Island Lake State Recreation Area	Ogemaw	Ogemaw Hills Pathway
Luce	Canada Lakes Pathway	Ogemaw	Midland-Mackinac Trail
Mackinac	Sand Dunes Ski Area	Ogemaw	Rifle River Recreation Trail
Macomb	Stony Creek-Metro Park Trail	Ontonagon	Bill Nicholls Trails
Manistee	Big M Bike & Ski Trail	Ontonagon	Porcupine Mountains Wilderness State PK
Manistee	North Country Trail (Huron-Manistee NF)	Ontonagon	Ehico Mountain Bike Complex
Marquette	Blueberry Ridge Pathway	Ontonagon	Bergland to Sidnaw Trail
Marquette	Granite Pointe Nordic Ski Center	Osceola	White Pine Trail State Park
Marquette	Anderson Lake Pathway	Oscoda	Hinchman Acres Resort
Marquette	National Mine Ski Area	Otsege	Pine Baron Pathway
Mason	North Country Trail (Huron-Manistee NF)	Otsego	Shingle Mill Pathway
Mason	Whiskey Creek Trail	Otsego	Midland-Mackinac Trail
Mecosta	White Pine Trail State Park	Otsego	High Country Pathway
Menominee	Cedar River Pathway	Ottawa	Bass River Recreation Area
Menominee	Felch Grade Rail Trail	Ottawa	Hofma Reserve
Midland	Pere Marquette Rail-Trail - mid MI	Ottawa	Musketawa Trail
Midland	Midland City Forest	Ottawa	Holland Lakeshore Bike Paths
Midland	Midland-Mackinac Trail	Prasque Isle	Sinkholes Pathway
Midland	Pine Haven Recreational Area	Presque Isle	High Country Pathway
Monroe	Pointe Mouillee Game Area	Presque Isle	Black Mountain Forest Rec Area
Monroe	Sterling State Park	Presque Isle	Clear Lake State Park
Montcalm	Fred Meijer Heartland Trail	Presque Isle	Ocqueoc Falls Pathway
Montcalm	White Pine Trail State Park	Roscommon	South Higgins Lake State Park
Montmorency	Buttles Road Pathway	Roscommon	Tisdale Triangle Pathway
Montmorency	Clear Lake State Park	Saginaw	Saginaw Valley River Trail
Montmorency	High Country Pathway	Schoolcraft	Seney National Wildlife Refuge
Muskegon	Hart-Montague Bike Trail	Schoolcraft	Fox River Pathway
Newaygo	North Country Trail (Huron-Manistee NF)	Schoolcraft	Bruno's Run Trail
Oakland	Ortonville Recreation Area	Schoolcraft	Indian Lake Pathway
Oakland	Highland Recreation Area	St. Clair	Bridge to Bay Trail
Oakland	Indian Springs-Metro Park Trail	St. Clair	Wadhams to Avoca
Oakland	Seven Lakes State Park	St. Clair	Ruby Campground
Oakland	Kensington-Metro Park Trail	Van Buren	Kal-Haven State Trail
Oakland	West Bloomfield Trail Network	Washtenaw	Pinckney State Recreational Trail
Oakland	Pontiac Lake Recreation Area	Wayne	Middle Rouge Parkway
Oakland	Proud Lake Recreation Area	Wayne	Willow-Metro Park Trail
Oakland	Holly State Rec. Area-Holdridge Lake	Wayne	Oakwoods-Metro Park Trail
Oakland	Novi North Park	Wayne	Maybury State Park
Oakland	Bloomer Park	Wayne	Lower Huron-Metro Park Trail
Oakland	Bald Mountain State Recreation Area	Wayne	Pointe Mouillee Game Area
Oakland	Clinton River Trail	Wexford	Cadillac Pathway
Oakland	Addison Oaks County Park	Wexford	White Pine Trail State Park
Oakland	Stony Creek-Metro Park Trail		

City	Pop.	Trail Name
Acme	❶	Vasa Trail
Adrain	❹	Heritage Park
Adrian	❹	Kiwanis Trail
Alamo Township	❷	Kal-Haven State Trail
Alanson	❶	Mackinaw City to Cheboygan Trail
Alanson	❶	Mackinaw/Alanson Rail Trail
Algonac	❶	Bridge to Bay Trail
Allegan	❷	Allegan State Game Area
Alpena	❹	Norway Ridge Pathway
Alpena	❹	Chippewa Hills Pathway
Andersonville	❶	Indian Springs-Metro Park Trail
Atlanta	❶	Sinkholes Pathway
Atlanta	❶	Clear Lake State Park
Atlantic Mine	❶	Bill Nicholls Trails
Augusta	❶	Fort Custer Recreational Trail
Avoca	❶	Wadhams to Avoca
Avocxa	❶	Ruby Campground
Baldwin	❶	North Country Trail (Huron-Manistee NF)
Baldwin	❶	Pine Valleys Pathway
Baldwin	❶	Sheep Ranch Pathway
Battle Creek	❺	Linear Park - Battle Creek
Battle Creek	❺	Fort Custer Recreational Trail
Bay City	❹	Sleeper State Park
Bay City	❹	Bay City State Park (Tobico Marsh)
Bay City	❹	Bay Hampton Rail Trail
Beechwood	❷	State Line Rail Trail
Beechwood	❷	Holland Lakeshore Bike Paths
Bergland	❶	Ehico Mountain Bike Complex
Bergland	❶	Bergland to Sidnaw Trail
Berlamont	❶	Kal-Haven State Trail
Beulah	❶	Betsie Valley Trail
Big Rapids	❹	White Pine Trail State Park
Bloomfield	❷	Clinton River Trail
Bloomfield Hills	❷	West Bloomfield Trail Network
Bloomingdale	❶	Kal-Haven State Trail
Boyne City	❷	Avalanche Preserve
Boyne Falls	❶	Spring Brook Pathway
Boyne Falls	❶	Boyne Mountain Resort
Bradley	❶	Yankee Springs Recreational Area
Brighton	❸	Island Lake State Recreation Area
Brighton	❸	Brighton State Recreation Area
Brohlan	❶	North Country Trail (Huron-Manistee NF)
Bruce Crossing	❶	Bergland to Sidnaw Trail
Cadillac	❹	White Pine Trail State Park
Cadillac	❹	Cadillac Pathway
Caledonia	❶	Thornapple Rail Trail
Caseville	❶	Sleeper State Park
Cassopolis	❷	T K Lawless County Park
Cedar Lake	❶	Fred Meijer Heartland Trail
Cedar River	❶	Cedar River Pathway
Cedar Springs	❷	White Pine Trail State Park
Charlevoix	❷	Little Traverse Wheelway
Cheboygan	❸	Black Mountain Forest Rec Area
Clare	❷	Green Pine Lake Pathway
Clio	❷	Clio Area Bike Path
Coleman	❷	Pere Marquette Rail-Trail - mid MI
Conklin	❶	Musketawa Trail
Copper Harbor	❶	Copper Harbor Pathway
Crystal Falls	❷	Lake Mary Plains Pathway
Custer	❶	Whiskey Creek Trail
Dearborn Heights	❺	Middle Rouge Parkway
Dexter	❷	Hudson Mills-Metro Park Trail
Disco	❶	Stony Creek-Metro Park Trail
East Jordan	❷	Warner Creek/Jordan Valley Rd Trail
Edmore	❷	Fred Meijer Heartland Trail
Elwell	❶	Fred Meijer Heartland Trail
Escanaba	❹	Felch Grade Rail Trail
Ewen	❶	Bergland to Sidnaw Trail
Farmington Hills	❺	Proud Lake Recreation Area
Felch	❶	Felch Grade Rail Trail
Flat Rock	❸	Oakwoods-Metro Park Trail
Flint	❺	Holly State Rec. Area-Holdridge Lake
Flint	❺	Seven Lakes State Park
Flint	❺	Flint River Trail
Frankfort	❷	Betsie Valley Trail
Gaylord	❷	High Country Pathway
Gaylord	❷	Pine Baron Pathway
Germfask	❶	Seney National Wildlife Refuge
Gladstone	❷	Days River Pathway
Gobles	❶	Kal-Haven State Trail

City	Pop.	Trail Name
Gogebic Station	❶	State Line Rail Trail
Grand Haven	❹	Bass River Recreation Area
Grand Haven	❹	Hofma Reserve
Grand Junction	❶	Kal-Haven State Trail
Grand Rapids	❺	Cannonsburg State Game Area
Grand Rapids	❺	White Pine Trail State Park
Grand Rapids	❺	Kent Trail - Grand Rapids
Grandville	❹	Kent Trail - Grand Rapids
Grayling	❷	Wakeley Lake Quiet Area
Grayling	❷	Hartwick Pines State Park
Grayling	❷	Hanson Hills Recreation Area
Greenland	❶	Bill Nicholls Trails
Greenville	❸	Fred Meijer Heartland Trail
Gregory	❶	Lakelands Trail State Park
Gwinn	❷	Anderson Lake Pathway
Hamburg	❶	Lakelands Trail State Park
Hamburg	❶	Brighton State Recreation Area
Hampton	❶	Bay Hampton Rail Trail
Hancock	❷	Bill Nicholls Trails
Hancock	❷	Maasto Hiihto Ski Trail
Harbor Springs	❷	Little Traverse Wheelway
Hart	❷	Hart-Montague Bike Trail
Hastings	❸	Yankee Springs Recreational Area
Hastings	❸	Thornapple Rail Trail
Higgins Lake	❶	North Higgins Lake State Parks
Highland	❶	Highland Recreation Area
Hillsdale	❸	Baw Beese Trail
Holland	❹	Holland Lakeshore Bike Paths
Holly	❸	Holly State Rec. Area-Holdridge Lake
Houghton	❸	MTU Trail
Houghton	❸	Maasto Hiihto Ski Trail
Howard City	❷	White Pine Trail State Park
Hudson Mills	❶	Hudson Mills-Metro Park Trail
Indian River	❶	Wildwood Hills Pathway
Interlochen	❶	Lost Lake Pathway
Ionia	❸	Ionia State Recreational Trail
Iron Mountain	❸	Merriman East Pathway
Iron River	❷	State Line Rail Trail
Ironwood	❸	Wolverine Ski Trail
Ishpeming	❸	National Mine Ski Area
Ithaca	❷	Ithaca Jailhouse Trail
Jackson	❹	Ella Sharp Single Track

City	Pop.	Trail Name
Kalamazoo	❺	Kal-Haven State Trail
Kalamazoo	❺	Al Sabo Land Preserve
Kalamazoo	❺	Fort Custer Recreational Trail
Kalkaska	❷	Sand Lakes Quiet Area
Kendall	❶	Kal-Haven State Trail
Kenton	❶	Bergland to Sidnaw Trail
Kentwood	❹	Thornapple Rail Trail
Kibbie	❶	Kal-Haven State Trail
LaBranche	❶	Felch Grade Rail Trail
Laingsburg	❷	Sleepy Hollow State Park
Lake Ann	❶	Lake Ann Pathway
Lake Orion	❷	Addison Oaks County Park
Lake Orion	❷	Paint Creek Trail
Lake Orion	❷	Bald Mountain State Recreation Area
Lakeland	❶	Lakelands Trail State Park
Land O' Lakes,WI	❶	Agonikak Trail
Land O'Lakes,WI	❶	Watersmeet/Land O'Lakes Trail
Lansing	❺	Rose Lake Wild Life Research Area
Lansing	❺	Lansing River Trail
Lansing	❺	Sleepy Hollow State Park
Levering	❶	Mackinaw/Alanson Rail Trail
Lewiston	❶	Buttles Road Pathway
Locata	❶	Kal-Haven State Trail
Mackinaw	❶	Mackinaw City to Cheboygan Trail
Mackinaw City	❶	Mackinaw/Alanson Rail Trail
Mackinaw City	❶	Midland-Mackinac Trail
Manistee	❸	Big M Bike & Ski Trail
Marenisco	❷	State Line Rail Trail
Marilla	❶	North Country Trail (Huron-Manistee NF)
Marine City	❷	Bridge to Bay Trail
Marquette	❹	Granite Pointe Nordic Ski Center
Marquette	❹	Blueberry Ridge Pathway
Marysville	❸	Bridge to Bay Trail
Mason	❸	Burchfield (Grand River Park)
Matchwood	❶	Bergland to Sidnaw Trail
Mears	❶	Hart-Montague Bike Trail
Mentha	❶	Kal-Haven State Trail
Middleville	❷	Yankee Springs Recreational Area
Midland	❹	Pine Haven Recreational Area

City	Pop.	Trail Name
Midland	❹	Midland-Mackinac Trail
Midland	❹	Midland City Forest
Midland	❹	Pere Marquette Rail-Trail - mid MI
Mildord	❸	Proud Lake Recreation Area
Milford	❸	Highland Recreation Area
Milford	❸	Kensington-Metro Park Trail
Mio	❷	Hinchman Acres Resort
Monroe	❹	Sterling State Park
Montague	❷	Hart-Montague Bike Trail
Mount Pleasant	❹	Deerfield County Park
Mt Vernon	❶	Stony Creek-Metro Park Trail
Munising	❷	Grand Island National Rec Area
Munising	❷	Bay De Noc (Grand Island National RA)
Munising	❷	Bruno's Run Trail
Munith	❶	Lakelands Trail State Park
Muskegon	❹	Musketawa Trail
National Mine	❶	National Mine Ski Area
New Baltimore	❸	Bridge to Bay Trail
New Boston	❷	Willow-Metro Park Trail
New Boston	❷	Lower Huron-Metro Park Trail
New Era	❶	Hart-Montague Bike Trail
Newaygo	❷	North Country Trail (Huron-Manistee NF)
Newberry	❷	Canada Lakes Pathway
Northville	❸	Middle Rouge Parkway
Northville	❸	Maybury State Park
Norway	❷	Fumee Lake Trail
Novi	❹	Novi North Park
Onaway	❷	High Country Pathway
Onaway	❷	Sinkholes Pathway
Onaway	❷	Black Mountain Forest Rec Area
Ortonville	❷	Ortonville Recreation Area
Osseo	❶	Baw Beese Trail
Ossineke	❷	Chippewa Hills Pathway
Oxbow	❶	Pontiac Lake Recreation Area
Painesdale	❶	Bill Nicholls Trails
Paynesville	❶	Bergland to Sidnaw Trail
Pentoga	❶	State Line Rail Trail
Petoskey	❸	Little Traverse Wheelway
Petoskey	❸	Wildwood Hills Pathway
Pinckney	❷	Pinckney State Recreational Trail
Pinckney	❷	Lakelands Trail State Park
Plymouth	❸	Middle Rouge Parkway
Plymouth	❸	Maybury State Park
Pontiac	❺	Pontiac Lake Recreation Area
Pontiac	❺	Bald Mountain State Recreation Area
Pontiac	❺	Indian Springs-Metro Park Trail
Port Huron	❹	Bridge to Bay Trail
Portland	❷	Portland Riverwalk Trail
Quinnesec	❷	Fumee Lake Trail
Rapid City	❶	Bay De Noc (Grand Island National RA)
Ravenna	❶	Musketawa Trail
Reed City	❷	White Pine Trail State Park
Rochard Lake Village	❷	West Bloomfield Trail Network
Rochester	❸	Addison Oaks County Park
Rochester	❸	Paint Creek Trail
Rochester	❸	Stony Creek-Metro Park Trail
Rochester	❸	Clinton River Trail
Rochester Hills	❺	Bloomer Park
Rockwood	❷	Pointe Mouillee Game Area
Rogers City	❷	Black Mountain Forest Rec Area
Rogers City	❷	Ocqueoc Falls Pathway
Romulus	❹	Lower Huron-Metro Park Trail
Roscommon	❶	Tisdale Triangle Pathway
Rose City	❶	Rifle River Recreation Trail
Saginaw	❺	Saginaw Valley River Trail
Sanford	❶	Pere Marquette Rail-Trail - mid MI
Saranac	❷	Ionia State Recreational Trail
Sault Ste Marie	❹	Pine Bowl Pathway
Sault Ste. Marie	❹	Algonquin Ski Trail
Schaffer	❶	Felch Grade Rail Trail
Seney	❶	Fox River Pathway
Sharps Corner	❶	South Higgins Lake State Park
Shelby	❷	Hart-Montague Bike Trail
Sidnaw	❶	Bergland to Sidnaw Trail
Silver City	❶	Porcupine Mountains Wilderness State PK
South Haven	❸	Kal-Haven State Trail
South Lyon	❸	Huron Valley Trail
St Charles	❷	Saginaw Valley River Trail
St Clair	❸	Bridge to Bay Trail
St Ignace	❷	Sand Dunes Ski Area
Stager	❶	State Line Rail Trail
Stambaugh	❷	State Line Rail Trail

City	Pop.	Trail Name
Stickley	❶	State Line Rail Trail
Stockbridge	❷	Lakelands Trail State Park
Suttons Bay	❶	Leelandau
Sylvan Lake	❷	West Bloomfield Trail Network
Taylor	❺	Oakwoods-Metro Park Trail
Thompson	❶	Indian Lake Pathway
Thompsonville	❶	Betsie River Pathway
Thompsonville	❶	Crystal Mountain Resort
Thompsonville	❶	Betsie Valley Trail
Three Rivers	❸	T K Lawless County Park
Traverse City	❹	Muncie Lakes Pathway
Traverse City	❹	Vasa Trail
Traverse City	❹	TART & Boardmand Lake Trails
Traverse City	❹	Lake Ann Pathway
Traverse City	❹	Leelandau
Trout Creek	❶	Bergland to Sidnaw Trail
Vandalia	❶	T K Lawless County Park
Vanderbilt	❶	High Country Pathway
Vanderbilt	❶	Shingle Mill Pathway
Wadhams	❶	Wadhams to Avoca
Wakefield	❷	State Line Rail Trail
Watersmeet	❷	Agonikak Trail
Watersmeet	❷	State Line Rail Trail
Watersmeet	❷	Watersmeet/Land O'Lakes Trail
Wayland	❷	Yankee Springs Recreational Area
Wellston	❶	Big M Bike & Ski Trail
West Branch	❷	Ogemaw Hills Pathway
Westchester Heights		
	❷	Sleepy Hollow State Park
Wetmore	❶	Bruno's Run Trail
White Cloud	❷	North Country Trail (Huron-Manistee NF)
Whitehall	❷	Hart-Montague Bike Trail
Williamsburg	❶	Sand Lakes Quiet Area
Wixom	❸	Huron Valley Trail
Wolverine	❶	High Country Pathway
Wolverine	❶	Lost Tamarack Pathway
Wyoming	❺	Kent Trail - Grand Rapids

POPULATION CODE

❶=under 1,000 ❷=1,000-4,999 ❸=5,000-9,999
❹=10,000-49,999 ❺=50,000 and over

Mountain Biking Trails

Addison Oaks County Park
Agonikak Trail
Al Sabo Land Preserve
Algonquin Ski Trail
Allegan State Game Area
Anderson Lake Pathway
Avalanche Preserve
Bald Mountain State Recreation Area
Bass River Recreation Area
Baw Beese Trail
Bay City State Park (Tobico Marsh)
Bay De Noc (Grand Island National RA)
Bergland to Sidnaw Trail
Betsie River Pathway
Betsie Valley Trail
Big M Bike & Ski Trail
Bill Nicholls Trails
Black Mountain Forest Rec Area
Bloomer Park
Blueberry Ridge Pathway
Boyne Mountain Resort
Brighton State Recreation Area
Bruno's Run Trail
Burchfield (Grand River Park)
Buttles Road Pathway
Cadillac Pathway
Canada Lakes Pathway
Cannonsburg State Game Area
Cedar River Pathway
Chippewa Hills Pathway
Clear Lake State Park
Copper Harbor Pathway
Crystal Mountain Resort
Days River Pathway
Deerfield County Park
Ehico Mountain Bike Complex
Ella Sharp Single Track
Felch Grade Rail Trail
Fort Custer Recreational Trail
Fox River Pathway
Fred Meijer Heartland Trail
Fumee Lake Trail
Grand Island National Rec Area
Granite Pointe Nordic Ski Center
Green Pine Lake Pathway

Hanson Hills Recreation Area
Hartwick Pines State Park
Heritage Park
High Country Pathway
Highland Recreation Area
Hinchman Acres Resort
Hofma Reserve
Holly State Rec. Area-Holdridge Lake
Indian Lake Pathway
Ionia State Recreational Trail
Island Lake State Recreation Area
Ithaca Jailhouse Trail
Lake Ann Pathway
Lake Mary Plains Pathway
Lakelands Trail State Park
Leelandau
Lost Lake Pathway
Lost Tamarack Pathway
Maasto Hiihto Ski Trail
Mackinaw/Alanson Rail Trail
Maybury State Park
Merriman East Pathway
Midland City Forest
Midland-Mackinac Trail
MTU Trail
Muncie Lakes Pathway
Musketawa Trail
National Mine Ski Area
North Country Trail (Huron-Manistee NF)
North Higgins Lake State Parks
Norway Ridge Pathway
Novi North Park
Ocqueoc Falls Pathway
Ogemaw Hills Pathway
Ortonville Recreation Area
Pere Marquette Rail-Trail - mid MI
Pinckney State Recreational Trail
Pine Baron Pathway
Pine Bowl Pathway
Pine Haven Recreational Area
Pine Valleys Pathway
Pointe Mouillee Game Area
Pontiac Lake Recreation Area
Porcupine Mountains Wilderness State PK
Proud Lake Recreation Area
Rifle River Recreation Trail

Rose Lake Wild Life Research Area
Ruby Campground
Sand Dunes Ski Area
Sand Lakes Quiet Area
Seney National Wildlife Refuge
Seven Lakes State Park
Sheep Ranch Pathway
Shingle Mill Pathway
Sinkholes Pathway
Sleeper State Park
Sleepy Hollow State Park
South Higgins Lake State Park
Spring Brook Pathway
State Line Rail Trail
Stony Creek-Metro Park Trail
T K Lawless County Park
Thornapple Rail Trail
Tisdale Triangle Pathway
Vasa Trail
Wakeley Lake Quiet Area
Warner Creek/Jordan Valley Rd Trail
Watersmeet/Land O'Lakes Trail
Whiskey Creek Trail
White Pine Trail State Park
Wildwood Hills Pathway
Wolverine Ski Trail
Yankee Springs Recreational Area

Leisure Biking Trails
Addison Oaks County Park
Baw Beese Trail
Bay Hampton Rail Trail
Bridge to Bay Trail
Clinton River Trail
Clio Area Bike Path
Flint River Trail
Hart-Montague Bike Trail
Holland Lakeshore Bike Paths
Hudson Mills-Metro Park Trail
Huron Valley Trail
Indian Springs-Metro Park Trail
Kal-Haven State Trail
Kensington-Metro Park Trail
Kent Trail - Grand Rapids
Kiwanis Trail
Lansing River Trail
Leelandau
Linear Park - Battle Creek
Little Traverse Wheelway
Lower Huron-Metro Park Trail
Mackinaw City to Cheboygan Trail
Maybury State Park
Middle Rouge Parkway
Oakwoods-Metro Park Trail
Paint Creek Trail
Pere Marquette Rail-Trail - mid MI
Portland Riverwalk Trail
Saginaw Valley River Trail
Sterling State Park
TART & Boardmand Lake Trails
Wadhams to Avoca
West Bloomfield Trail Network
Willow-Metro Park Trail

Trail Index

Find me a place, safe and serene,
away from the terror I see on the screen.
A place where my soul can find some peace,
away from the stress and the pressures released.
A corridor of green not far from my home
for fresh air and exercise, quiet will roam.
Summer has smells that tickle my nose
and fall has the leaves that crunch under my toes.
Beware, comes a person we pass in a while
with a wave and hello and a wide friendly smile.
Recreation trails are the place to be,
to find that safe haven of peace and serenity.

By Beverly Moore, Illinois Trails Conservancy

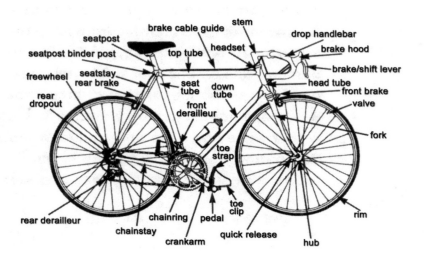

Tires and Wheels

Inspect your tire's thread for embedded objects, such a glass, and remove to avoid potential punctures.

Carry with you a spare tube, a patch kit, tire levers for removing the tire, and some duct tape.

Don't reassemble the wheel when fixing a flat until you have felt around the inside the tire. The cause of the puncture could still be lodged there.

Adjust your tire inflation pressure based on the type of ride. Lower pressure is better for off road biking or riding in the rain. A higher tire pressure is best for normal road biking or racing.

Sometimes a clicking sound is caused by two spokes rubbing together. Try a little oil on the spokes where they cross.

Reflectors

Have at least a rear reflector on your bike. Reflectors on the back of your pedals is an effective way of alerting motorists' to your presence.

Pedals

A few drops of oil to the cleat where it contacts the pedal will help silence those clicks and creaks in clipless pedals.

Saddles

Replace an uncomfortable saddle with one that contains gel or extra-dense foam. Select a saddle best designed for your anatomy. Women generally have a wider distance than men between their bones that contact the saddle top.

Chains and Derailleurs

Avoid combining the largest rear cog with the large chainring or the smallest cog with the small chainring.

Noises from the crank area may mean the chain is rubbing the front derailleur. To quiet this noise, move the front derailleur lever enough to center the chain through the cage but not cause a shift.

American Bike Trails

American Bike Trails publishes and distributes maps, books and guides for the bicyclist.

For more information:

www.abtrails.com